Beyond Individualism

Beyond Individualism

Michael J. Piore

HARVARD UNIVERSITY PRESS
Cambridge, Massachusetts
London, England
1995

Library of Congress Cataloging-in-Publication Data

Piore, Michael J.
    Beyond individualism / Michael J. Piore.
        p.   cm.
    Includes bibliographical references and index.
    ISBN 0-674-06897-1
    1. Individualism—United States.   2. Political participation—
United States.   3. Social movements—United States.   4. United
States—Social policy.   I. Title.
    HM136.P63   1995
    302.5′4—dc20   94-34909
                            CIP

To Iris and Paul Brest

Acknowledgments

This book was a long time in the making, and I am indebted to an unusually long list of people who read various portions of the manuscript and helped me to formulate and then reformulate my ideas. My colleague Rudi Dornbusch got me started on this project by suggesting that I turn an essay on Reaganomics into a short book. It would never have been completed without the help of Duncan Foley, who often seemed to grasp what I was trying to do better than I did myself and who was instrumental in helping me to define the issues I had to address in order to complete the argument. I am also indebted to Richard Locke, Jonathan Silin, Suzanne Berger, and Charles Sabel, all of whom offered advice and criticism at many junctures, and to Alice Amsden, Eli Ginzberg, Martin Krieger, Martin Rein, Peter Temin, and Eric Lindblad.

My sojourn at the Stanford Law School in the spring term of 1990 had a major impact upon my thinking about these issues, as did my colleagues and students at MIT in economics and in industrial relations. The central theoretical ideas were developed in collaboration with Fred Kofman, Richard Lester, and Kamal Maleck in a project on industrial design sponsored by the Sloan Foundation through the Industrial Performance Center at MIT.

I was particularly fortunate to have the support of John Arditi and Linda Woodbury, who not only managed the endless drafts of the manuscript but also made substantive suggestions as the argument developed, and the editorial support and assistance of Michael Aronson and Camille Smith at Harvard University Press.

The two people to whom this book is dedicated, Iris and Paul Brest, have done more than anyone else I know to try to understand the many groups into which American society has divided and to create space for them to talk with and listen to one another.

Contents

Introduction

For more than ten years now, economic policy in the United States has been preoccupied by the federal budget deficit. Behind this deficit, however, and until recently almost completely eclipsed by it, there has emerged an enormous social deficit, a pent-up demand for spending to redress income imbalance, to support health care, child care, and the care of the elderly, and to finance expenditures for a host of festering social needs: the rehabilitation of drug addicts, AIDS prevention and education and the care of people with the disease, public access for the disabled and handicapped, and the like. These needs are now being recognized by the Clinton administration, but the administration faces a dilemma: the budget deficit severely limits its ability to address the social deficit through government programs. Furthermore, the very recognition of the social deficit is likely to inflate the demands associated with it. This was certainly what happened in the 1960s in the last transition of this kind, when power shifted from the Republicans under Eisenhower to the Democratic administrations of Kennedy and Johnson.

The 1950s, not unlike the 1980s, was a decade of apparent prosperity and political complacency, but with a growing list of social problems that were barely acknowledged, let alone addressed. The shift from Eisenhower to Kennedy in 1961 was largely one of tone and style. The major substantive innovation in the early Kennedy years was a tax cut designed to stimulate the economy and reignite economic growth. The tax cut represented the triumph of Keynesian economics. It was sustained by a broad consensus in the economics profession, comparable in many ways to the one that sustained the movement toward deregulation in the 1970s and the one that is generating the pressures to control the deficit today. But it was successful in a way in which neither deregulation nor budgetary responsibility has been successful, not simply in that it was fully implemented but also in that the policy produced the intended results. It generated a period of growth and prosperity then unprecedented in American history.

The problems that dominated national politics in the following decade, however, turned out to have virtually nothing to do with the problems addressed by the professional consensus. The actual problems revolved around issues of the distribution of income and social status that went beyond economic growth and prosperity. Indeed it was almost as if the Kennedy rhetoric encouraged people to reevaluate their position in American society, raising questions they had not really thought about before, and the growing prosperity and declining unemployment freed them to express the anger and resentment that emerged in the process. And the country erupted in protests, marches, demonstrations, and ultimately in riots, first in the central cities, then on college campuses and in scattered factories, which at the beginning of the period were completely inconceivable.

A similar transformation of American politics occurred in the 1930s under Franklin Roosevelt. Roosevelt was elected, of course, at the nadir of the Great Depression, and we tend to attribute the social mobilization of the period to the conditions that brought him to power. But in fact the mass social protests, waves of sit-down strikes and spontaneous labor unrest that in retrospect seem to characterize the politics of the period actually did not occur until late in 1935, almost three years after Roosevelt had come to power, at the very moment when economic recovery had finally begun.

The mobilization and protest of the 1930s seem to have been brought to an end by the country's entry into the Second World War. Nobody really knows how to account for the end of the mobilization of the 1960s. Part of the explanation—in my own case, a very large part—is that people simply became tired. What had initially been experienced as an enormous release, spontaneous, even fun, became gradually over time somewhat boring and repetitive. And it became increasingly frightening and threatening as well, especially in the ghettos and universities where most of the property damage and the life threatening physical injuries were experienced by the protesters themselves. The movement was dominated by youth who wore themselves out and in the process grew up.[1]

If this is indeed what happened, it has ominous implications for the current period. The groups that protested in the 1960s are now populated by a new generation, much of which had not yet even been born in that earlier period, a generation that has inherited much of their parents' anger but have experienced neither the exhilaration nor the disappointment of its release.

Objective conditions also changed through the social reforms of the Kennedy-Johnson years and in the period of "normal" electoral politics under Carter, Reagan, and Bush. It is not simply that the reforms of the 1960s worked to redress social imbalances that were reintroduced and aggravated in the 1980s to generate a new social deficit. People's perceptions of their own personal responsibilities also came full circle. In the early 1980s, when the draconian welfare reforms of the Reagan era were coming into effect, I asked a friend of mine who was an organizer in the inner city why the cutbacks were accepted passively in neighborhoods that had once been so aggressive in the pursuit of welfare as a basic right. His answer was that the poor felt guilty. The system in the 1970s had lent itself to cheating and the people living under it had exploited the opportunities it offered. It was not that they lived particularly well; they were still recognizably poor, in many ways even desperate. But they *had* tried to beat the system; in their own mind they had cheated. They, more than anybody, recognized the truth of the charges leveled by the critics of the system; this led them to feel guilty, and in a not wholly logical but nonetheless real and profound way, they had come to feel responsible for their own poverty. Much the same sense of guilt and personal responsibility was evident in talks I had with union leaders and even with the rank-and-file during the period of concession bargaining in the 1980s. They actually thought that their high wages and rigid work rules *were* responsible for the competitive problems of American industry, and, if they resisted concessions, they did so halfheartedly, accepting the justice of their own defeat.

The conditions that sustained such resignation and acquiescence are gone. The opportunities to exploit the welfare system have been curtailed to a point where charges of cheating and abuse can no longer distract the

clients from the reality of their own poverty. American unions have conceded so much in terms of wages and work rules and the relative pay of
U.S. workers in the international marketplace has fallen so far that these
can no longer plausibly explain the country's continuing competitive dis-
advantage. The notion that anything that workers could realistically do,
individually or through their unions, would in itself save their jobs is simply
no longer believable. The deprivation they and their families have suffered
in the attempt to shoulder responsibility for the country's problems is now
what dominates their perception of the economic policy debate. Bush's
defeat was a clear mandate for a government that would assume responsibility for the economic welfare of its constituency.

The political rhetoric had in fact already begun to shift before Clinton's
election. Bush's campaigns—epitomized by the Willie Horton ads in 1988,
playing on racism by focusing on a black convict released in the Massachusetts prison leave program of his Democratic opponent, and the 1992
"family values" attacks upon working women, abortion, and gays—could
not have been more in the spirit of the Reagan years. Indeed nothing in
Reagan's own campaigns was quite as extreme in tone and tenor. But Bush's
speeches also contained a secondary theme. That theme was never developed in his campaigns, but he made it the centerpiece of his acceptance
speech at the 1988 convention and his victory speech the following No-
vember and periodically returned to it throughout his administration. This
was the theme of a kinder, gentler society. It recognized the excess of the
Reagan policies and the legitimacy of the social grievances associated with
them. The failure of the "family values" theme in 1992 and the open support of the Democratic Party for feminist and gay issues was the final blow
to the old political rhetoric.

The shift in the mood of the country, moreover, is not just rhetorical.
Signs of a new political and social mobilization, of a renewed willingness
to go outside the normal bounds of the electoral process, began to appear
even before the end of the Reagan era and accumulated throughout the
Bush years. Jesse Jackson's presidential campaign attracted a following of
social grievants and fed them into the political process in a way in which
no comparable candidate had done since McCarthy and McGovern cam-
paigned against the war in Vietnam. The war in the Gulf generated a much
greater protest movement on college campuses than the President, or the
press for that matter, was prepared to recognize; the comments of the

protesters revealed precisely the hunger for meaning and participation in history a surfeit of which had led to the retreat of their parents in the early 1970s. The Supreme Court's decision on abortion in 1989 reactivated both the women's movement and an even more militant movement of harassment and civil disobedience among the anti-abortion groups. Militant protest among gays and lesbians has branched out from AIDS activism to broader social issues, crystallized by the formation of the group Queer Nation, whose name symbolizes its aggressive stance on gay rights. A new militancy among the deaf was revealed in the protest against the hearing president of Gallaudet University. And even the labor movement has emerged from a period of quiescence to wreak vengeance on management in strikes that nearly drove the *New York Daily News* into bankruptcy and did in fact kill Eastern Airlines, and to overturn their own leadership in national elections in trucking and in a number of local elections in the automobile industry.

How can society deal with the emerging conflict between social demands and economic constraints? The preferred solution among politicians and policymakers has been the development of some kind of political consensus. The search for such a consensus actually began around the budget deficit in the waning years of the Reagan administration. The model for, and most successful example of, such consensus building was the Greenspan Commission, which had addressed the impending deficit in the social security system. A similar commission composed of leaders of important economic interests—trade unions, labor, agriculture—and representatives of the major political parties and congressional leaders was proposed to address the deficit in the overall federal budget by New York's governor, Mario Cuomo. Such a commission was actually set up in 1987 under the leadership of former party chairmen Drew Lewis and Robert Strauss. Its recommendations would undoubtedly have served as the fulcrum for a budgetary compromise in the early Bush administration had not budget policy been preempted by Bush's famous read-my-lips campaign pledge of no new taxes.

Clinton's town meetings can in many ways be understood as a much broader and more open attempt to produce essentially the same thing, a broad consensus that would break the political impasse over budgetary policy and allow the country at last to address its economic and social problems in a deliberate, systematic way. Its most ambitious goal is the "new covenant" the President called for in his acceptance speech to the Democratic National Convention.

The town meeting approach has the distinct advantage over the commissions of the 1980s of being more open, in terms of both its agenda and its representation. It admits all sorts of groups that had no seats on the commission—women, gays and lesbians, the handicapped, environmentalists, consumer advocates—and brings to the table the whole variety of social claims that would have to be deferred to reduce the federal deficit. But, its strength is also its weakness. It seems too amorphous to produce a structured political coalition or a systematic approach to policy. And it risks enlarging the set of demands with which the political process is forced to deal and reinforcing them through the legitimacy it confers not only upon the groups' demands but also on their spokespersons as they appear before the President on national television. In any case, Clinton has proved no more successful than Bush in constructing a consensus about the budget.

Nonetheless, the contrast between the commission and the town meeting reveals how much the American political process has changed in recent years, how far we have moved from a well-structured set of political claims and political claimants into a world where both claims and claimants are in a state of flux and uncertainty. In this new situation, things that were once unmentionable, like homosexuality, condoms, and hypodermic needles for drug addiction, have become the focus of political organization and the subject of public debate. But commissions and town meetings have one thing in common: they both constitute attempts to resolve political problems outside established governmental institutions. They supplement, even sidestep, the official electoral process. They create alternative channels of debate and compromise in which we are represented not as individuals and voters but as members of various groups, economic interest groups in the case of the commission, but in the case of town meetings also groups defined by social roles and social stigmas, biological traits and physical characteristics. The commission at least gave a certain deference to the official channels, working off-stage almost surreptitiously. But the town meetings are ostentatiously open and public.

How are we to think about political processes of this kind? Why are they necessary? What precisely are they attempting to accomplish? How should we judge the results? Will they eventually be able to reconcile social claims and economic constraints? Indeed, where do the claims and the constraints they are attempting to reconcile come from? How do we know that the constraints are real and the claims legitimate? Could there be a substitute for the extra-electoral politics of marches, demonstrations, sit-ins, strikes, and civil disobedience? Why, in fact, do social demands tend to intensify and manifest themselves in these ways even as they are being addressed?

These issues are not easy for us in the United States to recognize and deal with. The extra-electoral tactics of demonstrations and civil disobedience are manifestations of cohesive social groups, and the extra-electoral structures are attempts to accommodate groups in politics, economic groups in the case of the commissions, a less well defined set of social groups in the case of the town meeting. But we as a society are committed to individualism. Our commitment in this regard is both positive and normative. We take the individual as the basic building block of socioeconomic systems. We try to understand society as an aggregate of its individual members and the economy as a collection of individual producers and consumers. We believe that the society and the economy *ought* to be organized in this way and understandable in these terms. There is no place in this vision for cohesive social groups, groups that are more than the sum of their individual members, and no legitimate place in the political processes that arise from this vision for group representation. Hence it is no accident that the commissions operate behind closed doors and that the role of group representatives in the town meetings is obscured in a sea of other people appearing in the guise of individual citizens randomly selected by television news organizations or by operators taking telephone calls from the outside.

This book constitutes an attempt to broaden our concept of individualism in a way that will enable us to recognize and come to terms with these groups, to better understand the origin and nature of the social claims they make and of the way those claims are related to, or can be reconciled with, the ability of the economy to generate the productive resources required to meet them. Its argument about the relationship between groups and individuals and the process through which that relationship has been played out in American politics hinges on meaning and understanding.

The cohesive groups into which society divides form communities of meaning, social spheres in which a common set of understandings emerges and evolves over time. Our economic institutions define communities of meanings as well. Communication within such communities is easy and natural. But communication across their boundaries is problematic, and in recent years social and economic structures in the United States have developed in ways that make such communication increasingly difficult. The social groups into which the society is dividing are less and less capable of understanding and talking to one another. They are also less and less interested in the economy and able to appreciate the ways in which it conditions and constrains the country's capacity to respond to the claims they assert in the political process. Our economic institutions face parallel problems: their competitive position in world markets depends increasingly upon cooperative arrangements and strategic alliances that span institutional boundaries and demand patterns of trust and communication that are foreign to American managerial practice.

This recent evolution of the relationship among communities of meaning, in both the economy and the society, is in no small measure the product of the political process, of the way political leadership has been exercised, and of the social and economic policies the country has pursued. To the extent that our problems are the product of politics and policy, we should in principle be able to reverse them through politics and policy as well. But our capacity to think through and appreciate how this might be done is limited by the framework of liberal social theory. The immediate limitation is the theory's emphasis on the individual, but the more fundamental limit is its account of the way in which the individual comes to understand and interpret the world. In effect, the theory assumes that understanding and interpretation are self-evident. In other words, it sidesteps the problem of understanding altogether. To work our way out of the immediate problems the country faces in social and economic policy we are forced to reconceptualize the relationship between the individual and the social setting in which he or she resides; to incorporate explicitly the processes through which meaning and understanding are generated and evolve over time; and to recognize the way in which politics enters into that process. Our starting point in the immediate problems of contemporary American politics thus leads to a much broader and more ambitious excursion into social theory itself.

1

The Social Deficit and the New Identity Groups

That Presidents Reagan and Bush bequeathed to their successors a substantial social deficit is now conventional political wisdom. But the dimensions of that deficit and the problems it poses for the political process are not so fully appreciated. The social deficit is large: if its components were denominated in dollar terms and added together, it would dwarf the budget deficit; and, understood in this way, it is clearly in competition with reduction of the budget deficit for national resources. But it is not altogether meaningful to think about the problem in this way. The claims at stake are extremely diverse. That diversity gives rise to enormous confusion, confusion about what the claims really are, about who will represent them, and about how they translate into programmatic demands and public policy. Some of the claims are largely symbolic and could be met without any substantial expenditure of federal funds. Others could take multiple forms, giving rise to considerable controversy about who can legitimately represent them and generating increases in a number of spending categories at once.

At least two very different structures of representation, two very different kinds of demands and policy approaches, are incipient in the politics of recent years. One is the trade union movement, anchored in the work place. The other consists of a diverse set of groups defined by their social, as opposed to economic, identity: ethnic and racial minorities, women, the handicapped, the disabled, the aged, gays and lesbians. The nature of these two types of representation and the different challenges they pose for the political process are the focus of this chapter and the next.

The Social Deficit

In economic terms, what is most striking about the Reagan-Bush years is the changes in the distribution of wage and salary income and of employment opportunity. The Reagan administration permitted, even encouraged, a widening of the distribution of income. The shift in the income distribution was accompanied by an enormous deficit in the balance of trade, a growing gap between imports and exports, in effect a subsidy to the country's standard of living financed by borrowing from abroad. That subsidy went largely to those who were already well off, who experienced an increase in their standards of living while the incomes of the blue-collar labor force declined. Economic insecurity among low-income workers also increased; unemployment fell in the latter part of the 1980s but from record postwar levels and began to rise again with the onset of the recession in 1990. Full employment meanwhile came to be defined as a rate that had once been considered recessionary. The percentage of unemployment covered by insurance has fallen from 43.3 percent in 1980 to 30.6 percent in 1988.[1] The minimum wage was allowed to fall relative to the average wage, from 47 percent to 35 percent, the longest and most sustained decline since its introduction in the 1930s.[2] Wage differentials between high school and college graduates, which had narrowed progressively in the earlier postwar decades, began to widen in the Reagan years and continued to do so after he left office, this in the face of a shrinking supply of unskilled workers, which economists had generally predicted would push the differential in the other direction.[3] These changes in the wage and salary distribution were reinforced by changes in the tax structure that increased the dispersion of income even further. The population living in poverty grew and became more concentrated among particular racial, ethnic, and demographic groups.[4] Substantial pockets of the poor were bottled up in the ghettos of our central cities, increasingly beset by street gangs, drug addiction, and hopelessness, which we have come to think of as so many manifestations of social disintegration.

Meanwhile, there was a dramatic increase in the labor force participation of women, especially young women with children. In the Reagan years alone, according to the Bureau of Labor Statistics, participation rates jumped from 42 percent to 57 percent for mothers with children under age 6 and from 39 percent to 51 percent for those with children under one year. This is creating a large and growing deficit in custodial care, reflected in the expanding demand for child care and services for the aged, the handicapped, and the sick, and a decline in the welfare of all of these groups who used to be cared for by women in the home. The deficit in custodial care has in turn interacted with the deficiencies of a medical care system financed primarily through employment-based insurance. The medical care system has absorbed part of the demand for custodial care, driving up costs that were already prone to rise more rapidly than the general price level. The increased precariousness of employment threatens, where it does not actually compromise, medical coverage and has been one of the factors driving secondary earners into the labor market. Costs have been further inflated by expanding poverty and unemployment, which have augmented the pool of medically indigent persons whose care is subsidized by increases in the prices of services to the insured population. And these cost increases, reflected in insurance rates, have forced employers to limit coverage further, jeopardizing the medical welfare of the population and the financial stability of the insurance system.

Social Claimants

It is one thing to draw up a list of the social needs and neglects of the Reagan-Bush years, to identify the potential for social mobilization and the economic dilemmas that are likely to constrain the country's response. It is quite another to foresee the precise form in which the social deficit is likely to present itself in the political process or how the society might realistically attempt to accommodate it. The problem is precisely that in a period of social mobilization grievances cannot be reduced to a list of particular items: such items are at best so many markers of the position of whole groups in the social structure; and the demands that are really being made, the changes that would have to take place to assuage the anger and resentment that are being expressed, are in the social structure itself. In the current situation, moreover, it is not at all clear what groups, what social structure, we are talking about.

Trade Unions

The most obvious representative for the grievances associated with the social deficit is the trade union movement. The people most adversely affected by the changes in the income distribution of the Reagan years and the collapse of employment opportunity were blue-collar workers concentrated in the historic bastions of union strength and marginal workers trapped in low-wage jobs to which the labor movement looked, when in its ascendancy, as the frontiers of union organization.[5] Because they are already strapped to support their families, the deficits in custodial care for young children, aging parents, the handicapped, and the chronically ill are most acute for these groups as well.

Trade unionism is the form of social mobilization with which American society is most familiar. Unions were the vehicle for protest throughout the late nineteenth and the greater part of the twentieth century. Explicit recognition and legitimation of unions as a continuing institutional form are products of the Great Depression, probably the single most "mobilized" period in American political history. Since the Depression, we have learned to accommodate unions within regular political and economic processes. Even in the last decade, when "normal" electoral politics have prevailed and individualistic approaches to economic and social problems have predominated, a group politics revolving around organized labor and the organized business community has, as I noted in the Introduction, operated behind the scenes through the Greenspan Commission on Social Security and the Lewis-Strauss Commission on the Federal Budget Deficit.

American trade unions have historically been organized from the shop floor, and their primary locus of operation is the workplace. This suggests that in the hands of the labor movement the claims associated with the social deficit will be largely economic and will make themselves felt in demands upon particular employers for wages and benefits. This has the advantage from a political point of view that grievances will be diverted from the federal budget itself to the productive sector, where the grievants · will be forced to face directly the limitations imposed by productivity and by the competitive environment. If they do not take cognizance of these constraints, their employers will be driven out of business and they will lose their jobs. But it would be a mistake to think that the social claims expressed through the labor movement will be primarily for *increases* in wages and benefits. American unions, possibly because they are centered in shops and, therefore, sensitive to the economic environment in which their demands must be met, have historically been at least as concerned with justice and equity in the workplace as with the level of compensation as such. From this point of view, the salient feature of social policy—or the lack thereof—under Reagan and Bush was a statistic not included on the list just enumerated: the increased variance of wages *within* labor force groups. The dispersion of wages increased, in other words, not only across categories into which workers are generally classed (by age, education, experience, industry, and occupation) but *within* each of these categories as well.[6] This apparently arcane statistical finding translates into a dramatic decline in the ability of economists, but also, and much more important, of workers themselves, to understand and justify differences in incomes in terms of any of the attributes that differentiate one worker from another.

The growing "residual" dispersion actually began in the 1970s and is closely related to the decline in union strength. Although even at their peak in the 1950s American unions represented a minority of the labor force, the labor movement remained central to the wage-setting process until well into the 1970s. The wages that unions established for their members through collective bargaining set a pattern for compensation and benefits that generally extended to the unorganized workers as well. The labor movement itself operated to extend the pattern in the political process through social security, minimum wage, and labor standards legislation, which it periodically upgraded to keep pace with gains in the private sector. And the threat of union organization forced employers above the legislated floor to follow the union pattern even when they were not themselves organized. The result was a well-established, orderly, and visible set of wage and employment relationships in which the disparities among industries and occupations nationally and among particular work sites within any local community were limited and confined by a set of historically sanctioned customs and traditions.[7] That order was strained by the first oil shock and the increased competition unleashed by deregulation in the latter part of the 1970s, but it was completely upset in the course of the Reagan years.

The pivotal event in the process through which this occurred was Reagan's response to the 1981 strike of the federal air traffic controllers. Because the strikers were federal employees, their strike was illegal, and contingency plans for manning the airports with military personnel had already been developed under Carter. But Reagan went much further. In a highly publicized set of moves, he broke the union. He dismissed the strikers, hired new workers to replace them, and kept the military on the job for over a year until the replacements had been fully trained. The President's action galvanized anti-union managerial factions in a whole variety of industries and occupations where union organization had previously been unassailable. And it set the stage for a prolonged period of union givebacks and concession bargaining.

Economists and, to some extent, the business community have perceived this as a return to a market economy. But this is hardly the way it is understood by the people whose work lives are governed by the new arrangements. These workers find it increasingly difficult to perceive the rationale for the conditions to which they are subjected. Unionized workers have been led to believe they were making temporary compromises to restore the competitive position of their industry and the American economy. This interpretation becomes less and less plausible as the period of time is extended and the industries and the economy regain their health. At the same time, the practices employers have instituted in place of the structures and procedures the unions have "conceded" are so various that workers cannot figure out why they are treated in one way and their counterparts next door in another. In some companies, practices vary in an erratic way from shop to shop or even within the same shop from one year to the next, thereby heightening the sense of the essentially arbitrary nature of employment practices. Since much of this variation is the product of confusion and debate among managers themselves—fairly typical of the last decade but rare in the earlier postwar period—about "best practice," one cannot even argue that prevailing conditions express a set of market forces whose logic and coherence workers themselves are simply unable to see.

For marginal groups within the labor force the problem is that the structures of employment have not kept pace with the changing nature of these groups or of their employment commitments. The relative number of such jobs has grown in recent years, but the quality of the wages and working conditions has deteriorated substantially. These trends partly reflect structural shifts involving particular industries and technologies. But they have been heightened by a tendency of employers generally to segment their labor force, creating a permanent core of workers to whom they are prepared to develop extensive, strong commitments in terms of fringe benefits and job security and a peripheral group to whom their commitment is contingent although the employment relationship may last just as long.

These peripheral labor forces include a number of people who in fact have a temporary commitment to the labor market (students, housewives, retirees) but they also include many whose commitment is long term. The commitment of many others, most especially of young women, became more permanent in the 1980s. These people now find it difficult to understand why they should continue to be hired as part-timers or temporary help, at lower wages and without fringe benefits, when the work they do is often the same as that performed by their permanent colleagues. Thus it is very likely that a resurgence of trade union organization would involve enormous pressure to restore equity in the compensation structure.

The least disruptive way to do this would be to select a set of standard jobs and equate the wages of comparable jobs to that standard. When this is done in a relatively centralized wage-setting regime the process is managed so that nobody experiences a decline in income. Either the best-paying jobs are used as the standard and other jobs are raised to meet those levels, or the wages of the incumbent are frozen and downward adjustments are made only when the job becomes vacant. This is how the U.S. wage structure was initially ordered in response to pressures from the industrial unions newly organized in the Depression under the aegis of the War Labor Boards, which set government wages during World War II and through centralized collective bargaining in the early postwar period.[8]

In a decentralized wage-setting regime or when the pressures to rectify inequities are spontaneous, the process is very different. Workers in the low-wage sectors, driven by newly awakened feelings of anger and resentment about the injustice of their position, create pressures through strikes and other job actions to increase their wages to what they see as the prevailing standards. But the higher wages they generate relieve competitive restraints that hold the wages of other enterprises in check, leading their workers, who often feel the initial wage disparities were in fact just and equitable, to press for higher wages in their turn. This second round of wage increases restores the initial wage disparities, resurrecting feeling of inequity and injustice, reinforcing the original anger and resentment, which are then expressed in a new round of job actions and strike threats, culminating in further wage increases. This, of course, again releases their competitors from market restraints, enabling them to pay higher wages to their workers and so on. A process of this kind becomes an engine of inflation.

This wage-wage inflation, as it is called, can in principle be contained by the monetary authorities if they restrain the expansion of the money supply and limit the resources required to finance the process. The precipitous decline of the rate of inflation in the early Reagan years under the stringent policies pursued by Paul Volcker as Chairman of the Federal Reserve Board is a clear demonstration of this effect and has reinforced this lesson among professional economists, bankers, and policymakers, making it quite likely that the Fed would indeed move to restrain the process were it to begin again. But Volcker's monetary policy was implemented under what were probably the closest thing economists (or bankers for that matter) will ever see to pure laboratory conditions. He imposed monetary restraint in the social vacuum created by the resurgence of individualism and Reagan's election when organized labor was in full retreat. The pursuit of such a policy in a period of incipient social mobilization, when anger and resentment are already extreme, is quite another matter. It risks aggravating a set of social tensions that are themselves a threat to economic stability and expansion. In addition, it is likely to provoke a political challenge to the capacity of the Federal Reserve Board to pursue an independent monetary policy. Faced with similar challenges in the past, the Fed has chosen to compromise its policies in the light of social and political realities.[9]

The advantage of the labor movement as a vehicle for protest is that trade unions are precisely the kind of social actors it is easy to compromise with. They are established organizational entities with experienced leaders who are sensitive to economic reality, accustomed to negotiation, and skilled at leading their constituencies into a settlement. At critical historical moments—in the aftermath of the Depression in World War II, in the Korean War period, and through the systems of wage and price controls imposed by Presidents Johnson and Nixon in the late 1960s and early 1970s—the country has been able to construct around trade unions an orderly process through which social pressures could be translated into public policy. These earlier periods offer a model of a process of negotiation and accommodation for the coming decade.

The problem with the model is that it is not clear that the labor move-ment any longer has the stability or the coherence to assume the role it has played in the past. Popular attention has focused upon the declining pro-portion of the labor force represented by trade unions and the weakness of the union organization that remains. The decline in union membership in the Reagan years was indeed dramatic: it fell from 23 percent of non-agricultural employment in 1980 to 16 percent in 1989.[10] What is not perceived are the internal divisions within the labor movement itself, and these may have an even more dramatic effect on the role trade unions play in a period of renewed social mobilization. As president of the AFL-CIO, Lane Kirkland has managed to maintain labor unity, but he is over seventy years old; people are anticipating his retirement, and the struggle to succeed him has already begun among national leaders from very different indus-trial backgrounds and with divergent views about the roles labor ought to play in American society, indeed about American society itself. Meanwhile many of these leaders are vulnerable to challenge within their own unions. Most of them have led their organizations to bargaining concessions that are bound to be challenged in any revival of militancy among the rank and file, especially one that comes to be perceived in terms of opposition to the policies and tactics of the Reagan-Bush period. For example, New Di-rections, a dissident group within the Automobile Workers that has con-sistently opposed labor relations reform within that industry, gained con-trol over the local union at the Nummi plant in California, which has served as a model for labor-management cooperation within General Motors. Of even greater import in terms of national union politics, a dissident candi-date won the presidency of the Teamsters, one of the largest national unions and perhaps the biggest wildcard in the struggle for leadership succession within the AFL-CIO.[11]

The problems of labor leadership, moreover, are not transitory; they reflect structural characteristics of the economic and political environment that have undermined union organizational more generally. Deregulation and the expansion of international trade have made that environment not only more competitive but more unstable, unpredictable, and in terms of the fate of particular business enterprises apparently more capricious as well. The increased dispersion of earnings noted above—and of the terms and conditions of employment—is one manifestation of these trends. The trends increase the opportunities for invidious comparisons among different groups of organized workers, which opposition candidates can exploit to mount challenges to established leaders.

In this environment, moreover, particular enterprises are subject to sudden, and frequently extreme, fluctuations in profitability and market share. Management has tended to respond to these fluctuations with abrupt changes in labor strategy, implemented without warning or consultation. The most notable of these was the shift at Caterpillar from a policy of cooperative and consultative labor relations to a confrontational strategy of radical cuts in employment and wages; this case achieved high visibility when the UAW tried to forestall the new approach in a long, bitter, and ultimately unsuccessful strike, which attracted the attention of the national press and, even more, of the labor relations community.[12] But it was not unique or even particularly unusual. The effect of such shifts is to compromise the reputation of the leaders who participated in the original cooperative strategy, and of cooperation itself, in the eyes of the rank and file and to make other officers reluctant to move out in advance of their members and exercise leadership in collective bargaining.

The legal and political dynamic that has weakened the protection afforded to union organization in the face of employer opposition has also undermined the security of the leaders in the remaining unions and made them increasingly vulnerable to challenge from insurgents. Driving these changes is a shift in the balance among competing constitutional principles and social claims. Since the passage of the Wagner Act of 1935, the existence of trade unions and the stability of their organizational structure has been secured at some cost in terms of the rights of both employers and individual workers. At various times, the law forced workers to join unions and/or to pay dues even when they actually opposed the unions' policies, and employers were severely restricted in the actions they could take to oppose union organization, including their right of free speech regarding the expression to their employees of views opposing trade unions.

One could argue that these restrictions had been imposed under the threat of anarchy and revolution in the Depression years of the 1930s and that in the first two postwar decades the courts were by and large willing to accept them under the commerce clause of the Constitution as the price of an orderly system of industrial governance, necessary to social stability and economic progress in advanced capitalism. Beginning in the late 1960s, however, and increasingly in the 1970s and 1980s, these restrictions on individual rights came to be viewed with increasing suspicion and concern by the Courts.[13] Employers' freedom to resist union organization drives and collective bargaining demands were gradually enhanced, and workers' rights to deal with their employer directly were extended. The rights of members to dissent within union organizations were also strengthened and the internal procedures of unions came under increasing scrutiny. The insurgent victory of the Teamsters is the leading example, in fact, of the way the legal evolution is affecting the leadership structure; it is a product of changes in the internal organization of that union and of a shift to direct election of the union president imposed by federal regulatory agencies and the courts.[14]

These changes make the union more responsive to its members, more democratic internally. But they do not enhance the ability of the unions to promote social stability. The limitations on individual rights that have now been lifted served to insulate the older trade unions from their adversaries in management and from internal political dissent. They produced as a result a set of structured institutions directed by experienced leaders, backed by knowledgeable professional staffs, and secure enough in office to commit their organizations to stable, long-term agreements. It was these unions that were so successful in reconciling workers' demands with other social claims and with the requirements of productive efficiency. The organizations that are likely to be successful in the new climate will undoubtedly be a good deal more responsive to the demands of their constituencies and a lot less responsive to the economic constraints that limit the society's capacity to meet them.

Finally, and most important for an understanding of social policy at the current juncture, among the structural changes that have worked to undermine the position of trade unions in American society has been the gradual emergence of strong organizations and group affinities based on sex, sexual preference, racial and ethnic ties, religion, physical handicap, and the like. These new affinities have severely compromised the status of trade unions as representatives of social grievances of any kind. They no doubt reflect long-term social trends: we have progressively stigmatized and ghettoized the aged, the handicapped, the medically ill, the mentally ill, and so on, in separate institutions and corners of society. But these new groups have also been fostered by governmental and business policies designed escape the constraints of existing social structures, particularly unions.

Federal labor policy, for example, has substituted legislative remedies to the particular grievances of all of these groups (the handicapped, the aged, the racial minorities) for collective bargaining, and in the process has encouraged people to define their grievances and to organize in this way. At the same time, private employers have tended to encourage such organization in the workplace as an alternative to unions: Digital Equipment Corporation, for example, which is aggressively anti-union, has within it organizations of women, blacks, and gays, among others. The company advertises its openness and sympathy for these affiliations to the point of a whole corporate page in the program of the Boston Gay Rights parade.

New Social Groups

For the newer non-union groups, it is harder to discern the form their social claims are likely to take because, despite their lobbying efforts for legislative remedies and despite efforts of companies like Digital, they still have only a kind of *de facto* status. Their capacity for sustained organizational existence is unclear.

Pluralist and Corporatist Groups

Perhaps the best way to think about these groups is in terms of the basic individualism of traditional Anglo-Saxon social theory, or what the Europeans call *liberalism*. In that theory, the individual is the basic social unit, and the society is viewed as simply a coalition of individuals. Each individual is both unique and multidimensional, with a variety of interests. Individuals may come together into coalitions to pursue one or another of these interests. But since individuals are so different and have so many separate interests, the groups represent interests rather than individuals. Any particular individual will need to join many different coalitions to be adequately represented, and in each coalition will be allied with a different set of others. Groups exist, in this liberal conception of society and politics, but they are *pluralistic,* not in the sense that there are many groups but in the sense that each individual is associated with many groups and group memberships are only marginally overlapping. A corollary of this way of looking at the world is that an individual's commitment to any particular group is limited. Heavy demands on time and resources are likely to interfere with the pursuit of other interests. The problem of aggregating the claims of different groups and rationing scarce resources is more easily solved in a society of this kind because individuals themselves can readily be made to see that allocation of excessive resources to one of the groups to which they belong will limit the resources available to groups representing their other interests.[15]

The characteristics of the kinds of groups identified above is that they all have the potential for violating the liberal conception of society. Many of an individual's interests are bound up and represented by a single group. Indeed, the number of interests associated with a single group is so large that it defines the person. Because they seem to represent the whole person, such groups are often termed *identity groups*. The group is associated with and tends to represent the individual's lifestyle, to use a term whose current popularity may reflect the fundamental problem of social organization that the country is about to face. Such groups are *corporatist*, rather than pluralist. The same individuals are grouped together repeatedly in one organization after another, and groups competing for resources tend to be mutually exclusive in that the interests of one group's members do not overlap and coincide with those of the members of another.

In recent years there has been a renewed interest among political scientists in this form of social organization, which is now termed *neo-corporatism* to distinguish it from older theories tainted by association with fascism and nazism in the 1930s. In some European countries neo-corporatism is even a part of the political vocabulary and a subject of public debate.[16] But there is a critical difference between the corporatist groups that are potential players in the politics of the coming decade and the groups of corporate and neo-corporate theory. The latter play functional roles in the economy: the structure is modeled on the corporate estates of medieval Europe. The political structures of Franco's Spain and fascist Italy were composed of industrial and professional representatives. And the neo-corporatist debate is largely about the delegation of state power to trade unions who represent the working class and can enter into negotiations with similarly constituted groups of businesses to formulate and ratify national economic policy.

The U.S. labor law as originally written and interpreted by the courts, at least until the middle 1970s, is neo-corporatist in this sense,[17] and the national economic commission envisaged as a way of resolving the political impasse of the budget and trade deficits is prototypical of the neo-corpor-

atist approach in that the groups it draws to the negotiation table are defined by economic roles and functions. It is no accident that the commission was the brain-child of the governor of New York. Apart from the
Greenspan Commission on Social Security, the last effective use of this
approach was in the New York City financial crisis of the mid-1970s, when
the city's banking community collaborated with its municipal unions to
fashion and implement a remedy. That settlement created a quasi-govern-
mental organization that continues to oversee the city's finances even today,
and that gives the old-style corporatism a continuing reality in New York
life.[18] Elsewhere in American life, it is a largely forgotten form.

The New Corporatism

The groups that are now emerging on the political landscape are not corporatist in the old sense. There is no obvious relationship between these
new social groups and the roles their members play in the economy. This,
as we will see, constitutes a real problem because it is the economy that
generates the resources with which the demands of these groups are going
to be met. And because the groupings are defined independently of the
economic structure there is no straightforward way for them or their members to comprehend how economic resources constrain the satisfaction of
their demands.

   Indeed, if one traces the evolution of the social structure out of which
these groups are emerging, the groups can be seen as a product of the
breakdown of the very worlds that corporatist theory sought to capture. In
the medieval world, corporatism (as opposed to pluralism) was a meaningful depiction of the social structure because of an integration of production and consumption within the household, or more precisely, the
extended family. Households were differentiated functionally so that they
played specialized roles in the economic structure (at least if one is prepared
to accept nobles and the clergy as having economically valid functions),
but these functionally differentiated corporate groups were made up not
of individuals but of households. Within the household, consumption and
production were not conceptually distinct.[19]

   One of the basic transformations that took place along the way to
modern times was the separation of consumption and production: pro-

duction moved outside the home and consumption remained an activity associated with the family. This situation is still compatible with a functionally defined corporate political structure so long as the consuming family derives its income from a single, unambiguously defined position within the economic structure. The urban bourgeois family of Victorian novels and television sitcoms, headed by the male breadwinner and managed by the female wife and homemaker, constitutes precisely this construction.[20]

In the nineteenth and early twentieth centuries, that type of family was more of an ideal than a reality for most Americans. But the institutional reforms and innovations that shaped the structure of the labor market in the course of the twentieth century—restrictions on female and child labor, compulsory school attendance, secondary education, the minimum wage, restrictions on industrial work at home, trade unions, and the like—were conceived with this ideal in mind. In the 1930s the New Deal labor market policy was quite consciously intended to reserve jobs for full-time adult male workers.[21] And in the 1950s, when the women who had been drawn into the market by the demands of war production were driven out again by returning male veterans and the New Deal social programs combined with the wages of the newly organized manufacturing workers to provide income security for most adult males, that model became the norm of middle-class American life.[22]

Many of the new groups seem to have grown out of the decline of the family as an integrating social institution. A key aspect of this decline has been a process in which categorically defined financially and/or emotionally burdensome members have been encouraged to leave the household unit and move into living arrangements where they associated with other people categorized like themselves. The process, which began with the aged, the sick, and the handicapped, has been extended to single parents, gays, the blind, the hearing-impaired, and so on.

The rapid rise in female labor force participation rates in the last twenty years has been an additional, perhaps final, blow to the family as the critical integrating social institution. In the Reagan years, the rise in female participation was the consequence—given the pro-family rhetoric of the administration, probably unintended and certainly unforeseen—of Reagan's economic and labor policies. By driving down the wage rates of unionized male workers, these policies forced women to remain in the labor market to supplement household earnings during the critical years of family formation when income demands tend to rise. The increase in participation rates has been particularly dramatic, as already noted, among women with small children. These women are now no longer free to assume full responsibility for child care, let alone to care for the aged and the handicapped. And the economic fate of the family is no longer identified with a single earner who can be represented by one workplace-based union organization. In fact, labor market deregulation under the Reagan administration, from the abolition of restrictions on industrial work in the home to the creation of a subminimum wage for teenagers, worked across the spectrum of New Deal reforms to undermine the dominant-wage-earner model and to create space within the labor market for the multi-earner household.

The disintegration of the old corporatist structure of interest groups, however, does not in itself explain the new corporatist structure that seems to be emerging in contemporary politics. Indeed, one might have expected the breakdown of such cohesive social groupings as the extended and then the nuclear family and of workplace-based trade unions to make way for a new pluralism. This outcome would seem all the more likely given the American attraction to individualistic social theory, from which pluralism derives, as an ideal of how a just and good society ought to function. In certain respects, the thrust of public policy was in this direction: the corporatist framework of U.S. labor law was, as suggested earlier, progressively weakened by court interpretations resting on individualistic and pluralistic social theory.

But here a deep paradox of Anglo-Saxon social thought came into play. While we find it very difficult to think of society as anything more than an aggregation of individuals and reject social theories predicated upon the idea that human beings understand themselves only as part of cohesive social groups, we have an apparently irresistible attraction to the notion of fundamental physical and biological distinctions among human beings. We seem prone to understand social groups, and to justify their recognition in public policy, in biological terms. We tend, moreover, to do this much more often and much more readily than other Western cultures, which are less committed to individualism as an analytical or normative principle. It is as if, lacking a way to understand how the society might generate cohesive social groups but faced with a world in which such groups exist, we are forced to assume that they are somehow inherent in nature.

Nowhere is this tendency more obvious—or in terms of the recent evolution of American society·more important—than in terms of race. Anglo-Saxon culture, or at least its American variant, makes·a sharp distinction between black and white. We see the world as divided into these two fundamentally distinct groups and every individual as falling into one category or the other. This construction stands in sharp contrast to that of Latin countries, which recognize a whole spectrum of different racial characteristics and possess a vast vocabulary for distinguishing subtle variations along it.[23] This does not necessarily mean that U.S. society is any more racially discriminatory than the societies of Latin America, but it does give a distinct character to the structure of our institutions and ideologies. In particular, it led to the sharp dichotomies first between slave and free and subsequently in Jim Crow segregation.[24] It also proved to be the vehicle of black liberation. The civil rights movement essentially took the category of black, which had been the fulcrum of social oppression, and, by organizing around it politically and defining social and economic policy through it, changed its value from negative to positive. This change is suggested by such phrases as Black Power and Black Is Beautiful. In Latin culture, where the people whom we would lump together as a single type are spread out over the whole color spectrum, the notions of black power and black beauty are inconceivable. In this sense, blacks are the first of the new noneconomic corporate groups in American society, and the other groups that emerge out of the breakup of the family, and that have a similar physical or biological core to their definition, have drawn upon the black model.

The parallel is complete in the case of two of these groups: gay men and lesbians. For Americans, homosexuals as a distinct group of people, defined by their sexual orientation, seems to be a natural category. It created the potential for oppression and discrimination. And because these people were well defined, and confined, socially, it led to the development of distinct gay and lesbian cultures. But building, in many cases quite consciously, upon the black model, those categories and the cultures created by the people forced to live within them became the vehicles for gay liberation. Latin cultures make a sharp distinction between the individual and the sexual acts in which he or she engages; a whole spectrum of individual behaviors can thus be socially recognized; gays do not exist; and gay lib-

The Divorce of Economic and Social Structures

Because economic and social structures are dissociated, demands that the social claimants make upon the nation's resources are formulated independently of the nation's capacity to meet them. The constraints upon the ability to meet these demands are not directly perceived or understood by the claimants. There is no reason to expect such groups to generate a leadership that can understand or evaluate the cost to society of the claims they are making. But even if the leaders, through some kind of negotiating process with public policymakers, business leaders, or other groups, came to understand the constraints, they would probably not be able to convince their constituencies to follow them. Indeed, the way these groups are constituted, there is no natural context or vocabulary in the experience of the membership to talk about, let alone evaluate, compromises imposed by resource constraints.

From this perspective, at least, trade unions are clearly the preferable channel for the expression of social grievances. The burden of the social deficit will be easier to the extent that remedies for it can be negotiated in collective bargaining and provided in the workplace.

Clearly this will not be possible with all social demands, but the two principal items on the current social agenda, daycare and medical care, do appear to lend themselves to such solutions. The difficulty is that individual workplaces, and a trade union structure anchored within them, appear to be less and less coherent as social or economic units. They are less coherent economically because they are becoming smaller and more dependent upon outside suppliers, consultants, subcontractors, temporary help services, strategic alliances, and collaboration to perform productive operations once provided by their own employees. Many of these relationships, moreover, have loose institutional boundaries and confused legal status, making them a difficult target for trade union organization and bargaining. They are less coherent socially because both dual-career households and the long-term personnel strategies of major companies imply that work lives will involve considerably more interfirm mobility, and that occupationally and geographically defined labor markets may become increasingly important relative to markets internal to particular enterprises. Were social services tied to the firm, people would have to change daycare and medical arrangements each time they changed jobs.

These considerations suggest that the reintegration of social and economic life requires a detailed examination of the evolution of the economic structure as well as the social one. That problem is examined in Chapter 3. In the short run, however, we are more or less stuck with the social and economic structures (or lack thereof) that we have and the politics of social mobilization toward which they seem to be leading. The next chapter explores the nature of that politics.

2

Politics and Policy

A period of social mobilization would seem, at first blush, to play into the hands of the Democratic Party. It was in the period of Republican rule that the social problems of the country were allowed to accumulate and the new identity groups and their associated grievances emerged on the political scene. The Republicans have resisted the claims these groups have made. They have gone out of their way, moreover, to do so on principle, calling into question the legitimacy of the demands when they could as well have appealed to the budgetary constraints within which they were obliged to operate.

But, at least until the 1992 presidential campaign, the Democrats seemed unable to construct an opposition policy that would enable them to lay undisputed claim to the allegiance of the aggrieved. The party was divided between a self-styled "moderate" wing, represented by the New Democratic Coalition, which wanted to dispute the Republicans for what it conceived of as the broad middle ground of the electorate, and the "traditionalists," who sought to preserve the party's historic commitments to the programs and policies of the past and/or to particular groups and social problems. Neither of these factions managed to articulate a clear alternative to the Republican program. The "moderate" Democrats seemed to define themselves essentially in opposition to others within their own party. They were not clearly differentiated from the Republicans except possibly in terms of honesty and integrity, virtues that speak hardly at all to the issues that

29

would be raised in a period of social mobilization and protest. The traditionalists were in many ways equally unprepared to command the historical moment. They were actually split—or maybe just confused—by commitments to traditional programs on the one hand and traditional constituencies on the other, and they were leery of building the new identity groups into the party's coalition and incorporating their demands, especially when these came into conflict with the claims of older ethnic and union constituencies. The defection of their traditional electorate to Republican candidates, which was in no small measure the product of the party's ineptness in the face of newly conflicting demands, left them hurt and bewildered.

In the face of this division, the Democratic Party seems to have generated its electoral strategy by stitching together the two approaches. It has sought to appeal to the disadvantaged and socially stigmatized groups one by one, finding for each some particular demand that it could endorse without antagonizing the others. But it has also tried to select from the historic repertoire of Democratic programs those, such as medical insurance and social security, which have broad appeal. It has tried to minimize electoral slippage among its traditional adherents through appeal to tradition, and to attract enough Republican middle-ground voters, by appealing to morality, decency, and competence, to constitute a majority.

It has now been doing this for so long that it has lost a clear image of who it is and what it is about—in its own eyes and in the eyes of its electorate. Its image is particularly confused in comparison with that of its adversary, which was completely refurbished and sharply defined by the Reagan presidency and has survived, surprisingly untarnished, the compromises of practices and rhetoric under Bush. What is left of the Democratic Party is clearly enough to win an occasional election, with luck, as Clinton demonstrated in 1992, even a presidential election, just as the Republicans were able to elect Eisenhower despite the hegemony of New Deal liberalism in American politics. But it is doubtful that it is enough to sustain the party in power over the long term. Nor is it likely to be enough to capture the allegiance of the mobilizing grievants and channel them into the regular political process.

What the Democrats fail to recognize, it would seem, is that politics is not always a matter of piecing together a winning coalition out of bits and pieces of the electorate. At certain times it is a battle for hearts and minds. It is about the dominance of contesting, basically contradictory beliefs that

Americans, at some level, all share. These contradictions are enduring themes in American politics. To the extent that party politicians are more than professional vote-getters, to the extent that they are committed to principled philosophical positions, the Democrats and Republicans represent different sides of these contradictory beliefs.

The basic contradiction revolves around the origin of the socioeconomic order and the fate of particular individuals within it. Republican politics in the last decade has played upon the idea that there is a natural order and the individual is basically responsible for his or her own portion. The attempt to improve upon nature through policy and absolve the individual of responsibility for his or her fate, they have argued, will only interfere with nature and reduce the size of the pie that "nature," left alone, would generate. Particular individuals may advance in the process, but the society as a whole will be made worse.

The Democratic position, to which the party has been committed at least since the New Deal, is that there is no such "natural" world. Socioeconomic structures are inevitably the product of policy and can be improved through politics. But the party has been unable to distinguish this position, let alone separate itself, from the particular structures that it created in the 1930s.

These opposing positions actually involve two sets of propositions, one about the responsibility of the individual and another about the mutability of socioeconomic constraints. The relationship between them is, as will become apparent in subsequent chapters, potentially quite complex, and logic allows a variety of intermediate positions. But politics has not been about the resolution of the conflict but rather about an oscillation between the two extremes, and the logical possibilities for an intermediate position have never been developed. Reagan tipped the balance in one direction in the 1980s; social mobilization is part of the process through which the balance is shifting in the other direction, and if the Democrats could only reassert their historic commitments they could recreate a secure electoral base.

The nature of the inner conflicts at play here is epitomized by the way welfare mothers and unionized workers relinquished in the 1980s what they had so aggressively demanded as their just rights in the 1960s and 1970s. But the internal conflicts and the way they are played out are not fully, or even mainly, objective. Governor Ann Richards of Texas spoke to these conflicts in her keynote speech to the 1988 Democratic Convention when she read a letter from a working mother trying to balance her children's need to have her at home with the family's dependence on her income from work. "They say it is your fault," Richards said in her speech, "and that is wrong." This is the schizophrenia in the American electorate: the simultaneous belief that our dilemmas are our own personal failings and would somehow be resolved if we only tried harder, and that these dilemmas are actually socially created and could be relieved by public policy. Republicans have succeeded by playing upon the idea that it is our fault, and the Democrats have failed because they have been unable to convince us that the Republicans were wrong.

At some level this inner conflict, or something like it, characterizes all the aggrieved groups in American society: working mothers who feel guilty about their children; blacks fighting their own belief in their inherent laziness or, worse still, in their biological inferiority; workers fearing that their wages are putting them out of a job; gays struggling against their inner conviction that AIDS is God's retribution for their sins. The anger that these groups express when they do mobilize and demonstrate is directed as much at themselves as at their adversaries. It is an effort to suppress the feeling that it is their own fault, to convince themselves that "that is wrong." But in the 1980s the Democrats were simply unable to commit themselves to a candidate who developed in his campaign the theme that Richards laid out in the convention.

The candidate who has come closest to catalyzing the new constituencies and incorporating them into the electoral process is Jesse Jackson, and his 1988 presidential campaign is a prism through which to view the challenge they pose to conventional politics. Jackson's key asset in the campaign was the sense he had engendered among the aggrieved that he understood and sympathized with their concerns and was committed to their cause. He alone, not only among politicians but among national figures of any kind, had consistently appeared at the events through which these minorities tried to evolve and organize in the face of the oppression of the lean Reagan years. He was the only national politician who had the courage to appear at the Lesbian and Gay march in Washington in October 1987 and to speak out openly before 600,000 people at an event that obtained (albeit somewhat belatedly) national media coverage. His appearance there was dismissed by the political establishment as a thrust for media attention, an interpretation that missed the fact that he had also been the only national politician to travel to Jay, Maine, where, in an obscure town with no national media coverage at all, he spoke to strikers at the International Paper Company. And he had been the only politician to interrupt his campaign to speak to the mechanics at Eastern Airlines when the courts vacated the injunction against Frank Lorenzo's sale of the Eastern shuttle and opened the way for the dissolution of the company and the total elimination of their jobs.

Pundits would probably say that Jackson was the only person who could "claim" to have supported all of the aggrieved groups of the Reagan era, but they would miss the point. When a busy man travels to a place like Jay, Maine, to speak to people who are fighting a lonely and forgotten battle for jobs to which they know they will never return, he does not have to "claim" anything of these people or of their brothers and sisters who read in their union papers and parish newsletters what is not reported by the national media.

But Jackson did more than simply put in time on an unusual political circuit. He also managed to find a language that expressed the feelings and articulated the thoughts and convictions the newly formed constituencies had barely managed to formulate themselves. In this respect, it was no accident that Jackson was a southern black man, for, as we have seen, the ideological structure that creates identities based upon gender and physical handicaps is, at root, the same structure that defines blacks as a separate group. And, in the South, where blacks were an integral, if distinct and subordinated, part of the social structure, they experienced the same desire to be admitted to equal status without giving up the community of separateness from which they derived the dignity, identity, and security that the larger society denied them and which, when fully developed, enabled them to assert their demands in a commanding way. Thus Jackson understands why gays might no longer seek freedom in the privacy of their bedrooms or the deaf seek salvation in hearing aids. Moreover, blacks, because they were the first of the new identity groups to emerge upon the political scene, became the model for the movements that followed, and others have looked to them as the pioneer and exemplar.

Jesse Jackson was the protégé of Martin Luther King and claimed his mantle. But Jackson is not King. The difference between the two political leaders is indicative of how far American politics has come since the 1960s and is the source of many of Jackson's political problems. Emblematic of

that difference is Jackson's reluctance to distance himself from the Muslim
leader Louis Farakhan and the militant black nationalism he preaches. King
made his appeal for blacks on the basis of human rights and individual
liberties. King's imagery was an amalgam of the Old Testament and the
New; he likened blacks to the biblical Jews and the Jews to Jesus, who
through his death created a path to individual salvation. King made the
struggle for black rights the struggle for the rights of each and every human
being.

Jackson seems, in contrast, to be battling for the rights of groups as much
as the rights of individuals. He has been preoccupied by the image, not of
the oppressed Jew, but of organized Jewry. The rainbow coalition he
formed was a coalition of different-colored groups, not different-colored
individuals. In this kind of coalition, it is not inconsistent for the leader to
have special commitments and particular allegiances.

This difference between his view and King's is something that Jackson
has been unable or unwilling to articulate. It is unclear how much of the
difference he himself recognizes or understands. But it is obviously sensed
by the public at large. It is part of his appeal to people who realize themselves as individuals in the context of one of these groups, as Jackson
apparently does himself. But it is also part of what makes him so threatening to those who are still committed to the original American ethos of
autonomous individualism and remain distrustful of group allegiances and
ambivalent about their own group commitments.

Given the problem that Jackson presents, it is not surprising that most
Democratic politicians have tried to distance themselves from him. The
tragedy is that in so doing they distance themselves from an understanding
of the forces in American society that he, and his appeal, represent. The
failure to take the lesson of the Jackson candidacy was most apparent in
the 1988 Democratic Convention. There, Jackson withheld support for
Dukakis in a prolonged set of negotiations over personal recognition, platform concessions, rights to speak on the convention floor, and what airline
equipment and accommodations the party would allot to him in the campaign. With the help of the national press, the party leadership trivialized
these maneuvers, attributing them to Jackson's hurt pride and the wounds
of childhood. Jackson's maneuvers could as well have been understood as
a strategic effort to convert a series of mass movements, relatively inchoate
with little formal organization, for which he served as a symbol and

spokesman, into the kind of alliance of structured groups that could sustain the bargains into which his adversaries in the nominating process were asking him to enter. Having resisted such a sympathetic interpretation of Jackson's dilemma, the Democratic leaders also eschewed the rallies and marches through which they might have learned to understand his constituencies directly and laid their own claims to their support.

Finally, with the nomination of Bill Clinton, the Democrats fielded a candidate who seemed to understand some of these lessons. The rapport Clinton established in the town meetings and voter forums around which he structured his primary campaign had much of the same flavor as the rapport Jackson built with his constituencies, although perhaps without the endorsement of their concerns that Jackson's more selective audiences implied. Clinton called in his acceptance speech at the Democratic Convention for a New Covenant. The terms of that covenant clearly recognized the social grievances of the Reagan-Bush era but demanded that the aggrieved commit themselves in turn to accept greater personal responsibility for their own welfare and that of the country. The proposed covenant represented an attempt to break out of the frame in which the party had cast its 1980 campaigns and define his candidacy in a way that would appeal to the social grievants without making him hostage to them in the eyes of the electorate.

But the campaign as it played itself out after the Democratic Convention never put this new approach to the test. The family values theme around which the Republicans built their national convention, with its strident attacks against working women, abortion rights, and gays and lesbians, drove all of the new identity groups into the Democratic party by default. Even Republican organizations of women and of gays and lesbians endorsed the Democratic candidate. He garnered the support of blacks and of the labor movement in much the same way. The bargain that Clinton offered in the New Covenant was never struck. The strategy after the convention was largely the same strategy—if it can be dignified by that term— that the Democrats had pursued throughout the Reagan years.

Clinton presented himself as a candidate of the "establishment" wing, dedicated to winning back the "middle class." He had in fact been a prominent member of the New Democratic Coalition. He distanced himself from the traditional Democratic constituents, especially from blacks and trade unionists, but carefully so as not to alienate them to the point where they would boycott the election. His speeches and public appearances were skillfully crafted to resonate with the country's concerns about the economy, medical insurance, crime, and the deep conflicts of values occasioned by the shifting social structure—the very issues that underlie the social deficit. But he managed to do this without at the same time offering proposals specific enough to evoke anxieties about his solutions that might undercut the concerns about the problems themselves.

The Democratic victory had much to do with luck: a lackluster economy that fell back into a recession, leaving the incumbent who had expected a robust recovery dogged by renewed economic decline; Bush's persistent refusal to address the electorate's concerns; a third party that cut more heavily into the Republican electorate than into the Democratic constituencies. But the campaign Clinton himself conducted was, from a professional viewpoint at least, "flawless," and in the postmortems on the day after the election drew expressions of admiration and acclaim even from his adversaries.

It was a measure of the mood of American politics, however, that the campaign so admired by the political community was viewed by the electorate in quite a different way. For once, people seemed to see through the hollowness of the rhetoric. They voted without enthusiasm for any candidate. And the new approaches and understandings that Clinton seemed to promise in the convention were left to be tested not in electoral politics but in his capacity to govern the country.

Governance

The problem of governance arises because a period of social mobilization is, by definition, one of extra-electoral politics in which people do not respect the rules and procedures that in normal times define the boundaries of acceptable activity, one in which they engage readily in tactics outside regular electoral politics. Historically, such periods—the labor militancy of the late 1930s, for example, or the black civil rights movement of the 1960s—have been marked by strikes, demonstrations, civil disobedience and, occasionally, riots bordering on rebellion and revolution but without the sustained anarchy and violence that revolution usually entails. In normal times, governance is a question of forming electoral alliances and legislative coalitions, but in periods of social mobilization it becomes one of modulating protest, channeling it toward demands with which the legislature is accustomed to dealing. It is about opening up space within the legislative process for groups that are not among the recognized constituencies and inducing politicians to think about issues they find strange or even repugnant.

The problem is likely to be complicated in the current period by four specific factors. The first, already mentioned, is the divorce between the economic and social structures: because the new social groups are not embedded in the economy, they are not fully cognizant of the constraints the economy imposes on society's ability to meet their demands. This is particularly true of the new identity groups. The difficulty is much less acute within trade unions; but an insecure trade union leadership, challenged in a period of social mobilization by these new identity groups for the allegiance of the aggrieved, and accused by many within union ranks of caving in too readily to employers' pressure in the recent past, may be a lot less willing to remind their membership about how the economy constrains their freedom of action.

The second complicating factor is that the demands being pressed are associated with identity. In normal politics, compromise is felt as an accommodation within the framework of a larger community and is made in the interest of preserving a long-term relationship that might at some future time be renegotiated. But when the issues are attached to identity, they touch upon the very core of people's self-conception. Demands are made as much for their symbolic value as for their practical impact upon daily life. Politics becomes a matter of principle, or even worse, of the integrity of the self, and compromise becomes an externally imposed hypocrisy, a violation, denial, or betrayal of self. Thus, for the women's movement, abortion comes to symbolize women's right to have control over their own bodies, and it becomes difficult to make concessions about age, time since conception, parental consent, and the like without seeming to concede the independence and integrity of a woman as a person. A similar issue arises in terms of public access for the physically handicapped, a demand that involves the physical modification of public accommodations and might lend itself to a wide range of compromises on the basis of cost if it were not perceived as symbolic of the right to citizenship.

In the face of a profusion of ever expanding claims that would overwhelm federal resources even without an inherited budget deficit, the pre-

ferred economic solution would be to transfer what resources are available
to individuals, families, and local communities. The claimants would then
face the resource constraints directly and could pick and choose among
competing demands themselves. The transfer of funds could presumably
be accomplished through direct payments to families and individuals,
through a tax reduction, through federal grants-in-aid to local communities, or through some complex combination of these approaches.

But this solution is also foreclosed by the symbolic importance of the
claims being made. Working women want, and many of them desperately
need, child care and easy access to birth control information and abortion
facilities, but they are also asking for the legitimation of the role in society
that generates these needs. And the federal provision of these services provides legitimacy in a way in which their own private expenditures on the
same services cannot. They want, in other words, Ann Richards's affirma-
tion that it is not their fault if they cannot afford to stay home and take
care of their children. Gays, in the same way, want and need funding for
AIDS education to prevent infection and research to cure the disease. But
they desire at least equally—indeed in some ways even more strongly—
legitimation for the sexual practices that define them as a social group and
absolution from the guilt associated with the disease. And public funding provides those things in a way in which funding through individual
purchases and private contributions, were these a realistic alternative,
would not.

To recognize this is also to suggest the possibility of an alternative
strategy, one that attempts to separate the symbolism from the substantive
claims and attach it to acts that do not absorb economic resources. In
American society the President can provide this kind of purely symbolic
recognition acting alone without congressional sanction. Clinton clearly
grasped this point. Once he assumed office he moved almost immediately
to divert social demands in this way, composing his Cabinet to provide
unprecedented representation for excluded minorities and women, focusing women on abortion rights, some of which he could extend through
executive order, and his gay constituents on the military service, which he
thought, in this case naively, that he could open to them in the same way.

One problem with this strategy is that symbols can come to play real
roles in social processes, although those roles are often hidden and little
understood. This was a considerable part of the problem in the attempt to

open a place for gays in the military. The resistance was undoubtedly based upon fears and prejudices that went beyond any reality. But a number of military leaders also articulated a very explicit theory of the way homophobia served to motivate the troops. The military, they argued, was dependent upon the capacity of men to drive themselves to exceptional feats of performance, and for this it drew upon recruits' needs to prove their own masculinity. It was, in other words, as if all soldiers kept a piece of their inner selves hidden in the closet and presented a masculine front to the world that differed from what they knew themselves to be. With gays in the ranks, competing and possibly outperforming other soldiers, no feat of physical prowess, however extreme, would prove that one was really "masculine," and this motivating drive would be removed.

The other problem with the symbolic strategy was that Clinton was not alone in recognizing its potential. His Republican predecessors had used the powers of the office in much the same way but to opposite effect. Both Reagan and Bush mixed together, and deliberately confused in the public mind, their opposition to the substantive claims that were being made and the budgetary constraints that made these claims difficult to meet. They resisted claims on resources in ways that enhanced rather than diminished their symbolic value, and they asserted the older vision of society in which the members of the aggrieved groups occupied subordinate, pitiful, and/ or outcast positions. They did this most obviously and conspicuously through the politics of abortion rights. Reagan and Bush managed the issue of AIDS funding in much the same way. Bush's offhand response to the news that Magic Johnson had AIDS, "He is a *good* man," with the not so subtle implication that gay men were not, served by itself to raise the stakes in the battle for AIDS funding, and for drug rehabilitation programs as a complement to enforcement, in a way that should have made his budget director blanch.

The ways in which the Republican White House orchestrated the politics of race and equal employment opportunity cannot be simply reduced to these terms. Neither Reagan nor Bush sought to reestablish the old structures of Jim Crow. But in a variety of actions ranging from the Willie Horton ad in the 1988 campaign to the nomination of Clarence Thomas to the Supreme Court, the Republicans sought to enhance the self-esteem and assuage the wounds of those groups who felt threatened by the black drive for upward mobility and social equality. The struggle has now developed to a point where it is very difficult for any president to redefine its terms by himself, independent of other political actors, as Clinton learned on the issues of gay rights, governmental funding of abortion for the poor, and several of his more outspoken and hence symbolically most important appointees.

All of this is the more unfortunate because, even without the deliberate manipulation of social symbols, the clash between the new identity groups and the older social structure provides plenty of room for the kinds of misunderstandings that inadvertently hurt and anger and undermine the government's capacity to control events. This was most painfully and publicly evident in the Senate's treatment of the sexual harassment charges brought by Anita Hill against Clarence Thomas when he was a candidate for the Supreme Court. The Senate leadership, in fact most members of the Senate, saw the issue raised by Hill's charges in procedural terms. They focused first on the impossibility of judging what ultimately reduced to the word of one person against the word of another and then on the question of how and why regulations had been violated and the charges leaked to the press. But for women, or at least a large and vocal segment of the female population, the issue was the willingness of the society to recognize their integrity and come to grips with the ways it was compromised by the power men were able to exercise over them through sexual harassment in the office. The fact that the exclusively male senators of the committee ignored the issue of sexual harassment in favor of rules and procedures seemed only to strengthen the determination of the women to confront the substantive issue. That some of Anita Hill's most aggressive questioners subsequently stood up and condemned sexual harassment served to inflame the situation still further, compounding, in the eyes of the women, male chauvinism with hypocrisy. Had the charges been handled somewhat differently, the issue might indeed have been sexual harassment, but in the end this was not the issue for either side. For the senators it was the issue of rules and procedures. For the women it became the integrity of self.[1]

An even more dramatic example of the potential for confusion and misunderstanding was the confrontation over the presidency of Gallaudet, the federal college for the deaf. On the surface, the issue in the controversy was relatively straightforward. Gallaudet is an institution of higher learning for the hearing impaired chartered and financed by the federal government in Washington, D.C., and governed by a board that, while nominally appointed by Congress and the President, is in fact self-perpetuating. The board had only three hearing-impaired members; its chair was not deaf and did not even know sign language. The president of Gallaudet, who also was not deaf, retired, and the board selected as a replacement another non-deaf candidate with no previous experience in deaf education, who also was unable to sign. A student, and eventually faculty, protest developed: the protesters demanded the appointment of a deaf president. The protest received national attention; it was followed daily by television news and received front-page newspaper coverage throughout the country. It attracted almost immediate and virtually universal support from the editorial writers, political figures, and apparently the general public. The chair of the board and the newly appointed president tried to defend themselves but received no sympathy from any quarter. Within two weeks they had both resigned, and a deaf president was appointed to head the university.

But what exactly was the Gallaudet controversy about? What did the appointment of a deaf president represent? How could a situation that was universally repudiated once it was recognized have arisen in the first place and continued for so long? How did the board come to take and then defend a series of actions that found absolutely no sympathy in any corner of American society? What exactly was demanded at Gallaudet, and what conceded?

The chair of the board of directors maintained that the primary function of the college president was to raise money to finance the institution. The ability to communicate internally with the students and faculty, she argued, was thus much less important than the ability to speak with outside funding sources. In terms of the role of college presidents in general, she was certainly correct. And there is every reason to believe that the students and faculty at Gallaudet heard and understood her argument. The unspoken implication was that the hearing impaired could not communicate well with the outside world and were not well qualified for the presidency. In these terms, the confrontation was really about the nature of the relationship between the hearing impaired and the larger society. It was about whether the deaf were obliged to find ways of relating to the outside world on its terms or whether the larger society was obligated to find ways of relating to the deaf in the terms in which the latter lived and functioned in their daily lives. Understood in this way, the confrontation redefined the whole relationship, not only between the deaf and the hearing worlds, but between the society at large and all of the enclaves defined by social and physical disabilities.

Because the sympathy for the students' demands was so complete, it is hard to see exactly how the issues were defined by the majority of the country. But it seems doubtful that most people saw the episode as one in which the hearing world accepted the responsibility to make the adjustments required to communicate with deaf people on their own terms. And it seems even more doubtful that they saw it as one in which the society agreed to create a physical environment in which the blind and the crippled would feel as at ease in public as in their own institutionalized settings. They would almost certainly have resisted extending the principle still further to free black teenagers to behave in the White House as they do on the streets of Harlem or gays and lesbians to walk on Main Street the way they do on Castro in San Francisco. Indeed, the question of what adjustments to truly accommodate the deaf as full citizens in everyday life would imply, in terms of the cost of redesigning public facilities and social and educational processes, was never considered.

It seems more likely that the editorial writers and journalists thought they were reporting a confrontation about job discrimination or, because of the symbolic importance of the particular job involved, about self-government and bureaucracy. Defined in these terms, the concessions of principle made by the larger society were at most concessions about how the enclaves of stigmatized peoples were to be allowed to function internally. The reason the students and faculty failed to see it in these terms is not simply, as the chair of the board so cogently argued, that that is not the role of a college president. The protesters failed to see it in this way because they understood—as do the members of all these communities—that true internal independence is simply not possible so long as they are obliged to exist in, and are ultimately dependent upon, a larger society that defines the interactions with the enclaves in terms of its own tastes and convenience. For the deaf, therefore, even a concession about civil rights and democracy implied a shift in the mode of accommodation in the broadest sense.

The critical point, however, is not whose interpretation was right or wrong in this confrontation. It seems difficult to deny the ultimate humanitarian validity of the claims of the students and faculty once the social structure comes to be defined in this way. But it seems absurd to accept these claims without thinking through the implications for the reorganization of the physical and social environment and envisaging the process through which such a reorganization ought to be carried out. The real issue posed by the confrontation is the political implications of the radically different and inherently incompatible interpretations and their potential for creating disarray in a period of general social mobilization.

The potential for disarray is present first and foremost in the fact that the events at Gallaudet demonstrated the effectiveness of direct confrontation. It produced immediate attention, universal sympathy, and total victory. But it worked too well. Its success encouraged a political approach that almost by its very nature cannot be effective if it becomes routine, an approach that, moreover, provides scope for an emotional acting out (to use a term that one organization devoted to civil disobedience actually adopted as its name), for an expression of anger, unrestrained by tactical considerations, that is as likely to harden the opposition as it is to produce concessions. In this particular case, moreover, it encouraged this mode of confrontation while at the same time creating expectations that will eventually compound the hurt and anger generated by a lifetime of social stigma with a feeling of betrayal when the deaf try to collect on the promises they thought were made at Gallaudet about their position in society at large. When this happens, it is likely to justify in the minds of the deaf even more extreme political acts at the very moment when the society at large is becoming increasingly intolerant of the acts in which they have already engaged.

Just how great the gap in understanding can be is well illustrated by an article that appeared in the *New Republic* shortly after the Gallaudet settlement. The author crafts an elaborate argument about the difference between the deaf and ethnic and racial minorities, and then quotes one of the student leaders at Gallaudet to show how militant and absurd they have become: "If I had a bulldozer and a gun, I would destroy all scientific experiments to cure deafness. If I could hear, I would probably take a pencil and poke myself to be deaf again."[2]

The *New Republic* missed the point.[3] The deaf are exactly like blacks. Perhaps not what blacks were, but certainly what they have become. We have created a social structure in which an individual's entire identity comes to be bound up with a single physical characteristic. Any attempt to alter that characteristic then becomes a threat to the individual: it operates at once to stigmatize and to threaten his or her individuality as a human being. Curing deafness is like straightening black hair.

This makes the deaf a cohesive social group. And it makes for a politics that is less and less about control over economic resources and more and more about their symbolic content, a contest over interpretation in which economic resources are increasingly about the meaning they confer upon the victors. In the longer run we may be able to reintegrate the social and the economic structures in a way that will make them more manageable politically. To do this, we will have to move beyond an individualistic conception not only of social activity but of economic activity itself. That is the subject of subsequent chapters. But in the meantime we are stuck with these new categories.

Public Policy

Even if "normal" politics prevails and we manage to delay indefinitely the kind of social mobilization that characterized the 1930s and the 1960s, the newly emerging corporate groups are likely to create increasing confusion in law and social policy. Indeed, they have already begun to do so. The effects are most prominent in educational policy, but their impact is also apparent in at least two other major areas of public policy: medical insurance and equal employment opportunity.

Education

Here, the force of the new identity groups and the politics of social stigmatization have crystallized in the debate about multicultural scholarship and education. In a sense this is the culmination of a campaign against what these groups perceive as the dominance of the white, Anglo-Saxon perspective in the academy. What began as a movement to legitimize first black and women's studies and then scholarship associated with virtually every stigmatized minority grew into an attack on the conventional curriculum itself, first at the college level and subsequently at all levels of education. Pushed to the extreme, it seems to call into question the very notion of objective scholarship and universal education, to argue that what is taught in the schools ought to be tailored to the backgrounds of the students. As applied to pedagogical technique, this is hardly a controversial proposition, but the focus of the new, multicultural movement is not on technique. It is on the *content* of education itself.

In this extreme version, the "multicultural" education movement is ultimately an attack on the Lockean view of knowledge that lies at the core of American individualism. It challenges the very notion of an objective reality, separate and distinct from the observer and assessable through systematic inquiry. But it is almost inevitable given that the new identity groups see their struggle as about the interpretation of the social categories with which they are associated. Liberation has become an effort to gain control over and give new meaning to the terms that define them as a group, to make black beautiful or gay proud.

The perspective out of which this view emerged is easiest to understand, and least challenging to notions of scientific objectivity, in the field of history. Here, in the form of the "new social history," it has probably exerted its greatest influence on the discipline as a whole. In this field, too, it can be understood as an attack upon the integrity of conventional scholarship in terms of its own canons of objectivity rather than as calling into question the notion of objectivity itself. The historian's view has been eloquently articulated by Joan Nestle, curator of the Lesbian Herstory Archives, in an introduction to a collection of her writings:

> History, like so many other things, has been redefined in the past two decades. More and more we are learning to listen to the individual and collective voices of the people who were once seen only as the victims of history, or as the backdrop for the drama of the rich, the powerful, the heads and tails of state. Like pointed trees in robust operas, the baker and the housewife, the whore and the clerk just stood there while Kings and Queens sang their dreams and dirges around them. Now we have grassroots history projects documenting a vast range of human life . . .
>
> "I am glad the time has come when the—lions write history—" Wendell Phillips wrote to Frederick Douglass in 1845. "We have been left long enough to gather the character of slavery from the evidence of the masters." The Lesbian Herstory Archives is all about lions writing history. It is about a people's refusal to live within the dirty jokes and folklore pathology of a controlling society. To deprive a people of their history, or to construct one for them that immortalizes humiliation, is a conscious cultural act of the powerful.[4]

Joan Nestle is Jewish, and in her emphasis on history as a story that gives meaning to a people she echoes a theme central in the literature about the

Holocaust and especially prominent in the stories of Elie Wiesel, who writes to give meaning to the Holocaust experience and to build a Jewish identity that will sustain resistance and survival.[5] But her themes are, of course, most prominent in the black history movement, to which Nestle alludes when she quotes Wendell Phillips.

Although the themes about the politics of scholarship seem least challenging to conventional notions in history and the social sciences, they are in no sense confined to these disciplines. Because so many of the new social groups are defined by their physical and biological characteristics, the movement inevitably extends to the exact sciences as well. It is reflected in the debate about the legitimacy of research and teaching about genetic differences in I.Q., or even, as the deaf student in the Gallaudet confrontation made so clear, of medical research about the causes and cure of any number of physical and mental conditions. It brings back to the fore, from an unexpected quarter of the political spectrum, the issues once thought laid to rest in 1925 by the Scopes trial on the teaching of the theory of evolution in the Tennessee public schools.

In some sense these debates in American education never went away. They are raised not only by Darwinian theory but equally by the question of bilingual education, also a much older theme in American education than is generally believed (the bilingual movement originated among Germans in the Midwest in the late nineteenth century and continued there until it was abandoned in the First World War out of fear of the doubts it might cast upon the national loyalties of ethnic Germans).[6] The basic themes of current debate have been prominent in discussions about minority education among professional educators at least since the late 1960s. But the debate really came to the attention of the general public and began to be played out in the popular press only with the reform of the core curriculum at Stanford University in 1989. The 1991 report of the Social Studies Syllabus Review Committee in New York State has now extended the public debate into secondary and primary education and, in proposing reforms within the *public* school system, has brought it into the political arena.

At one level the text of the Review Committee report is uncontroversial. It seeks, in the approving words of one of its most articulate critics, "to diversify the syllabus in order to meet the needs of a more diversified society";[7] to recognize the enlarged perspective created by the civil rights movement of the 1960s and the new non-European immigration of the 1970s and 1980s; to encourage, in the report's own words, "a more tolerant, inclusive and realistic vision of American identity than any that has existed in the past." The specific reforms range from the fundamental (Columbus did not "discover" America; he revealed to Europeans the existence of a continent already populated by native groups to whom his "find" was hardly a discovery and ultimately proved a disaster; Africans found out about America in still another way) to what will seem to most readers the essentially trivial (Africans were not "slaves" in the American South; they were an "enslaved people").

At another level, however, the traditional curriculum can be seen as an attempt to impart to all students a single, common culture, and from this perspective the report disputes both the approach to education and the culture itself. Viewed in this way, its argument is that "the main objective of public education should be the protection, strengthening, celebration and perpetuation of ethnic origins and identities"; that "previous ideals of assimilation" should be put aside and the curriculum should highlight instead "the racial and ethnic pluralism of the nation." This second message may be less a product of the report than of the debate it has engendered. Even the critics have admitted that it is more a question of emphasis than of specific words and phrases, that it is "assumed rather than argued." But by reading it in this way, the critics have used the report to catalyze a national debate.[8]

Pushed to the background in that debate is the question of historical fact itself. Indeed it is unclear whether *real* history is relevant at all. Schlesinger suggests that, for his adversaries at least, it is not: "Am I wrong in sensing a certain artificiality and inauthenticity in all this? If the ethnic subcultures had genuine vitality, they would be sufficiently instilled in children by family, church and community." The prominent role that the new politics of identity gives to history in both oppression and liberation would certainly justify improvisation and invention. But the opponents of cultural pluralism see history in equally instrumental terms. The role of the curriculum is to maintain national unity; the single (and Eurocentric) interpretation of history creates the nation. And in its defense they freely invoke the image of the balkanization of American society or the disintegration of the Soviet empire (which in other contexts they applaud). For Schlesinger, the problem is that the report "reverses the historic *theory* of America" (emphasis added), not the historic facts. And another critic, Kenneth Jackson, in his dissent, asserts that a "viable nation has to have a common culture to survive in peace."[9]

These debates are troublesome in and of themselves, but they are especially difficult to address because lurking behind them is the central question of American educational policy in this century, the integration of the public schools. They come at a time when the goal of school integration is increasingly under attack, not only from the right, which is suspected of trying to perpetuate a white supremacist social order, but in the minority communities themselves, disillusioned by the costs that they have incurred in the pursuit of this goal and by the results it has achieved in terms of the educational attainment and social advancement of their children. The original 1954 integration decision of the Supreme Court rested in large measure on scholarly research that indicated that black students performed better in integrated schools, a conclusion that has been called into question by subsequent findings, some of which suggest just the opposite.[10] The costs of the integration process—a process that seems never to come to an end— in hostility and harassment faced by young black children are increasingly recognized in black writing.[11] And "own" institutions—women's colleges, traditionally black colleges and universities, Gallaudet for the deaf, Jewish yeshivas, and Catholic and Protestant parochial schools—have experienced a resurgence of popularity and are increasingly valued for the opportunity they offer for minority self-government and independence that cannot be obtained within an integrated public school system.

The implications of the movement for multicultural education, or for segregation for that matter, are quite ambiguous. The movement can be read not so much as an attempt on the part of the identity groups to control their understanding of themselves as an effort to change the way they are understood by others in the larger society. The latter objective would be best accomplished in a unified school system, not in a segregated system with the potential for each school to choose its own syllabus. But the view of education emerging in the multicultural debate certainly does make segregated schools a very different proposition from what they were in *Brown v. Board of Education*. And in any number of ways a good deal more attractive even for the advocates of *unum*, as the opponents of the New York Review Committee's report have styled themselves. Kenneth Jackson's notion of nation building is undoubtedly simplistic, but if the politics of identity groups were allowed to play itself out within an integrated system, some issues of interpretation would have to be resolved to preserve a semblance of national unity. One cannot imagine Jews accepting as fact that their ancestors were not slaves in Egypt, as one black-oriented text book has asserted, or that people who see themselves as victims of the Holocaust in Europe and slavery in America will accept Arthur Schlesinger's dictum that "Europe is the unique source of [democratic] ideals."[12] Thus, whatever its intent, the debate clearly forces us to abandon the framework in which we resolved the issues of educational policy in the past.

These debates concerning public education are particularly difficult for Americans because the public school system is a communal institution. It is supposed to bind the society together into a coherent whole. Integration has been urged in terms of the values of nation building. And opposition to it has crystallized around more local notions of community, first in the form of the neighborhood school and now in terms of the identity groups. Nobody is arguing that compulsory education or public schools should be abandoned. The closest thing to a proposal that can be understood according to the classic liberal notion of society as an aggregation of individuals is the idea of some kind of voucher system that would give individual families a "freedom of choice" among competing schools. But this proposal has actually attracted surprisingly few adherents. In many ways, moreover, it fails to address the debate about the *content* of education; virtually all proposals envisage a certification procedure that would imply public regulation of the content of the curriculum. The newest and, in terms of the politics of identity groups, most significant issue in education is thus not addressed by freedom of choice at all.

The deep paradox of American education policy is that as a nation we are committed to public education as an expression of identity and community but we subscribe to an individualistic social theory in which that commitment has no meaning. Faced with a conflict about what that commitment implies and how it is to be fulfilled, we are once again without an apparatus with which to think it through.

Medical Insurance

After education, medical care is probably the most politically sensitive area of public policy, and in recent years concern has reached crisis proportions.

Medical expenses have risen progressively over the last three decades; in the late 1980s and early 1990s the cost of medical care was rising at close to twice the overall rate of inflation; real medical expenditures have been rising as well, so that the medical care sector absorbs a progressively larger share of the nation's income. The reasons for this are not well understood. It no doubt reflects in part the complex institutional structure of the industry, the byzantine financial structure in which fiscal responsibility and control are widely diffused, and the peculiar place of health in the national psyche. Were American society suddenly homogenized and the complexity of identity politics by some miracle made to disappear, we would still face a crisis in the medical care sector.

But medical care is also a prism through which the contradictions in contemporary social and economic policy have come to be refracted. And it reveals clearly the underlying challenge to our traditional modes of thought posed by the new identity groups in the current economic and budgetary crises. The key to the way broader issues of public policy come to be reflected in medical care is the medical insurance system. That system has two major components: Medicare, the public system through which the federal government provides medical insurance to the elderly; and a private system in which most of the remainder of the population obtains medical insurance directly or indirectly through employment. A substantial portion of the population, however, is excluded from both of these insurance systems. These people, the medically indigent, obtain care largely at public expense. Some of that expense is absorbed directly through federal government programs and appears explicitly in the federal budget, but the cost of care for most of the uninsured is hidden. They are treated by private providers who then inflate the rates paid by insured patients to cover the expense.

As the costs of medical care have risen progressively in recent years, the insurers have sought to limit their liabilities, and, because the system is interconnected in this complex way, these efforts tend to transfer charges around rather than actually reduce expenditures. Both the public and the private insurers are guilty in this regard. In the public sector, the size of the Medicare program makes it an attractive target for policymakers attempting to control the federal budget, quite independently of any increase in the cost of the program itself. And private insurance payments are a target of employers seeking to cut labor costs in the face of international competition, separately from the fact that insurance costs have been rising at a disproportionately rapid rate.

The public Medicare program is directed at the aged, who, as already noted, constitute the first and, politically at least, the most cohesive and powerful of the groups to emerge in the breakdown of the dominant-earner model of the family. The continued degeneration of that model through increasing labor force participation has created a deficit of custodial care for the aged, an unknown but possibly large portion of which has been transferred to Medicare. In the budgetary politics of the last decade, the aged have managed to place a lock on the programs especially directed toward them, and, hence, despite the very large portion of the total budget absorbed by social security and Medicare, *benefits* have been protected from the pressures to control government expenditures. Policymakers have reacted to the lock on benefits by seeking to control instead the *cost* of specific services, limiting payments to providers. Providers have in turn reacted by raising charges to other customers. The burden of the federal deficit is in this way transferred to other parts of the medical care system and, in particular, to private employers who provide insurance for the non-aged population.[13]

This private, employer-based insurance is also built around the dominant-earner model: primary wage earners obtain coverage for themselves and their families through their places of employment. Primary wage earners tend to work in relatively high-wage industries. In low-wage industries, insurance coverage is much less common. But since these industries disproportionately employ secondary earners, many of their employees obtain medical insurance indirectly through other family members. The net effect of the private system is thus that high-wage industries subsidize low-wage industries. That effect too has been enhanced in the past decade by the increase in female labor force participation. The effect is, of course, further exaggerated by the tendency for providers to inflate the rates charged to the insured to cover the cost of care for the medically indigent, who also are disproportionately employed in low-wage industries.

In virtually every other industrial country in the world, medical costs are socialized. One could say that our system effectively socializes costs too. But the fact that we do so in this indirect and surreptitious way means that the labor costs of our high-wage industries are inflated relative to those of our principal industrial competitors. The automobile industry estimates that medical insurance adds $500 to the cost of producing a car in Detroit relative to Windsor, Ontario, across the river in Canada.[14] The other side of the coin is that production costs in low-wage industries are low in the United States relative to other industrial countries. Unfortunately, in these industries we tend to compete with the developing world, whose cost advantage is already so great that subsidies to medical care provide little competitive thrust.

In the face of competitive pressures in world markets and rising costs and growing demands for medical care, those private employers who do provide insurance are making a variety of efforts to redefine their responsibilities and limit their exposure. These efforts, recently catalogued in the *New York Times,* are remarkable, first, in the very wide diversity of approaches and in the contradictions among them, but also in the way they reflect the fault lines in the emerging socioeconomic structure.[15]

One approach is to tie coverage to a specified group of doctors and facilities so as to capture economies of scale. The logic here is to maximize the client base, which would seem to imply more extensive family coverage, but it flies in the face of the demise of the dominant-earner family. The completely opposite approach, which is also being tried, is to individualize insurance. This is leading a number of companies to restrict coverage to the individual employee, and/or to impose additional charges for workers who elect family coverage. This is consistent with the disappearance of the dominant-earner family. But individualization is a limited solution if in fact the society ends by picking up the tab for care of the medically indigent and loading the cost onto the newly individualized rates.

Individualization is also inconsistent with the very notion of insurance. This is apparent in another cost-cutting trend that grows out of this approach, one that according to the *New York Times* is becoming even more pervasive: the redefinition of insurance categories by various markers of health risks and the imposition of a separate rate for each category. An employer no longer pays a standard rate for each worker but instead is charged—and presumably passes on to the worker—differently depending on the worker's age and any other characteristic that can be shown to affect health. The problem is that insurance is basically an effort to escape individuality; it only works by treating the individual as a member of a group in terms of which he or she can diversify personal risk. But almost any group that is not arbitrary in either a physical or a social sense is bound to have distinct medical risks. And this is certainly true in a society where so many of the key groups are coming to be defined by biological traits.

Thus this approach must inevitably lead to different insurance premiums for women and men, for blacks and whites, for gays and straights, indeed, ultimately for each and every ethnic group identified in the Immigration Commission's *Dictionary of Races*. And we will be forced to face directly the question of whether these definitions are equitable or desirable, and if they are not, how exactly we expect employers to handle the rising costs of medical care. The problem we are encountering becomes obvious when one raises the question of whether blacks constitute a legitimate risk group, especially if they have higher medical expenses than whites. Given the way in which we have tried to deal with racial discrimination, this is a question that will find its way to the Supreme Court. It is hard to see how we can allow experience rating in medical insurance based on race if we will not allow racial segregation in the public schools. But if not race, why sex, sexual orientation, hearing impairment, physical handicap? And if employers cannot control medical costs in this way, how can those costs be limited?

Employment Policy

A third area of public policy that has been complicated and confused by the emergence of the new identity groups is equal employment opportunity. The history of this endeavor stretches back into the 1930s, when the Roosevelt administration issued the first executive order mandating "fair employment practices" within the federal government and among government contractors in the private sector. Similar orders were issued in every subsequent administration. The policy was finally codified in the Civil Rights Act of 1964. Title VI of that Act forbade the use of federal funds to finance organizations, governmental or private, that engaged in racially discriminatory practices. Title VII established an administrative agency to protect equal opportunity in the private sector and created a judicial remedy for employment discrimination.

Until 1964, however, the national commitment to equal employment opportunity was almost entirely rhetorical. Title VII of the Civil Rights Act as originally conceived was essentially symbolic as well. It sailed through Congress without discussion or debate; there is virtually no legislative history. The Title was written by the AFL-CIO, and the labor lobbyists who later came to oppose and resent many of the specific policies with which it became associated were largely responsible for its passage. The black organizations that were influential in the later evolution of employment policy were preoccupied at the time with school segregation and public accommodations. The women's organizations, which became the other pillar of support for equal employment opportunity, were for the most part nonexistent. The original policy was not conceived in terms of the tight budgetary constraints under which the Clinton administration is currently operating, but if anybody had been looking for the kind of symbolic gesture with minimal real impact upon government activity or the operation of the economy around which Clinton has sought to build his social policy, Title VII would certainly have been high on their list.

Once it was seriously pursued, however, the logic of equal employment led both administrative agencies and the federal courts to review an expanding list of employment practices. The control they imposed over those practices became progressively more invasive as well. The policy now limits permissible hiring criteria, educational requirements, and testing, aspects of the employment relationship over which the employer previously exercised unilateral control. It also places limits on job allocation, promotion decisions, wage determination, and employee grievances, which had previously been governed by collective bargaining arrangements but had not been subject to review by government. Those arrangements were protected by federal labor legislation but the courts had scrupulously refrained from review of their substantive content. At the same time, the number and kinds of people protected either by amendment to the original legislation or by supplementary legislation modeled upon the original law have also expanded. The criteria for protection now include, in addition to race and sex, physical handicap, and, in some state and municipal legislation, sexual orientation. The administration of the law has become hopelessly entangled in the question of targets and quotas.[16]

In contrast to education and health, the problem in employment is not the pursuit of communal goals in a society pervaded by an individualistic ethos. The goal of equal employment policy is preeminently individualistic: it is the distribution of jobs and work rewards on the basis of the personal merit of each employee. The problem is that, contrary to expectations, the labor market does not work even approximately in this way. The law was designed to sanction exceptional departures from meritocracy. But the administrators discovered that they were operating in a system where jobs were distributed and wages determined, regularly and systematically, not on the basis of individual characteristics but on the basis of group affiliations. Employers turned out to know virtually nothing about the causal relationships between job performance and even apparently objective criteria like test scores or educational credentials, and proved incapable of defending such selection criteria when they turned out to discriminate against particular groups in the labor force.

Our problem in sorting through these issues is that we began the process with no clear understanding of the nature of the private employment relationship. To the extent that there has been a clear model, it is the economists' model of the private business firm. That model assumes that the firm maximizes profits, and that its employment decisions are made on the basis of the worker's contribution to this goal. That contribution is in turn generally assumed to be related to individual characteristics, basically natural endowments (physical prowess, native intelligence), skill and knowledge acquired through some kind of replicable process (education, on-the-job training), and personal effort and commitment.[17]

There are any number of reasons why the assumptions in the economists' model may not be realized in practice: firms may not actually maximize profits; law or social custom may mandate discrimination, foreclosing certain profit-maximizing strategies; work may be a group process in which individual merit is much less important than whether the individual fits with and is accepted by co-workers; individual traits, either natural or acquired, may be highly correlated with group membership and either difficult to access directly or not directly observable at all; employers may be prejudiced and believe any of these things to be the case although they are not; one or more of these factors may enter into decisions in other parts of the social system that feed into employment—in the schools, for example, or in the choice of technology (and if they do, their effects may be easily remedied by the employer through, for example, on-the-job training, adding a ladies' room, or adjusting a seat, or they may be irremediable). The effort to work through these factors and sort them out in administrative and judicial practice and through academic research suggests that each of them is at work in one or another part of the system, but that when and where a particular one will be important is difficult to predict.

The economists' model could be dismissed as merely one particularly abstract and academic way of thinking about the problem were it not for the fact that it has actually served as a framework through which employment policy is formulated and disputes adjudicated. It also embodies a set of assumptions, not all of them clearly explicit, reflecting a way of thinking about social policy that is very widespread—I am tempted to say universal—in American society, a way of thinking that I have alluded to before and will return to in subsequent chapters. These include the ideas that the individual is a meaningful unit of analysis and the group, per se, either is not or should not be; that one can separate reality from the perception of reality; that the natural world as expressed in innate characteristics or basic technology is distinct from the social world in which skills are acquired and basic technology is brought into production and the work it entails assigned. All of these assumptions are called into question by the role the stigmatized groups are coming to play within the social structure. It is not clear that we would be led to question these assumptions by employment policy alone, without the broader challenges that such groups present. Nor is it clear that the assumptions can be worked through and revised in the context of employment policy in isolation, without reference to the other issues raised in this book.

In any case, rather than examine the fundamentals of the economic model upon which the goal of equal employment opportunity is predicated, we have tried to force practice to fit the model. The courts and administrative agencies have judged practices by the results they achieve and, when the results are biased against the stigmatized groups, have demanded that employers show that their actions are grounded in meritocratic practices. Given the new presumptions, managers find that they can avoid administrative and judicial scrutiny simply by insuring that they have a sufficient number of previously excluded groups on their payroll. This has encouraged, if not actually forced, businesses to make employment decisions that *favor* members of these groups and disfavor other applicants, generating as it were reverse discrimination.

These developments in employment policy have created a backlash among people who are not members of the newly favored groups. Even some of those who have benefited from the policies resent the fact that such employment practices deny them the opportunity to prove their worth as individuals.[18] But the policies have also reinforced the new group structures. Before 1964, employment disputes were resolved through collective bargaining and trade unions were the only officially recognized form of group representation. Legislated labor standards existed, but they were an extension of the system of collective bargaining. Trade unions were the key actors in the politics that governed the evolution of such standards, and the standards expanded, when they expanded at all, only in response to union pressure. Title VII created a second mechanism for the pursuit of employment rights, one responsive to a different set of group affiliations. Legislated standards became an independent factor in the evolution of employment standards. Title VII itself became a model for addressing the employment grievances not simply of blacks and women but of all the socially stigmatized and underprivileged. And as this model was developed and expanded, it further encouraged people who understood themselves in terms of social stigmas to organize politically and seek political remedies not only at work but in other areas of social and economic life as well.

In employment policy itself, these developments are in some measure responsible for the sense of chaos that surrounds the distribution of wages and employment opportunities. The emergence of this second system of employment rights has diverted people who might otherwise have sought to organize unions and has encouraged them to seek legislation instead, thus weakening the labor movement and making it vulnerable to the attacks that Reagan, through his treatment of the air traffic controllers, encouraged. And the remedies imposed under the civil rights legislation have added to the distortions of accustomed wage relationships that the Reagan-Bush economic and social policies initially introduced. The standards associated with civil rights legislation would immensely complicate the task of making economic policy if trade unions were again to become an important vehicle for social mobilization and if their efforts to represent social grievances were to generate wage-wage inflation. They will be especially important if trade unions and the new identity groups mobilize simultaneously and compete for the allegiance of aggrieved individuals, each adversary trying to assert its own distinct set of wage standards.

Conclusion

We have seen that the social deficit is really a marker of deeper and more fundamental deficiencies: deficiencies in our structures of group representation; a growing disjuncture between our economic and social structures; and the declining capacity of our conventional party politics to aggregate interests and mediate among conflicting claims. The claims associated with the social deficit, as we saw in Chapter 1, might be represented in the political process by two very different social movements, the labor movement and the new groups of those who have been socially stigmatized.

Unlike the labor movement, the new identity groups have no recognized institutional existence, and one has to imagine the process through which their claims might be resolved. That exercise underscores the disjuncture between the social structure in terms of which we understand and experience our personal lives and the economic structure that provides the resources that sustain us as we do so. In contrast to the labor movement, the new social groups have so little to do with the structure of the economy that it is difficult to see how they would ever be led to respect the economy's constraints when formulating their demands or to accept the compromises necessary to reconcile competing claims for economic resources.

The claims of these groups might conceivably be channeled through the electoral process, but here the limits of conventional party politics come into play. The Republican Party has articulated and embraced a version of individualism that denies the legitimacy of cohesive social groups, let alone the claims they are making on the society. It has opposed the policies and programs that the newer groups have sought to use to change their social status, and it has used the symbolic power of the Presidency to reinforce traditional roles and social stigmas. The Democratic Party has historically articulated a philosophy that recognizes the political origins of social structure and appeals to group identities, but it has been paralyzed by its commitments to the particular programs and the particular groups with which it has traditionally been identified, and it has proved unable to reformulate its policies and programs to fit the new social reality.

Understood in these terms, the relationship between the political and the social structures is only half of the deficit problem. The other half is the economy. The economy not only generates the resources with which the social demands, however they are articulated, must be met; its social architecture also determines the degree to which the constraints imposed by those resources are likely to be recognized and respected in the political process. The next chapter, therefore, turns to an examination of the economy and the policies that have governed its evolution.

The examination of specific policy issues at the end of this chapter, however, leads one to wonder whether the problem is after all one of material resources. Additional resources would not change the challenges the new social groups create in education and employment policy and would certainly not resolve them. With additional resources, the structure of medical insurance could be altered so as to alleviate the problems that social groups now pose in that domain, but the issues of social groups might simply crop up in a different guise under the new structure. The underlying problem in all three of these areas is that we are prisoners of the individualistic framework through which we are accustomed to consider social policy and lack an intellectual apparatus with which to sort out the roles played by such groups.

Once the problem is stated in these terms, it becomes apparent that the political impasse is in large measure also a product of the way we are accustomed to think about society. The Republican Party's success in generating a coherent political program and maintaining it even in the face of mounting social difficulties derives from the way it draws on the individualistic framework that is so widely shared. The inability of the Democratic Party to separate itself from its historical commitments reflects the lack of an alternative representation of society, a model in which its past commitments might be seen as particular applications and which could be applied to generate new programs more appropriate to the current historical moment. I shall argue that a good part of our problems in economic policy can also be traced to the deficiencies of that intellectual framework.

3

Economic Constraints and Social Demands

How should we think about the economic constraints upon the country's ability to meet social demands? From one perspective, the constraints and the demands are totally distinct, linked only by the fact that the one determines what resources are available to meet the other. But from a broader perspective the two are interrelated. That interrelationship is twofold: first, as we have seen, the way social groups are embedded in the economy determines their ability to recognize and accept the constraints it imposes. But second, as I shall argue here, the social structure may be an important determinant of long-term economic growth. Even in the short term the two may not be as easily separated as discussions—particularly recent discussions—of economic policy presume, and it is instructive to examine these short-term relationships first, for they underscore the need to manage the long-term evolution of the socioeconomic structure.

Short-term Economic Policy

The conventional economic wisdom is that the deficit is a short-term problem. In the long run, if we can get the economy to expand, incomes will rise, the tax system will generate more government revenue, and we will "grow our way out of the deficit." Indeed, in the most optimistic scenario, the declining deficit will itself spur growth by freeing funds for growth-generating private investment, funds that at present government

60

borrowing squeezes out of the financial markets. All of this assumes, however, that the social claimants will sit quietly in the wings waiting for the
economy to free up the resources necessary to meet their demands. If they
do not, things become a great deal more complicated and the presumptions
about the debt may actually be reversed.

The problem is that in the short run the binding constraint upon government spending is the willingness of investors, many of whom are now
foreigners, to hold U.S. government securities. The real fear about the deficits we have been running both in the federal government budget and in
our balance of international trade is that at some point foreign investors
will lose confidence in our willingness or ability to divert resources to pay
the interest on our debt and, as a result, will demand exorbitant returns to
continue to hold our securities or, worse still, will withhold their funds
entirely. We take some comfort from the fact that they have not already
done so, despite the fact that the debt has been accumulating for over a
decade.

But the tolerance of foreign markets for American debt is actually something of a mystery. The various budgetary compromises, it would seem,
limited though they were, however precarious politically and however dis-
appointing in the eyes of the technicians who fashioned them and the
domestic press that reviewed them, were nonetheless sufficient to reassure
foreign investors about the country's intent. The difficulty with this view
is that it is hard to see how we were so successful in convincing foreigners
when we could not convince ourselves. A somewhat more plausible explanation is that increasing insecurity in the rest of the world, especially in
Eastern Europe and the Middle East, has heightened the attraction of the
United States as a politically stable haven for funds.

If this is what has maintained the flow of foreign investment, social
mobilization will be doubly dangerous: the chaos and anarchy that mark
the politics of such periods will make the country look more and more
like those parts of the world from which foreign funds have been fleeing,
reducing the attractiveness of American financial instruments, tightening
the budgetary constraints, and making the kinds of spending commitments
that might alleviate the social pressures and calm the society increasingly
difficult. The economic and social deficits, in other words, are in danger
of coming together in a vicious circle in which the social crisis aggravates
the economic crisis and each forecloses the policies that would resolve the

other. This is admittedly an extreme scenario. But it does make clear that as social claims expand and intensify, the choice between spending and debt reduction becomes increasingly complex, even in the short run.

That choice is further complicated by the impact of social mobilization upon wage determination and the trade-off between unemployment and inflation. As we saw earlier, the wage structure is doubly determined, once by the market forces that economic models typically take into account, and then again by a set of social standards. The latter have been largely dormant in the last decade, with the result that the wage structure, judged by any consistent set of social norms, is now seriously distorted. These norms are likely to be reasserted in a period of social mobilization, setting off a conflict between economic and social standards that could have serious inflationary consequences.

It may still be possible to impose "economic" discipline upon social forces in wage setting, as Federal Reserve Chairman Paul Volcker did in the early years of the Reagan administration, but, because from the perspective of social norms the wage structure is now so much further out of line, it will take a lot longer for that discipline to have its effect. It may also take a lot more discipline, a much greater decline in the level of economic activity, and much higher levels of unemployment. And, as the 1992 election clearly demonstrated—and as politicians and policymakers will not soon forget—the American electorate is not nearly as tolerant of that discipline today as it was in the early 1980s. An additional problem would be the impact that the prolonged stagnation necessary to control social pressure would have on the size of the budget deficit and the prospects for growing our way out of it.

For short-term economic policy, as for social policy itself, we need, it would seem, to better understand social forces so that we can manage them. But, of course, the real hope is that in the long run we can move to a socioeconomic structure that is inherently more manageable and in which resource constraints are less binding. From this point of view, the real problem with our economic policy is that it has been much too narrowly focused upon macroeconomic aggregates in the short term. What we really need is a long-term structural policy.

Even this, however, is a misreading of the underlying problem. The preoccupation with macroeconomics and with the economic short run is a relatively recent development. The early Reagan policies that generated the budget and trade deficits in the first place grew out of a structural diagnosis of the country's economic performance and sought to provide a long-term, microeconomic remedy. That remedy is the common source of both our social and our economic difficulties. In both areas of policy, moreover, the problem lies less in the specific remedy that was prescribed than in the intellectual framework in terms of which it was conceived. In economics, as in social policy, the basic problem is a commitment to an individualist ethos and an inability to recognize and accord a legitimate place to organic groups and cohesive social organizations. In this, there is a basic continuity between the economists who inspired Reagan's original policies and their more orthodox colleagues in the latter Reagan years and under Bush who saw their job as one of dealing with the macroeconomic consequences of the earlier structural reforms. There is actually a continuity between Reagan's advisors and the economic advisors in the preceding Carter administration as well.

The Intellectual Framework

The key economic policymakers under Carter, Reagan, and Bush all understood economic growth as generated by the actions of private individuals, motivated by the pursuit of personal gain, responding to price signals generated by their collective interaction in a competitive marketplace. The problems of the American economy, in this view, were the result of two factors. First, government had blunted motivation by high marginal taxes and redistributional programs that provided income and services independent of work effort. Second, government had distorted price signals through regulation and restraints upon the play of market forces so that even motivated individuals were led to waste resources by selling them to the wrong people and using them in inefficient combinations.[1]

Where Reaganomics and the more orthodox economics of the Bush and Carter administrations differed was in the emphasis placed upon the two aspects of the underlying diagnosis. Reagan's people placed heavy—in some cases, exclusive—emphasis upon motivation, to the point where they believed that the increased effort released by the lower tax rates and the income it generated would be so great that the total tax yield would actually increase.[2] Deregulation and competition to correct the price signals that directed this effort were decidedly secondary. For more orthodox econo-

mists, on the other hand, these were the most important determinants of
the country's economic performance, and the focus, especially under the
Democratic Carter administration, was on the institutional structures that
would make the price signals right. But all of these analysts had very much
the same vision of the economy, as a collection of private and basically
autonomous individuals. Among individuals, moreover, they saw managers
and entrepreneurs as the key actors.

   The plausibility of this characterization of the economy is enhanced by
the fact that the managers and entrepreneurs themselves appear to subscribe to it. They certainly do so in high rhetoric and in politics. A host of
autobiographies and private memoirs attest that it also corresponds to their
most deeply held images of themselves. But they exhibit some of the same
kind of schizophrenia, the same commitment to ideas that are logically
contradictory, as workers do when evaluating union rules and as welfare
recipients do in regard to public assistance. The policies that businessmen
and managers pursued as practitioners reflected a much more complex and
nuanced understanding of the social structure in which economic activity
is embedded and of social process in the generation of economic growth.
Their endeavors—the actions that they thought proved their *individual*
worth as entrepreneurs—were designed to create institutional structures
and organizational cultures that would generate growth and efficiency internally in a way that was dependent not on the individual character of
any particular member but on the institutionalized structure and social
relations of the enterprise. These efforts, furthermore, rested on understandings and theories very different from those of either orthodox or Rea-
ganite economic theory.

The Practitioners' Vision

When one looks at recent economic history in terms of the vision of the
practitioners themselves, it too involves a change in the kind of structures
that business believes will be effective. The differences between the new
vision and the old are in many ways much greater than the differences
between the economics of the Reagan administration and that of the administrations before and after it. The change does not bring the practice of
entrepreneurs and managers any closer to the visions of economists, and
thus it in no way bridges the underlying dichotomy between social and

individualistic theories. But it is fundamentally altering the terms on which the social structure and the productive structure can be reconciled.

The Old Practitioners' Vision

For the greater part of the twentieth century, the institutional model that guided practitioners was the classic corporate organization, vertically integrated, hierarchical, and bureaucratic. The work of the enterprise was carefully specified, divided into a series of distinct tasks and operations, and distributed among an array of separate divisions and departments, where it was further elaborated and assigned to particular jobs. Relations among the divisions and, where possible, the performance of the work itself were governed by explicit rules and procedures. Communication was channeled along a clear chain of command. Overlap and ambiguity were to be eliminated. Externally, the corporation operated to structure and organize its markets, securing suppliers of raw material and parts at one end of the production process and product distribution at the other through an array of strictly subordinated suppliers, subcontractors, agents, and distributors.[3]

The classic corporation was an outgrowth of a commitment to *mass production* as an approach to technological development and economic efficiency. The underlying theory of the approach can be traced back at least to Adam Smith and was elaborated and extended by subsequent analysts and practitioners over the course of the nineteenth and twentieth centuries, most influentially for modern business practice by Frederick Taylor and Henry Ford. The essence of the approach is captured by Adam Smith's famous pin factory in which the work of the master pin-makers is broken up and divided so that "one worker pulls the wire, a second worker cuts the wire, a third worker heads the pin, a fourth worker points the pin, etc." Such a division of labor is effective because it permits the development of specialized resources specifically adapted to each task, first narrowly trained workers who are adept at "wire pulling" and then dedicated machines that pull the wire automatically. As this form of development proceeds, the resources become more highly specialized and the economy progressively more productive. In the extreme—exemplified until quite recently by automobile parts production and assembly—the resources are dedicated to a specific make and model, and each time the model changes the workers must be retrained and the machinery scrapped and replaced.[4]

The price paid for this approach to development is rigidity. The resources gain their productive power from a degree of specialization that makes it difficult or impossible for them to move to other uses. When they are not deployed in the tasks for which they are designed or trained, they are idle and unemployable. As a result, mass production is possible only if there is a large, stable market for a single standardized product. For the progressive division of labor to generate the continuous gains in productivity associated with economic growth, the market must also be growing. If the market is too small, if demand fluctuates widely and unpredictably, if the output is perishable, or too bulky to inventory, if it is readily made obsolete by fads and fashions, if it needs to be adjusted specially for each customer or group of customers, the gains from the specialization of resources are dissipated in unemployment, and other approaches to the organization of productive resources are called for.[5]

A good part of the organizational effort of a mass production economy is thus devoted to creating and maintaining markets that have the properties requisite to sustaining specialized resources. In most industrial countries, including our own, these efforts left a fringe of small producers existing alongside the large corporations and picking up the unstable portion of demand for mass-produced goods and the demand for high-fashion items, luxury goods, new products, and specialized capital equipment, all of which were too small to sustain mass production. Many of these small fringe firms contributed to the dynamism of the economy through the products they produced for the large corporations, but they themselves tended to be technologically stagnant. They did not partake of the dominant technological dynamic—dependent as that dynamic was on the capacity to specify distinct tasks and operations and to adapt resources specifically to them—and innovation, when it occurred in the fringe, was perceived as accidental and fortuitous rather than systematic and progressive.

The proprietors of these enterprises on the fringe of mass production came closer to resembling the entrepreneurs of American ideology than the corporate leaders who cultivated that image of themselves. The enterprises came a good deal closer to the economists' model of a competitive firm. But managers in this sector subscribed to the same organizational model as the rest of the managerial community and viewed their own organizations as frustrating and retrograde.[6]

Individualism in Mass Production

Mass production is a preeminently *social* productive system. The individual worker is totally dependent upon the larger operation of which he or she is a part for the economic and intellectual meaning of the work.[7] Unlike the master pin-maker, the pin-header produces nothing by himself; what he does has content and meaning only when performed in cooperation with the wire-puller, the wire-cutter, and the pin-pointer. It is paradoxical that an individualistic country like the United States should have pioneered this approach.

But the organizational forms of mass production actually are protective of a kind of individual autonomy, although in ways very different from the competitive market. So long as nothing breaks down, the social character of mass production is realized completely by the way the work is organized. It does not actually require any direct interaction among the workers in the system. The demands made on the individual are stringent, in the sense that every one of the assigned tasks has to be correctly performed if the individual's responsibilities are to be fulfilled so that the product of his or her work will fit back into the whole. But the demands are also strictly limited in the sense that, in principle, the worker is not required to do anything beyond the assigned tasks or to make any further moral or intellectual commitment to the employer.[8]

Mass production appears to leave considerable individual autonomy in a second sense as well. As noted earlier, production is physically separated from consumption by being located outside the household in the factory or office, and the household is represented in the labor market by a single dominant earner. Thus, not only are the constraints upon the wage earner in the workplace limited, but outside the workplace the productive system apparently does not constrain the earner at all, and other members of the household are apparently free of any productive constraints.

In a larger sense, the autonomy of the individual in consumption is illusory. The whole productive system requires for its efficiency and growth the extension of mass markets for standardized products, and that requirement, at least in the United States of the twentieth century, seems to have implied a mass consumption in which uniformity is fostered by pervasive media advertising, politics, and social pressure.[9] But the pressure for uniformity in a mass consumption economy, like prices and income in a competitive market, is not perceived as a constraint on individual freedom.

Mass Production and Government Regulation

The American business community was never an enthusiastic supporter of the government policies dismantled in the 1970s and 1980s, but from the perspective of mass production those policies had a certain logic and coherence that they lacked according to more atomistic economic theories.[10] Mass production, as we saw, requires a large, stable market for a single standardized product. Much of the energy of the classic corporation is directed at creating and maintaining such markets through advertising, special distributors, the provision of consumer finance, elaborate strategies that segment the unstable portion of demand and subcontract it to fringe producers, and the like. A parallel effort is directed at the stabilization of inputs through vertical integration or long-term contracting in order to sustain the operation of machinery too specialized to absorb substitute materials or switch back and forth among sources of energy. The first third of the century was especially fertile and creative in the development of strategies of this kind.

In the context of corporate efforts to stabilize markets, the Great Depression seemed to demonstrate the inability of private strategies alone to validate mass production. And postwar regulatory policy, put in place largely in response to the Depression, was understood as the analogue at the national level of the policies the corporations had been pursuing in individual markets. The key policies in this regard were those which sustained aggregate demand, and among these the key was mass industrial unionism.

Unions operated to this effect on two levels. The wage policy they pursued in bargaining with individual enterprises insured that the expansion of purchasing power of organized workers, and workers whose threat of organization forced the employer to meet union wages, would keep pace with the expansion of productive capacity. And the support unions gave in the political arena to the minimum wage, social security, unemployment insurance, and the like, along with the pressure the labor movement generated in government to manage aggregate demand so as to ensure full employment, had a similar effect on the purchasing power of the unorganized labor force. Unions also operated to stabilize labor relations on the shop floor (although for this purpose, business preferred other strategies). Together these effects created a predisposition in the business community to acquiesce in the legal structures that protected union organization and collective bargaining.

A similar logic created a grudging acceptance of fixed exchange rates, the agricultural price support system, and the reserves of "militarily strategic" raw materials. Each of these government policies operated to help ensure steady supplies without extreme fluctuations of prices in more or less the same way that corporations had been seeking to do by themselves since the turn of the century.

But as a support to mass production, the complex of postwar regulatory policies had a fatal defect. It maintained the critical background conditions for mass production in an essentially closed national economy, but it did little to sustain stability and purchasing power for the international economic system as a whole. Therefore, as productive capacity outgrew our national markets in the late 1960s and 1970s, U.S. companies became more and more vulnerable. In international competition, in fact, many of the postwar institutions operated perversely. The wage rates that once had sustained purchasing power now hampered the ability of companies to compete abroad. The purchasing power they created was neither necessary nor sufficient to sustain domestic industry. It was not necessary because, with low enough wages, foreign demand could be attracted as a substitute for any domestic shortfall. It was not sufficient because too much could leak out to foreign producers. The decreasing relevance of the postwar regulatory structure to the strategic problems of business made attacks upon it—launched in the vocabulary of the individualism and the competitive ideology to which American managers subscribed, or at least thought they subscribed—increasingly plausible.

But whether one understood the problem in terms of the historic evolution of mass production or in terms of the artificiality of government regulations imposed upon the working of the natural market, the economy of the 1970s had clearly become inhospitable to the structures of mass production. The most acute problem was the heightened flux and uncertainty in the business environment and of the basic parameters of investment decisions. This came to be symbolized by the sudden variability in energy prices that began with the oil embargo in 1974 and rose and fell thereafter with events in the Middle East.

These fluctuations in energy costs translated into an oscillation in demand for automobiles between large and small cars that was particularly unnerving for that conical mass production industry. But similar fluctuations developed in the following decade in other business parameters as well—exchange rates, interest rates, a wide variety of raw material prices, and so on—setting off fluctuations in the composition of demand that clashed with the fixed assets and the specialized resources even of industries whose products were not so heavily dependent on energy. Demand also fluctuated as the developing world first expanded on debt facilitated by the recycling of oil profits and then, when interest rates rose and credit disappeared, contracted.

As these developments unfolded, uncertainty and variability were further compounded by competitive pressures. The newly developed countries of Southeast Asia adopted mass production techniques in a way that greatly expanded world productive capacity in consumer durables, but combined them with domestic policies that forestalled a comparable expansion of consumer purchasing power. The internal domestic movement toward deregulation intensified competition still further. Finally, consumer demand became increasingly heterogeneous and diverse, augmenting uncertainty and compromising economies of scale yet again.

In response to the changed environment, new, more flexible production systems have emerged. These systems have been greatly facilitated by information technology; it is now possible to obtain many of the advantages of specialized machinery through software programs attached to general-purpose equipment. But the new flexible approaches are associated with institutional innovations as well, and those innovations have begun to coalesce into a new organizational model. Although still somewhat inchoate, that model has already begun to replace the classic hierarchical corporation as the goal of managers and entrepreneurs. It is articulated in the United States in a burgeoning normative literature published under such expressive titles as *Thriving on Chaos, When Giants Learn to Dance,* and *Post-Modern Management.*[11]

The structures that this new literature champions are much leaner and flatter than the classic corporation of mass production. They emerge out of the old corporation by eliminating several levels in the managerial hierarchy, but their thrust is to eliminate the hierarchical chain of command altogether by encouraging lateral communication within the organization. To this end, they advocate reforms like matrix management, in which a single executive reports to several superiors, a structure that is so messy and complicated for the people who operate within it that they are virtually forced to try to resolve problems at lower levels of the organization to avoid passing them upward to several, possibly conflicting, superiors.

The new organizational form also makes extensive use of ad hoc teams continually reshuffled for each new project. In engineering, these teams, whose members work in tandem, replace the sequential engineering characteristic of mass production. Under the old system, the product is first designed and then passed to a process engineer who designs the manufacturing equipment and finally to an industrial engineer who lays out the plant floor. In the new system of engineering teams and parallel engineering, all aspects of design are done at once. The watchword in the new organizational jargon is *networking,* and much of the scholarly literature that is emerging is classified under this heading. Part of it has a very narrow, precise mathematical definition of a network, but in much of it the term is used as a metaphor in the same way it is used by the layman.[12]

The networks that the companies are creating in practice are not confined to the interior of their own organization but extend across its boundaries to subcontractors, to suppliers, and to the agents and dealers who handle its products. The highly publicized Kan-Ban system of on-time deliveries, borrowed from Japan, is actually designed to force a close collaborative relationship between the purchasing company and the supplier, which were previously insulated from each other by the buffer of inventories. When parts arrive just as they are needed in production, problems have to be resolved immediately through close, intense consultation. In another example of the same type of reform, potential parts suppliers actually join the engineering teams designing the product and participate in the design process. Sometimes retail dealers and even consumers are pulled into the design process as well in order to introduce the "feel" of the market and the "voice of the customer." Close networking of this kind is not possible when suppliers (or dealers) find themselves in intense competition with one another, and large companies adapting the new organizational styles have radically reduced the number of subcontractors and given permanent commitments to those which remain, commitments that extend in time to products as yet nonexistent.[13]

Parallel changes are occurring in the design of work, in the relations between managers and workers, and, more broadly, in labor-management relations. Most companies have sought to carry out these changes in what they euphemistically call a union-free environment. But the prototype of the new approach is the Saturn agreement between GM and the United Automobile Workers. In many ways, Saturn is to the new organizational form what Ford's Model-T was to the old. The thrust of Saturn is to break down the sharp division between workers and managers and among jobs and job assignments, and to increase the breadth of responsibilities of both workers and managers. In the volatile markets for which the new organizations are designed, the product shifts too radically and unpredictably for the production process to be broken up into a set of fixed components that are parceled out to individuals as clearly delineated tasks. Instead, the workers' practical knowledge and hands-on experience are required for quick response and improvisation, but the workers have to be well enough educated to communicate directly with technicians and engineers and relate to the technical and scientific issues they pose.

Thus workers are being drawn into consultation with management through such organizational innovations as quality circles and, where unions still exist, through representation on boards of directors and even, as in the well-publicized cases of worker buy-outs in United Airlines and Avis Rent-a-Car, through direct ownership. Compensation structures that were once based on job content are also being redesigned to reflect participation through bonuses and profit-sharing, and to reflect the importance of education through skill increments and pay-for-knowledge schemes.[14] Finally, to secure employee commitment, employment is often guaranteed.

This last, however, is a particularly tricky part of the new model and the uncertain business environment to which it is a response. Employment guarantees are thought to be required to induce workers' cooperation in adjustments to that uncertainty. But the uncertainty also makes employment guarantees very risky. Caught in this contradiction, companies have been moving toward a core-periphery model of labor relations. The collaborative relationship and the quid pro quo of employment security, profit-sharing, and participation in management are offered only to the core. A second category of workers is defined: the peripheral labor force, with whom the firm maintains a more or less traditional arm's-length relationship. For these jobs the company tries to hire temporary workers, part-timers, summer interns, employees of temporary agencies, and the like, or to subcontract the work to other firms.[15] But this core-peripheral distinction, as we shall see, is not always possible.

Elements of the new organizational model can be found in American companies as far back as the 1920s and, in the postwar period, have been particularly prominent in the major high tech companies such as IBM, Digital, and Texas Instruments. But organizational innovations in the 1980s have also been heavily influenced by foreign practices, particularly those of Japan and, for smaller companies, Germany and central Italy. These were the countries, or regions, that performed best in the late 1970s and early 1980s when American business was floundering. At first they were as startled by their own success as U.S. observers were, but gradually they began to reconsider their own practices and to trace their success in the new business environment to various compromises originally made with the American model in order to adopt it to the peculiarities of their own cultures. By the middle of the decade they had abstracted a distinctive theory and organizational model of their own. As a translator for Americans at a Japanese business meeting put it in 1986, "I am having a lot of trouble translating what they are saying, but I think you get basic idea. Japanese managers are pretty smug these days."

Possibly because of these translation problems, American business strategists were slow to absorb these new theories. Looking at foreign practices through the prism of the classic corporate model, they saw only the inconsistencies, and they attributed foreign success to special competitive factors, particularly low wages and restrictive trade practices. But with the shock of the 1981–82 recession—and, somewhat paradoxically, under the pressure of the overvalued dollar, which actually did give foreigners a substantial cost advantage—they began to look seriously at foreign practices for lessons that could be imported to the U.S. And it is from that process that the new managerial vision has emerged.

But the conflict between an individualistic and a communitarian understanding of economic and social processes poses a special problem for American management in the implementation of this new vision. The emerging organizational model is much more fundamentally social than the organizational models of mass production. It does not create clearly defined roles into which a person can step without compromising his or her autonomy or individuality. The roles and functions are constantly shifting as the product is redefined in continuous adaptation to the market.

What holds these new organizations together is less an organizational chart than a common language and culture. Culture and language have instrumental roles in that they are what enables the members to work out and implement quickly new solutions to business problems. But it is less clear that they can be created instrumentally. They grow out of the kind of allegiance the individual has to a society when he or she learns to speak its language and becomes integrated into its cultural community, and they grow up in organizations that are able to command that kind of commitment. This makes such organizations much less the instrument of economic success than was the classic corporation of mass production and much more an organic entity.[16]

The several countries that seem to have pioneered the new organizational model are so different as to preclude any simplistic theory of a cultural disposition to business success in the climate of our times. But the national ethos in Japan, Germany, and Italy is much more consistent with an organic notion of society and community than our own. In the United States, the business structures that most resemble the foreign models are not in fact any of the large corporate organizations but the garment and construction industries, where constellations of small firms are constantly being regrouped in response, in garments, to fashion and style, or, in construction, to the progression from project to project and within each project as building proceeds through stages from framing to finishing. These are the most networked organizations on our economic landscape. But these two industries have for some time been embedded in immigrant enclaves with a communitarian ethos comparable to those found abroad. In garments, as the older Italian and Jewish communities have been assimilated into mainstream American culture, they have tended to abandon the industry and their place has been taken by new immigrant groups. The story in construction is a little more complicated, but here too many members of the younger generation have left as they have become assimilated.[17]

Commitments to individualism have definitely *not* prevented American industry from adopting new approaches. Indeed, one would be hard pressed to find a major American company that has not attempted in the last decade what those within it perceive as fundamental changes in its internal organizational structure and its managerial practices. The reforms of the middle 1980s were followed in the late 1980s and early 1990s by a dramatic revival of the fortunes of U.S. manufacturing in world markets. A good deal of that revival, however, was generated by the correction in the value of the dollar, a swing from a substantially overvalued currency to an undervalued one. This has made our goods much cheaper than those of our foreign competitors and masks what organizational inefficiencies remain. It may be a long time before we find out how large these inefficiencies really are.

Obstacles to Organizational Reform

When one looks at the process of organizational reform from the inside, however, one can well believe that the inefficiencies are still substantial. That process has been seriously impeded by two very different sets of factors. One of these is contradictions internal to the new model as it is now conceptualized. The second is the lingering attachment of important factions of American management to the organizational structures and business practices of mass production. That attachment has been inadvertently reinforced by national policies that, especially under Reagan and Bush, were conceived in the framework of competitive economic theory and were designed in the pursuit, not of mass production, but of a more competitive business environment.

The distinction between competition and internal organizational reform seems to have been more clearly recognized within the Clinton administration, but national policies reinforcing management's commitment to old practices have persisted. The persistence reflects a third set of factors that have impeded organizational reform: a concern about the employment opportunities for the low-wage labor force that the organizational changes, and the policies that promote them, might eliminate. That concern itself reflects an overly individualistic conception of the nature of the low-wage labor market and is misplaced.

Internal Contradictions

The first problem in realizing the new organizational structures is that the new model that much of American management is attempting to implement is not wholly coherent internally or fully consistent with the social and economic environment. The biggest problem appears to lie with the core-periphery distinction. The distinction would be easiest to implement if the workers needed by the firm could be divided into a permanent set of skilled collaborators and a fluctuating set of supplemental, unskilled laborers. But the reality is a good deal more complicated. Many firms seem

to be cutting their activities back to a set of core competencies and sup-
plementing these with shifting resources that vary from project to project.
Computer or telecommunications systems, for example, must be designed
and built by people who are expert in the construction of the equipment,
but they also require people who understand the operation of the industry
that is buying the system; hence, the composition of the design and manufacturing team typically varies as the company shifts from, for example,
a bank to a hospital. The supplementary workers, the experts in banking
or hospitals, are often as skilled as the people associated with the core
activities, and the degree of collaboration required when they are engaged
is often every bit as great. Thus the firm faces a problem that has not been
discussed in the managerial literature: how to obtain the commitment of
workers who are *not* part of the organization.

This problem may not, moreover, turn out to be a secondary issue that
can be addressed once the loyalty of the core labor force is secured.
Searching for a core competency is often like peeling an onion: the firm
may have a generically defined mission, but the skills that it needs to fulfill
that mission may shift so radically across projects and the mix of projects
may become so unpredictable that it cannot make a permanent commitment to *any* set of workers. Manufacturing and service companies become
like the general contractors in construction who have virtually no employees of their own and draw on a progression of different skilled trades
to do the work. Automobile makers in their planning for the future are
contemplating a world in which a car might be made of plastic or fiberglass,
but they are not really thinking of a world in which the car would be
fiberglass today, metal again tomorrow, glass the day after, and fiber or
metal again the day after that. Nor are they thinking about one in which
all three of the materials might be used but in proportions that varied
radically from one year to the next.

A similar problem is inherent in the proposition that the pace of technological change is shifting in a way that will require that workers have
several distinct occupations or "skill structures" in the course of their work
lives. There is actually very little evidence to support this proposition. Most
of what makes it plausible is consistent with the idea that the demand for
labor is simply varying more widely across an otherwise stable set of skill
requirements. But if it is true—and it is certainly widely believed—it implies that even firms that can identify a set of core skills that are sufficiently

stable to build into their permanent staff may be loath to make permanent career commitments to the workforce, and such firms too will be seeking a close collaborative relationship with people who will not be able to identify completely with the organization.

The trends in the social structure discussed in the preceding chapter complicate the situation even further. At the very moment when the firm is demanding greater commitment on the part of the worker, the worker's outside commitments are making greater demands as well. Again there is a paradox: these new production systems themselves remove the pressures for mass consumption and foster the diversification of lifestyles and identity groups that compete with the firm for the individual's loyalty and attention. The increasing labor force participation of women is similarly creating dual-career households that cannot or will not move geographically to enable the firm to make good on its promise of employment security or to meet its needs for flexibility and skill.

Finally, the opening of the firm to the outside labor market is changing the basic incentive structure that underlies the country's system of education and training. Under mass production, when most jobs involved a series of firm-specific skills and many workers were expected to remain with their employer throughout their work lives, the firm had a strong incentive to invest in its workforce. But as interfirm mobility increases that incentive is greatly diminished. One might expect that under these circumstances the workers themselves would assume the cost of training and education. But the transition in responsibility might under the best of circumstances take some time. It is likely to take place, moreover, only if the kinds of skills required and the career paths with which they are associated are clear to the workforce and to the institutions to which they will have to turn to obtain their training. Under current circumstances, however, there is no such clarity. A real vacuum appears to be emerging in skill development.

What is true of education and training is true of other functions that the self-contained, mass production enterprise once performed for itself. Just as the firm once had the incentive to engage in training because the immobility of labor enabled it to capture the return, large firms had an incentive to engage in basic research and development. But they are now cutting back on these functions as well, and narrowing their activities to projects whose payoff is direct and clear. Industries that have a tradition of small competitive firms, such as the garment and building industries, have research institutes sponsored by trade associations or trade unions. And there is a strong tradition of institutes of this kind in countries like Italy and Germany, which have extensive networks of small firms. In the United States the universities have traditionally played something of this role. But industry seems to be cutting back its contributions to university research in parallel with its own activities. And this is occurring at the same time that the federal government's contribution to academic research, much of which was made under the umbrella of military preparedness, is also being reduced. Thus, although the new models involve much more co-operation and exchange among organizations, such critical organizational components for technological advance as education and research may turn out to be missing.

Managerial Factionalism

The unresolved contradictions and inconsistencies in the new organizational model play into and aggravate a second problem: the lingering attractions of the old managerial approaches. Until recently, at least, this has probably been the more serious impediment to the development of collaborative institutional forms..

In most companies, there are really two distinct business strategies still being debated, with separate managerial factions committed to each. One strategy is to create new, more flexible organizational and productive structures and use them to move up-market with more customized products, competing on the basis of quality and variety. These new structures are also less sensitive to variability and uncertainty since they permit the organization to move around more easily in response to market changes. The other faction, however, would compete on the basis of cost alone, preserving much of the old organizational structure and many of the practices associated with it, but driving down cost through increased pressure on workers and suppliers and the squeezing of wages, commissions, and subcontractor mark-ups. Its adherents plan, as in the past, to attract customers away from more customized goods through lower prices and to maintain their own demand in the face of market fluctuations at the expense of higher-cost producers. Quality versus cost: the high road and the low road.

The two factions often agree on specific organizational changes but understand them in different strategic terms and implement them in completely different ways. When this happens, the cost strategy usually undermines the quality one. An example of this process is the introduction of the Kan-Ban system borrowed from the Japanese. In Japan the thrust of this practice is to eliminate the buffer stocks that insulate the various stages of the production process from one another and mask problems of coordination. These stocks also, of course, reduce flexibility, since each time the product changes they must be either worked off or scrapped. To operate effectively, the system requires extremely close cooperation between the suppliers and the mother company, and when it is introduced in Japan it is the fulcrum for the development of a whole new collaborative relationship.

The quality faction of American management sees it in much the same way as it is understood in Japan. But the cost faction views the Kan-Ban system not as a way of eliminating in-process inventories but as a way of shifting the cost of carrying them to the supplying firm. This, of course, increases the suspicion and hostility that traditionally exist in American supplier relationships and poisons the atmosphere against the high-trust, collaborative relationship that the quality faction is seeking to create. In companies with more than one plant, the implementation of the reform often varies from one facility to another depending on the particular purchasing agent. In those companies one can sometimes spot the plants controlled by the cost-cutting faction by looking for the trailer trucks, housing the inventories still carried on the suppliers' books, which are parked at the edges of the parking lots. One wonders how the quality faction makes out with those same suppliers in the plants that it controls.[18]

The internal conflicts within management in the administration of the Kan-Ban system are easiest to describe, but conflicts in labor-management relations are more acute and more of an obstacle to success. This is especially so in unionized plants where suspicious union leaders see reforms (such as quality circles) as ways of winning workers' loyalty away from the union organization and the new wage structures as indirect ways of undermining union rules and lowering earnings. In these plants, the cost faction in management reinforces factions within the union itself that oppose these reforms; indeed, in several cases, the cost faction, administering reforms designed by its quality-faction adversaries, has actually crystallized opposition among initially undecided union leaders. Even in nonunion companies, the conflict is creating potential problems for the future. In one particularly glaring case, the plant manager of a company that guaranteed employment assigned his surplus workers to sit in a roped-off area next to the plant entrance where the rest of the labor force filed by at the beginning and end of the workday. Those who did not quit presumably served as an example that encouraged the effort of people who still had jobs. But the effects on cooperation and commitment were more problematic.

Public Policy and Cost vs. Quality

Public policy in the Republican administrations, in this case under both Reagan and Bush, enormously encouraged the cost faction. The critical juncture in this regard, as in much else that transpired in the economy in the 1980s, was Reagan's handling of the strike of federal air traffic controllers in 1981. Firing the strikers, barring them from subsequent employment, and training replacements signaled to the managerial community a fundamental change in labor policy. The episode served to encourage factions in management that advocated a tough stance toward unions and their demands, and in many ways it ushered in the era of concession bargaining. But, most important, it led American managers to believe that it was possible to conduct a strategy of progressively lowering labor costs. Reagan's first labor secretary, Ray Donovan, whom he supported in the face of major charges of corruption and against the advice of most of his inner circle, further encouraged this belief, not only through his public statements but through the relaxation of health and safety regulations, including a longstanding ban on industrial work in the home. Appointments to the National Labor Relations Board and to the courts worked to weaken legal protection for trade unions. And, as we saw earlier, the minimum wage was allowed to decline relative to the average wage and the coverage of the unemployment insurance system was permitted to contract.

The Bush administration softened the rhetoric of the Reagan labor policy but basically sustained, when it did not actively encourage, the cost strategy as an approach to the problem of American competitiveness. Bush's own predilections were clearly revealed in the campaign debate with Michael Dukakis when the issue of the Massachusetts system of compulsory health insurance arose. Bush made clear that he would like to provide universal health insurance but that the imposition of these costs on U.S. business was too dangerous. We cannot risk, he argued, the effects this might have on our ability to compete in world markets. The fact that universal medical insurance has, as we saw earlier, a perverse effect on the competitive position of our high-wage industries is in a certain sense irrelevant here. Bush was apparently ignorant of this fact. The basic message he sent to American industry was that his government was prepared to validate, indeed he seemed actually to encourage, business as it looked to lower cost as the first line of defense against foreign producers.

Much the same message was carried by Bush's aggressive advocacy of a free trade treaty with Mexico. What American managers see is the prospect of altogether new opportunities to reduce labor costs, both directly by actually locating in Mexico and indirectly through a new wave of wage concessions secured by the threat of moving there. A policy initiative of this kind, promising to open a labor market of 25 million workers where the average hourly compensation in manufacturing is 15 percent of that in the United States,[19] completely dwarfed the adjustments that had been made under Bush in the minimum wage levels and regulatory enforcement polices inherited from Reagan.

Policymakers' Myopia

The irony here is that neither Bush nor Reagan subscribed to the business strategies of either faction of American management. Certainly, the economists in their administrations did not. They remained committed to models of atomistic, individualistic competition in which the organizational structures at stake in the managerial debates did not appear. This made them virtually blind to the real effects of what they were doing. North American free trade is a case in point. The advocates of this treaty presented it as a counterpart to the Common Market in Europe as it moved toward full integration in 1992. But in fact the impact of 1992 on managerial policy in Europe is very different.

The move for European unity was guided by Jacques Delor, a Christian Socialist, and was advocated in a rhetoric that equated socialism with the humanitarian values of the European Enlightenment. Delor promoted European union as a way of preserving this value system in a world that might otherwise be dominated by the United States and Japan. The message to business was that social policy in Europe would, in the long run, preclude the low-cost strategy, and that if they were to produce and compete from a European base they must develop organizational structures that would be viable for the quality alternative. The short-run implications of specific measures of social and economic policy—Delor's inability to obtain the passage of the his "social charter," for example—were subordinated to this underlying message in the same way that renewed regulatory enforcement and an increase in the minimum wage were eclipsed in the United States by the very different message Bush was communicating by the terms in which he promoted NAFTA. Moreover, while American policymakers may be taken in by the analogy of the European Community, American multinationals are not. They are committing their European facilities to the quality strategy, because they understand that the business environment of even the low-wage sectors of the Community will prove inhospitable to the low-cost alternative in the long run. As they do so, their U.S. plants are being committed to the low-cost strategy by default.

A further irony is that the myopia of policymakers, the reason that they do not appreciate the effects of their policies on business decisions, and the tendency to see social service costs as overburdening industry and forcing back the *level* of activity rather than as exerting their primary effect on the *structure* of activity, is that in Washington they are cut off from the operational economy in a way analogous to the way social groups have become divorced from the economy that generates the resources that support them. This is particularly unfortunate because it is difficult to believe that the background conditions that permit the low-cost strategy in the United States can be sustained. The fact is that the productive and organizational structures involved in the efficient production of long runs of standardized goods have been successfully adopted by developing countries, not only the Koreas and Singapores of Southeast Asia but (recent studies suggest) our neighbors in Mexico as well. For standardized goods, these countries can now achieve output per man-hour and standards of quality and workmanship that are substantially equivalent to those of U.S. facilities, but they pay for the man-hours at much lower wages.[20] To compete with the developing world over the long run, therefore, U.S. wages for semiskilled production workers will have to fall to comparable levels. Thus the low-cost strategy commits the United States not only to wages that are comparatively low today but to wages at the bottom of the labor market that decline progressively over time. This would mean that the social disparities inherited from the Reagan years would be doomed to get even worse.

But this already bleak scenario may be even bleaker. The impact of medical insurance on the relative cost structures of the United States and Canada carries a profound and telling lesson. Our private insurance system, as we saw in the previous chapter, has the effect, relative to the social insurance of medical care in Canada, of raising the labor costs of our high-wage industries, which use skilled, educated labor relative to that employed by low-wage producers. It is thus part of the broader business climate that makes the low-cost strategy more attractive to managers in the United States than in either Canada or Europe (or Japan for that matter).

The effect ultimately derives from the fact that our social policy is premised on notions of individualism, which we may believe underlie the organization and operation of American society but which actually do not. Americans are not, in fact, prepared to let the medically indigent die in the streets, and the costs of caring for them eventually get socialized whether we like it or not. What we see in medical care is reflected in other aspects of social policy as well. Our high-wage producers make up for the deficiencies of public education by providing training on the job, and they are now moving to make up for the deficiencies of custodial care by providing daycare and even elder care. These efforts probably also increase the disparity between the cost of highly qualified labor between Canada and the United States, although they are as yet too limited to appear clearly in measures of cost differentials that also reflect many other factors. But they do suggest that the United States is in danger, even on our own continent, of being pinned between our southern neighbor who can beat us in the low-cost strategy and our northern neighbor who can beat us in the quality strategy. In the world market, where we must compete on the high road with Europe and Japan, things look even worse.

Of course, however long we manage to stave off the pressures inherent in the emerging social structure discussed in the earlier chapters, social mobilization would appear inevitable long before we get squeezed out of world markets. If we are going to have to face the consequences of cost-cutting strategies eventually, a change in public policy designed to encourage the alternative managerial approaches appears desirable now.

Clinton: The Failed Promise of a New Economic Vision

For a brief period, in the months immediately following Clinton's election in 1992, it appeared that a change in policy was at hand. As a candidate, the President-elect had endorsed a number of proposals that seemed to point toward a high-wage economy: an active trade and technology policy; continuous worker training financed through a payroll tax on employers; new forms of labor-management cooperation and participatory management; supplements to the North American Free Trade Agreement including enforceable guarantees of labor standards; an increase in the minimum wage and indexation to prevent it from slipping relative to the average wage; a work-oriented welfare reform package; mandated employer-financed medical insurance; enterprise zones in central-city neighborhoods. Each of these proposals was open to alternative interpretations, but Clinton had surrounded himself with a group of advisors whose economic views differed sharply from those around Carter, Reagan, and Bush, and, taken together and read against the background of their writings, the proposals were a prescription for the transformation of the low end of the labor market and a signal to management that over the long run a low-wage strategy would not be viable. This view was reinforced by the appointment of several of these advisors to prominent positions within the new administration, most notably Robert Reich as Secretary of Labor and Laura Tyson as chair of the Council of Economic Advisors.[21]

Once Clinton was in office, however, other messages seemed to take the place of an emphasis on high-wage jobs: the preservation of small business, the immorality of continued welfare for those who could work, the U.S. commitment to continuing free trade, the preservation of democracy in Latin America. Virtually every component of the labor market package was compromised or abandoned. The increase and indexation of the minimum wage were postponed; the training tax was shelved; the medical insurance package subsidized low-wage employment; the welfare reform package precluded the kind of long-term training necessary for high-wage employment; the labor standards provisions negotiated to supplement the North American Free Trade Treaty lacked real substance, and the enforcement provisions were cumbersome and without effective sanctions.

The Promise and Disappointment of
Low-Wage Job Opportunities

The reason of principle for abandoning the campaign program was the old fear of the revenge of the natural market: the attempt to drive up wages at the bottom of the labor market would increase unemployment and decrease opportunities for income, particularly among disadvantaged groups. These fears were reinforced by the lingering unemployment inherited from the 1990–91 recession and the unusually slow pace of employment expansion in the recovery. But they also reflected the continuing impact of the Los Angeles riots, which reminded the nation of the persistence of black poverty and revived memories of the 1960s. We may not have wanted the low-wage labor market, but we evidently feared to give it up, and that fear had become a further deterrent to a high-wage economic strategy. This fear too is misplaced.

The Ghetto Employment Problem

The concern that higher wages will aggravate the employment problems of low-wage workers grows directly out of competitive economic theory. In this theory unemployment represents a gap between demand and supply. Demand, in turn, reflects the productivity of the workforce relative to the wage. To eliminate unemployment, either the wage must fall or the productivity of the pool of unemployed workers must rise.

   The Great Society programs of the 1960s took the latter approach. The shift in strategy is a reflection of the broader shift from active government intervention to the withdrawal of government from the economy. But in the case of policies toward the black ghetto, it seems, an additional factor is involved. In the 1960s low productivity could be attributed to the rural background of black workers, most of whom had recently migrated from the South, and to the poor preparation they had received in the segregated southern schools. Most of the black labor force today, however, has grown up in urban industrial society. A substantial portion has moved into the middle class. Those left behind in poverty thus appear to be a residual that earlier public policy failed to reach. They are easily perceived as a kind of underclass, trapped in a culture of poverty.[22]

A very different perspective, however, is generated by the experience of employment and training practitioners, especially in the 1960s. Like the perspective of managerial practitioners, it suggests a much greater emphasis on the structures of mass production and upon group and communal effects, in this case groups and communities that develop in the ghetto itself. But as with the perspective of managerial practitioners, a commitment to individualistic social theory denies us a readily accessible vocabulary to express it and a conceptual framework in which to work through its policy implications.

Key to the practioners' perspective was the recognition that in the tight labor markets of the 1960s—in direct contradiction to the assumptions upon which the training programs were predicated—anyone who wanted to work was able to find a job. Thus it seemed unemployment was not a sign of exclusion. On the contrary, blacks participated in the economy in an active way; it was not clear how the economy would operate without them. Unemployment reflected the nature of the roles they played. There seemed, in fact, to be a *dual labor market* divided into what came to be termed a *primary* and a *secondary* sector. The white male labor force held jobs in the primary sector. These jobs were relatively high paying, high status, and offered employment security and advancement. Jobs in the secondary sector, where the bulk of the black labor force found work, were low paying, menial, insecure, and without opportunity for upward mobility. Workers were frequently laid off for economic reasons; discharge was the preferred instrument for discipline. Since they were quite likely to lose any given job sooner or later, they had no particular incentive to stick with a job, and moved frequently on their own, quitting to take care of a family emergency, to be closer to home, or to work with friends. The resulting turnover, voluntary and involuntary, produced high unemployment rates as a byproduct.[23]

The dual labor market structure reflected the mass production economy and the way it had been structured by the New Deal reforms in the 1930s and in World War II and the early postwar period.[24] The long runs of standardized products and the dedicated capital equipment in mass production generated both the need for stable employment relations and the possibilities for employment security associated with the primary sector of the labor market. The institutional reforms of the New Deal and its aftermath, especially the industrial union movement, reinforced these characteristics of mass production jobs. But there remained a substantial fringe of output which was too specialized, unstable, and/or unpredictable for mass production. The institutional arrangements for this output had to accommodate the instability and uncertainties associated with it, and, in the case of relatively unskilled work, this portion of demand was relegated to the secondary sector. As the institutional arrangements of the secondary sector had solidified after the war, the arrangements of the secondary sector had become more distinctive and their importance, in relieving pressures that the formal institutions of the primary sector could not accommodate, had grown.

The dual labor market structure obviously worked most smoothly when the labor force also divided into groups with sharply different labor force attachments. Hence the secondary sector tended to draw upon women whose primary allegiance was to the home and youth and students looking for part-time or summer jobs.

Black workers in the early postwar period fit the requirements of this sector because they were migrants from the rural South. They saw the North through southern eyes. The North was in many ways the promised land.[25] The society was open, racial attitudes benign; the jobs were better paying and, relative to southern jobs given to blacks, of higher status. Especially in the beginning, moreover, many were in the North only temporarily. They often left their children behind, or sent them home to be raised, returning frequently themselves or, at least, planning to do so. Migrants had played similar roles in the northern industrial labor market since the second half of the nineteenth century, and except for the enhanced institutional rigidities that had emerged in the 1930s, the way blacks entered the urban labor market was comparable to the way European immigrants entered the American labor market.[26] Indeed, blacks had only begun to move north in large numbers when European migration was cut off, and employers began to recruit actively in the South for a substitute labor force.[27]

In the 1940s and 1950s, when the European ethnic settlements were second-generation communities that had developed strong allegiances to industrial unionism, the black migrants were also particularly appealing to northern employers. They had southern mannerisms, they were extremely polite by northern standards, even among themselves, but they also had a subservient and ingratiating manner in dealing with whites, a manner cultivated over generations in the South to confirm whites in their sense of racial superiority and allay their fears of black aggression, a manner impressed upon the black community by cross-burnings and lynchings and passed on from parents to children by a strict upbringing in which children were severely punished for any breach in the behavior patterns demanded by the southern code.[28]

Both the underlying economic and technological pressures that the American economy seeks to accommodate and the characteristics of the black workforce have changed dramatically since the 1960s. The adjustments in the organizational structures of mass production have radically altered the architecture of the labor market and fundamentally changed the constraints within which policy operates. The weakening of the trade union movement has enabled management to use the core labor force in ways that in the past were possible only in the ghetto and comparable enclaves of the dual labor market. At stake in the debates among managers about business strategy is the need to use any of the labor force in this way. A shift toward a strategy of differentiated quality-oriented production and the perfecting of the flexible technologies and organizational structures that would sustain that strategy would make the entire economy less sensitive to the flux and uncertainties that the secondary sector absorbed.

In this sense, the concerns about the poor and disadvantaged that appear to constrain policies that would push management in this direction are misplaced. Such policies would actually contribute to the resolution of ghetto employment problems. By themselves, however, they could not constitute the solution to the employment difficulties today that they might have in the 1950s and 1960s. The other part of the story of the ghetto labor market is the dynamic through which blacks emerged as the first of the new identity groups that characterize our society today. This emergence had begun to change the available employment opportunities long before the demise of mass production.

Changes in Black Attitudes

The characteristics and attitudes that made black workers so appealing to northern employers changed radically and dramatically under the impact of the civil rights movement in the 1960s. These changes reflected in no small part changes in the black experience itself. By the middle 1960s the northern black labor force had come to be dominated by the children of the original migrant population, who had been raised in the North.[29]

Members of this new generation compared their parents' jobs and the jobs open to them not to southern black opportunities but to the opportunities open to northern whites, jobs available in the primary sector, and they found their own opportunities inferior and degrading. They were disillusioned by their parents' experience and had a keen sense of betrayal of the promise of the American dream. They had been raised in the fragmented structure of urban migrant communities without the kind of supervision and discipline provided to black children in the South, encountering experiences completely foreign to their parents, who often were unable to offer relevant advice or understanding. They had a new language and style cultivated in urban areas, in part in reaction to the style and mannerisms of their parents.

Other children and young adults who moved into this world from the South were teased and ridiculed by their northern-born contemporaries and tried, as a result, to adopt the new style. They fell into a pattern of anger and belligerence, especially in dealing with whites, in order to repress the instinctive subservience that had been beaten into them by their southern upbringing, and that anger and resentment became incorporated into the new styles of black youth.[30]

All of this was encouraged and ultimately crystallized by the civil rights movement, and by the demonstrations and riots that accompanied it. It was very much a part of the process through which the black community self-consciously sought to assert control over its own identity. But one of its results was that the labor force whose demeanor had only yesterday seemed exemplary to their employers suddenly seemed to turn surly and resentful, difficult or impossible to supervise, and prone to violence.

Employers began to say that black youth didn't want to work, but the truth was that black youth were ambivalent. Many actually wanted to work, and they certainly wanted the income, but they did not want the kind of work that was available to them. Because the late 1960s was a period of such full employment that the jobs they could get were plentiful and the employment and training programs made them even easier to get when income was required, there seemed no reason to make great sacrifices to keep a job when you had it. And the changing attitudes and styles of the ghetto made the sacrifices in terms of the behavioral code of most secondary employment seem very high indeed.

The result was that employers began to look for a substitute labor force, and they quickly found one in new immigrants, first from Latin America and later from Asia, whom they recruited in much the same way they had recruited blacks to replace European immigrants in World War I and their children during and after World War II. This is the beginning of another chapter in ethnic succession.[31]

The changes in attitudes that occurred among blacks in the 1960s were not unique; they are in many ways a continuing feature of the immigrant experience in industrial society. A comparable change in attitudes occurred in the United States among urban ethnic groups in the 1930s as the children of late-nineteenth- and early-twentieth-century European immigrants came to dominate the industrial labor force. It expressed itself in the New Deal urban ethnic machines and in the industrial union movement that was, in this sense, comparable to the civil rights movement of the 1960s. Because the country was so committed to interpreting the black experience in terms of the history of race relations, the parallel went largely unnoticed. Moreover, the shift in attitudes of earlier immigrants, insofar as it was responsible for the industrial union movement, also left its impact, as we just saw, on the structure of economic institutions in ways that were not very helpful to black mobility and were not easy to address either for the older ethnic groups or for the black leadership, which was allied with these older groups in the Democratic Party.[32]

This interpretation, like theories of the black underclass and the culture of poverty, places heavy weight for its understanding of current employment problems upon the culture and social structure of the ghetto; but because it sees that structure as continuously evolving, its implications are a good deal more open and subject to influence by policy and politics. If attitudes changed radically once, in a very short period of time, they might change radically and suddenly again.

The style of behavior that alienated employers may be more deeply ingrained among black youth; it is the way people in the ghetto grew up being, so to speak, not an affectation self-consciously and deliberately adopted in rebellion against their parents or in an attempt to overcome their own southern upbringing. But the fact that the style is now unconscious suggests that it has lost its original meaning to the people who display it. The racial caste system of the old South has also receded from active memory, and it should thus be easier to assume a purely instrumental attitude toward the behavior required to gain access to white-controlled employment opportunities. In any case, the way the ghetto style developed and spread in the 1960s reminds us how rapidly and radically styles of behavior can be abandoned and new styles generated to replace them. The programs that seek to "teach" black youth what behavior is acceptable and get them to adopt it, an approach that was typical of the early manpower programs, might thus elicit a very different response were they to be replicated today.

Employer attitudes would also have to change if these programs were to reopen the jobs that black youth once held, but the thrust of the argument I am developing is that, in the North, employers were a lot less prejudiced and a lot more attentive to the reality of black attitudes back then they are generally given credit for. That this remains true even today is suggested by the fact that black immigrants, who have both a different style and a different attitude toward work, have never had any problem gaining access to the menial jobs from which native-born blacks are now excluded.

All of this makes it seem likely that the old programs would operate differently today even if they were revived without any other changes in economic and social policy. The policies suggested above should, however, augment their effectiveness. Many of the measures whose basic rationale is to discourage the low-road strategy, for example a higher minimum wage and universal health insurance, will indirectly make the wages and working conditions of low-wage jobs more attractive. And the shift toward the high-road strategy will increase the opportunities for upward mobility of low-wage workers.

The shift will, of course, also reduce employment opportunities for unskilled workers. That effect might be a problem if ghetto workers really wanted these low-wage jobs, but, as we have seen, they basically do not. The newly created skilled jobs will not automatically go to disadvantaged workers, but other institutional changes associated with the shift toward the high-road strategy increase the opportunities for public policy interventions that affect the distribution of jobs. Most important among these are the movement away from training and job-security arrangements tied to individual firms, toward arrangements that operate through a community of enterprises. The kind of training and placement services that in the Great Society programs were specially designed for disadvantaged workers will be needed by all workers and will become critical to the success of the enterprises as well. The stigma once associated with them will disappear, and at the same time there will be pressures to make them work effectively that were never present under the old system.

I have argued that public authorities need to intervene to promote these arrangements, and if the new institutions arise in this way, public authorities will be in a better position to insure access for all workers. But even if the new institutions are privately controlled through some kind of co-operative arrangement among enterprises, or through trade unions, the fact that they are separate from the production process will make them easier to supervise and monitor.

It is more difficult to see how public policy interventions might effect the changes in the attitudes and behavior of the more alienated segments of the black workforce. But this is largely because our understanding of the processes of cultural change and evolution is so underdeveloped, and our view of the ghetto culture itself so distorted. The gang organizations among black ghetto youth (which are a relatively new phenomenon—or rather a recent revival of a type of social organization that in the 1960s and 1970s was largely absent from black urban life); ghetto music, of which rap is only the most recent development in a continuous musical tradition; the new wave of black-directed films drawing upon the material of ghetto life and attracting large audiences in the ghetto but also throughout the society; even the organization of drug delivery, all suggest a much stronger and more dynamic culture, and a much higher degree of social structure and organization than is implied by terms like the "culture of poverty" or the "black underclass."

They also suggest much stronger and more organic ties between the culture of the ghetto and that of upper-income blacks and between the culture of the ghetto and mainstream American popular culture. The question is how to turn these ties to advantage. How can we use them to give those who are now apparently trapped in the ghetto access to employment and careers on the outside? How can we use them to build faith in the capacity of the society to operate as a high-wage economy and overcome the inhibitions that the lingering problem of black unemployment seems to place upon the willingness of even a liberal, Democratic administration to pursue a policy that tilts the economic structure toward high-wage jobs?

Conclusion

The economic problems of the ghetto labor force bring us full circle, back to the new identity groups and the difficulties they pose for the political process. Indeed, as I have characterized them the two types of problems are really outgrowths of the same process. The attitudes and behaviors that now bar ghetto blacks from employment grow out of their attempt to redefine themselves as a group in American society; those same attitudes and behaviors have become the language and style through which they now define themselves as individuals within their own community. In a way, these attitudes and behaviors are like the deafness of the students at Gallaudet.

To break through the barrier these attitudes and behaviors pose to employment opportunity, we need somehow to break down cultural isolation, not simply the cultural isolation of the black ghetto but also, it should be emphasized, the cultural isolation of the community of potential employers, which now serves as a barrier to the reevaluation of the potential of these workers and the reconsideration of the policies and practices that exclude them from jobs. If gangs, movies, rap music, and fashion suggest that the isolation is not as great as we might think, we are still a long way from knowing how to turn these ties to advantage through policy. If we did know how to do this, it seems, we would also know how to manage the political process dominated by other identity groups for whom the black movement of the 1960s served as a model.

But while our examination of the economic problems of the black ghetto points backward toward the political and social phenomena that were the subject of the earlier chapters, those problems are not different from the other economic problems that have been the focus here. Indeed, the root of the problems the society faces in politics is exactly the same as that of the problems we face in adjusting the economic structure: the difficulty of communication across closed social boundaries. The economy, like the society more broadly, is structured around separate communities and institutions that have their own ways of thinking and understanding, ways that facilitate the ability of their members to relate to each other and limit their ability to communicate with outsiders. If there is a difference, it is that in politics the boundaries around groups that create the difficulties in communication and understanding are relatively new. In the economy, in contrast, it is not the new structures but those inherited from the past that are too closed, too self-contained, too wedded to their own approaches to form the networks and teams that are required to compete effectively in the current technological and competitive environment.

This is a problem most of all, moreover, because we do not know how to think about it; it requires us to recognize and understand community, and we are prisoners of a conceptual apparatus that recognizes only individuals. If our economic problems are more severe in this regard, it is only because our conceptual apparatus—for thinking about not only economic problems but wider aspects of society— to the extent that it is embedded in a coherent and articulated set of theoretical understandings, is economic theory itself. It is thus to economic theory that we turn in the next chapter.

4

A Cognitive Approach
to Economics

The tension between individualism and community is a continuing theme in American life. This is not the first time this tension has become entangled. in economics and the prescriptions for resolving it have been drawn from competitive economic theory. Why this attraction in the United States to economic theory? Why do the solutions drawn from that theory so often fail to solve even our economic problems? Why, despite those failures, do we still turn to the theory for solutions not only to our economic problems but to broader political and social problems as well?

At one level there is a direct and straightforward answer to these questions. The attraction of competitive economic theory lies in our attachment to liberal individualism and individual autonomy.[1] Individual autonomy constitutes at one and the same time a standard by which we judge how society *ought* to be constructed and the starting point from which we seek to understand how society does, in fact, operate. And competitive economics provides a theory which builds upon, and promises to realize, this ideal of the autonomous individual.[2] It does this, moreover, in a complex and sophisticated way. A society can be composed of individuals in a trivial sense if the individuals are simply added together. But the social system that emerges in a competitive economy is a good deal more than the sum of its parts; individuals are led to behave within the economy differently from the ways they would behave were they outside it, and the welfare of the community that emerges in the process is much, much greater. At another level, however, this direct answer masks a different and more fundamental question: Why are we in the United States so attached to this notion of individual autonomy? Where does that attachment ultimately come from? Why does it persist?

It is not as if a social theory built around the autonomous individual has been spectacularly successful in explaining the phenomena with which we in the United States have actually had to grapple. This is certainly the message of the preceding chapters. Neither the new social groups emerging in politics nor the organizational structures of productive enterprises that are effective in the current economic environment are comprehensible in these terms. But these facts only deepen the mystery of why we nonetheless persist in trying to understand them in individualist terms. If they cannot be understood in terms of liberal individualism, how else might we understand them?

In an earlier but not very distant time, an active intellectual alternative to liberal individualism was provided by Marxist social thought. That approach has now been discredited by events in Eastern Europe and the former Soviet Union. But the attraction of Marxism had been diminished even before those events by the same economic and political phenomena that are straining liberal individualism. The greatest strength of Marx's analysis was that it anticipated features of Western societies that liberal individualism seemed to deny. The dominant forms of corporate organization were essentially coincident with those Marx foresaw and analyzed, and political conflict was structured around the socioeconomic classes that Marx placed at the center of his analytical scheme. The new forms of business organization, however, confound the predictions of Marxist thought and are completely alien to its analytical apparatus, and the politics of the new identity groups is disturbing precisely because it eludes the familiar structures of class conflict.

In this context, the collapse of the old Soviet empire was less important than its aftermath, which has revealed problems that parallel those which strain Marxist and liberal theories in the West. The ethnic conflicts there are extreme versions of the politics of the new identity groups; the East is faced with an equally extreme version of the Western problem of converting bureaucratic productive institutions into business units that can compete effectively in the international marketplace.

If Marxism no longer provides an alternative to liberal individualism, is there perhaps some third way of understanding economics and politics? Might we not even find a mode of understanding that gives individual actors the role that Americans seem to want them to have, that recognizes the integrity of individual persons that Marxism, with its emphasis on class conflict, seemed to deny?

This chapter and the next explore various paths along which such a third way of understanding might be pursued. In this chapter we examine the behavioral foundations of conventional economic theory and trace its limitations for thinking about the issues of concern in this book to its theory of knowledge: the basic problem is that it views behavior as the product of an effort to organize a set of means to attain a particular goal. It assumes that we possess for this purpose a set of causal models that connect the one to the other. But it does not explain where those models come from, let alone how they change over time.

I argue that this limitation can be overcome through ideas drawn from cognitive psychology. Those ideas provide a place for society in the operation of the economy. They also explain how the structures of American society might make their role difficult to recognize and hence sustain a notion of individualism that seems to deny society's existence. By and large, these ideas can be grafted on to liberal theory, enriching it without fundamentally changing its analytical thrust. But they ultimately prove too limited to deal with the problems of social and economic organization American society faces today. The next chapter thus turns to a more radical approach. It is an extension of the principles of cognitive psychology with which this chapter deals, but it requires us to think about human behavior in terms very different from those in which it is conceived in conventional economic theory.

Rational Choice

Competitive economic theory tells two distinct stories. One is about individual behavior. The other is about the economy as a system of interconnected individuals.

In the first story, individuals *optimize:* each person behaves so as to maximize his or her own personal welfare. Behind optimization lie two further assumptions about how people make economic decisions. People are assumed to make a sharp distinction between means and ends, and they are assumed to possess a causal model about how the means affect the ends. To optimize, they organize the means at their disposal, in the way dictated by this causal model, in order to "maximize" the ends that they want to achieve.

The story about the economy as a whole emerges from the story about the behavior of the individual economic agents. Its basic outlines can be found in Adam Smith, although, of course, it has been greatly refined by subsequent analysts. In a competitive economy where there are many buyers and sellers who optimize, as the theory of individual behavior assumes, each making decisions autonomously but all responding to the same set of market prices, the individual optima achieved by the separate agents will lead to a social optimum as well. Each individual will be induced to do what makes the greatest contribution to the whole, and the system will produce the maximum possible welfare for its members taken individually and in the aggregate.

Strictly speaking, the theory of individual behavior is not necessary to produce this result. The same outcome would emerge in a competitive system through natural selection even if individuals chose what they were doing in a purely arbitrary way. The least effective producers would lose money and be driven from the market, and, in the end, the most effective producers would remain.[3] But in a market economy, composed of purposeful and even mildly self-reflective people, purely arbitrary behavior is extremely unlikely. People would anticipate the effect of the competition, and those who were unwilling or unable to behave as the market demands would drop out on their own. In a competitive market, in other words, competition should naturally select the behavior long before it had to naturally select the result.

There is thus a certain coherence to economic theory. The behavioral pattern it ascribes to the agents is not really *assumed,* it is imposed by the institutional arrangements within which they operate. There are institutions that promote similar behavior in certain other social settings. The politician seeking to retain office in a democratic electoral process, for example, might make decisions so as to maximize his expected vote. However, outside a competitive market, or some analogous institutional mechanism to enforce it, this model is considerably less plausible.

Nonetheless, analysts have not been content to limit it to such circumstances. Economists themselves have extended it to consumer behavior, where the individual is assumed to maximize utility, not profits. In recent years economic theorists have increasingly focused on the analysis of this behavioral pattern and its implications within the firm where there is no direct competition.[4] It has been extended—primarily by other social scientists and philosophers, but with the help of some economists as well—to human behavior in general. It is particularly influential as a model of policymaking and politics. In the United States it provides the basic analytical framework taught not only in business schools (where one might assume that the competitive pressures of the environment where the students are being trained to work makes it appropriate) but also in schools of public policy. In its generalized form, it is known in philosophy as *rational choice theory*.[5] Most rational choice theorists are American, and the theory's career within the social sciences seems to reinforce the idea that there is something peculiar about the American experience that makes it particularly plausible and appealing in this country.

The limits of competitive economics, both as a broad theory of social and economic organization and as a theory of individual behavior, are easy to identify. As a theory of how to construct an economic system, competitive theory fails because it is basically a story about efficiency, about how to do the best with what we have, given what we already know. But economic welfare seems to be much more dependent upon growth than upon efficiency in the narrow sense. Even today, when a slowdown in the growth rate is a central policy concern, the American economy grows at over 2 percent per year. In a ten-year period we increase our output of goods and services by over 20 percent. It is difficult to believe that we could generate this much increased output through improvements in efficiency. And even if we did, those improvements would be a one-shot deal. After they had been made, we would have to turn back to economic growth to increase our standard of living.

This logic is reflected in business practice. The theories that have had the greatest impact on practice, whether they be the mass production theories of Ford and Taylor or the newer networking theories derived from Japan, Germany, and Italy, were developed to solve the problem of growth, not the problem of efficiency.

The new networked organization, moreover, appears to conflict with the competitive market as a social form. The kind of technological change for which networks are valued involves intense, direct interaction among individuals and organizations. Networks are thus the antithesis of the isolated individuals acting independently, constrained only by income and prices, which constitute the nodes in the competitive marketplace.

It might conceivably be possible to use these two forms of organization simultaneously by assigning some kinds of problems to networks (for example, the problems of creating new products and methods of production) and other kinds of problems to markets (for example, the allocation of scarce resources) but even this is questionable. As Adam Smith pointed out at a very early point in the development of market theory, if you allow business people to get together to discuss anything, they will inevitably conspire to fix prices, forestall competition, and thereby compromise the efficiency of a market system. And if dynamic economic processes cannot be organized without direct communication among society's members, it is hard to see how society in general could be constituted in this way.

But the problem of rational choice theory is not limited to networked organizations. Rational choice is unable to explain technological change even in a competitive marketplace. Technology is "useful knowledge"; it is the body of theory, the causal understandings, which enable us to convert resources into goods and services. Rational choice theory assumes that we know these causal relationships. It does not explain where that knowledge comes from, let alone how it changes over time. It does not, for that matter, explain even how we identify the resources that serve as means, or the goods and services that are the ends, or how we distinguish between means and ends. It lacks an epistemology, a theory of knowledge. It begs the fundamental epistemological questions: What do I know? How do I know it? Do I know what you know? Do we know the same things? When you see a chair and I see a chair, do we see the same thing? When a tree falls in the forest and there is no one around to hear it, does it make a sound?

Classical American liberalism derives from John Locke and was built around the radically objectivist position that he adopted in response to these questions: There is an external world and we perceive it directly. When you see a chair and I see a chair, we see the same thing. When a tree falls, it makes a sound whether or not there is someone around to hear it. We intuit the causal relationship between the falling tree and the sound it makes directly from nature. Convictions like these are rooted in Locke's conception of the human mind as a *tabula rasa,* an empty slate upon which external reality is mapped through experience.[6]

This view may still dominate the kind of instinctive, unreflective liberalism that pervades American society. But the more considered and self-conscious liberalism of rational choice theory tends to rest more comfortably on an idealistic approach reminiscent—somewhat paradoxically, given the political ideologies with which this approach has been associated in the past—of Plato or Descartes: the critical behavioral patterns and the central conceptual understandings that underlie behavior are present in the mind prior to, and independent of, experience in the world. This view opens the door to an extreme solipsism in which knowledge is solely dependent upon our internal representations, and the chair you see is likely to have nothing to do with the chair I see.

Earlier versions invoked God to ensure some correspondence among the mental images possessed by different people and between the external world and our internal representations of it. In place of God, modern theorists invoke biology: the representations, or at least the mode of representation, they claim, are "wired into" the human system biologically. These can then be thought of as passed from one generation to another like other biological traits and as evolving through mutation and natural selection. Natural selection ensures compatibility.

This approach is used to "explain" not only the causal models we use to connect means and ends but also the behavioral pattern itself, the tendency to think in causal terms and to optimize. Biological structures and natural selection then substitute for the institutional structures that make this behavior pattern plausible in a competitive market. And it is the "sociobiology" of this behavior pattern that makes it plausible to use the theory of economic behavior as a theory of human behavior more generally.[7]

In principle, the sociobiology of human behavior could be separated from the sociobiology of the causal models we invoke to decide the substance of behavior in a particular situation. But this will not solve the problem with which we are concerned here, because it is precisely the way those causal models emerge and evolve over time that needs to be pinned down in a theory of technological change.

In any case, none of the extreme variants of sociobiology in which one might ground the behavioral assumptions of rational choice theory is consistent with the dominant trends in psychological research. This research suggests that what is interesting about human behavior is not the way it is biologically determined but precisely the fact the it is biologically indeterminate and open. Because much of this research has been generated by the effort to develop information technology and its results underlie computer science and are at the forefront of the technological revolution through which we are living, it is very difficult to ignore. We shall discuss it here under the heading of cognitive psychology.[8]

Cognitive Psychology

The dominant view in cognitive psychology starts with the proposition—which is in itself not inconsistent with sociobiology—that our relationship to the external world is mediated by a set of mental images. We see a chair because we have an image of a chair already in mind. These mental images are variously termed *paradigms, models, theories,* or *cognitive structures.* They lead us to see selectively. They enable us to focus, to screen out background noise from objects and events that are of no real interest or concern. In so doing, these structures equip us to operate effectively in the environment in which we live. All biological organisms have an equivalent set of mechanisms; without adequate mechanisms of this kind, the organism cannot survive.

But the structures at stake here can be generated in different ways. They can be innate, the product of the biological evolution of the species. But they can also be acquired through interaction with the external environment. Biological organisms differ in terms of the relative mixture of these two sources of mediating structure. Organisms that are hard-wired have difficulty adjusting to changes in the environment. Organisms that acquire more of the critical structure through interaction with the world are more supple. They can supplement their biological apparatus through experience, and this enables them to operate in various environments, environments that biological evolution did not "anticipate."

The different biological species are arrayed along a spectrum in terms of the degree to which the structures that mediate their relationship to the external world are innate or acquired. Human beings stand at one end of this spectrum. We are distinguished from other biological organisms—indeed one could say from all other things—by the degree to which we acquire the critical mediating structures through interaction with the environment after birth, and by the degree to which, once acquired, these structures can be modified, replaced, and/or abandoned. This gives us a unique capacity to adjust to a wide variety of worlds.

The classic illustration of this insight is the analogy between the beehive and a complex manufacturing system. The two may look alike. They may even be functionally equivalent. But the bees in the hive are specialized biologically. They cannot exchange roles and functions among themselves. And neither the bees individually nor the hive as an organizational structure can adapt to changes in the external environment. Human beings *learn* their specialized roles, and these roles, individually and collectively, can be changed as external circumstances require.[9]

The fact that our mediating structures are supple and adaptable in this way gives us an enormous advantage over other species, but it is also responsible for the basic human dilemma: our very capacity to adapt to changing circumstances makes our grasp upon external reality problematic. We cannot be certain about the external world. Meaning and interpretative capacity are always contingent. The fundamental epistemological puzzles are thus symptomatic of the nature of humankind as a species. We are fated always to wonder whether the tree makes a sound, whether a chair is a chair. Experience has the capacity at one and the same time to direct action and to so fundamentally call into question our ability to understand that it forecloses any action at all.

The contingency of our cognitive structures thus translates into a felt sense of the contingency of our grasp upon reality. While it is actually indicative of our ability to adjust and survive in a changing environment, it leaves us torn between what one sociologist characterizes as *anomie* and *alienation*.[10] We vacillate between the feeling that our grasp upon reality is dissolving and we are being lost in a sea of senselessness and confusion (anomie) and the attempt to pin down reality, to anchor it outside ourselves in nature or in God (alienation).

But if they do not adhere in nature or in God, where do these structures that pin down reality for us come from? Experiments in learning suggest that, at least in part, these structures grow out of experience, and evolve from simple, elemental representations to increasingly complex systems for organizing knowledge. Early experiences, which recur, are essentially memorized. We collect them in sequences of things that we learn to expect will be repeated one after another in time. Or we think of them against background characteristics of the environment, much as Pavlov's dogs learned to associate food with the sound of a bell. The initial order of experience may thus be termed *concrete*.

But as experience accumulates we begin to perceive more abstract relationships that are governing. As we do so, the abstractions replace the concrete experiences as the cognitive structures that are stored in our mind. Thus, in language acquisition, we may begin by memorizing a set of words or the sentences into which the words form. But we quickly acquire a set of grammatical rules that govern the generation of the sentence we speak and the interpretation of what we hear. Over time, as experience expands, these rules through which we understand experience and generate action become increasingly abstract, governing a wider and wider range of experience and increasingly far removed from any particular concrete situation or event.

In these respects, cognitive psychology is not completely different from liberal epistemology. It has a more complex and involved view of perception, but understanding is ultimately a reflection of an objective, external reality, albeit not always a direct and faithful one. The increased complexity is nonetheless significant. It has two important behavioral implications.

First, the distinction that cognitive psychology generates between abstract and concrete structures of thought suggests that economic agents and political actors do not always distinguish means and ends in quite the way that economic theory assumes. Agents will make this distinction when they understand what they are doing in abstract terms: the nature of abstraction is that it permits us to see that there are many ways to, for example, build a car or set wages for a job. We insert a bolt *in order to* attach the wheel to the car. A wage is paid *in order to* attract a supply of labor.

Engineers and craftsmen with high levels of education and/or a broad range of experience on the job may well perceive the world in these terms. But semi-skilled workers, especially those in assembly, have neither the training nor the experience that would enable them to understand what they are doing in this way. They tend instead to memorize their job as a sequence of operations performed one after another and repeated in a continuous cycle. Because they understand the job in this way, changes that the engineers view as improvements in the production process or a response to changes in the business environment are, for the production worker, inexplicable. They threaten his or her sense of control over the world, they generate the anxiety associated with anomie, and they are resisted as if the way the work is done, the memorized routine of the job, were an end in itself.

Often workers became attached to certain wage patterns in a similar way.

They come to expect wages to change regularly at a certain time of the year or a particular set of differentials to be maintained between jobs; they become uncomfortable when these patterns are threatened and act to defend them as ends in themselves. Managers who have a broader understanding of the process of wage setting see wages as a way of allocating labor or motivating workers, or, in more personal terms, as a way to support of consumption patterns, and can be persuaded to accept change in terms that have no meaning to the workers.

This distinction between concrete and abstract structures is important in understanding particular phenomena, especially in a mass production economy where the economies of scale associated with long runs of standardized products place a high premium upon stability. To achieve that stability, much of the variability in conditions that would lead economic actors to develop a broad understanding of the world in which they work is suppressed, and the range of experience that is understood concretely is greatly enlarged. But at the higher organizational level where the critical decisions governing the behavior of productive enterprises are made, the agents generally understand the relevant operations abstractly, and decisions are cast in terms of a distinction between means and ends.

The Social Foundations of Knowledge

The second, and for present purposes more important, insight of cognitive psychology is about society. The enriched understanding about the relationship between our mental images and the external environment provided by cognitive science generates an organic notion of society and its relationship to identity and individuality that liberal epistemology does not have.

Human beings acquire these cognitive structures through their interaction with the external environment. That environment is not given by the physical universe. It is generally a social environment in which even physical objects derive their meaning from the social context in which they appear. Much of what we need to know to operate effectively, indeed in many cases even to survive, is purely social. Chairs are classified as barstools and thrones, and barstools are reserved for one use and thrones for another. Because so much of what we know is specific to particular social contexts, moreover, our grasp upon reality, our ability to operate effectively, meaning, understanding, interpretative capacity, are all socially de-limited. Beyond the boundaries of these accustomed social settings, experience is meaningless; it is largely noise. Our capacity for rationality in the sense that we understand that term in liberal theory is socially bounded. Society then becomes a precondition for rationality: we could no more think of disobeying the rules that constitute its structuring principles than we could think of disobeying the laws of gravity.

Actually, our dependence on society extends even to the laws that govern the physical universe, to the laws of the natural world that are in fact independent of society, for most of these laws are too complex to be grasped by induction solely from our own personal experience. Clinical evidence suggests that the simplest principles governing the physical world—the law of the conservation of matter, for example—are induced or intuited in this way.[11] Perhaps we also induce an intuitive version of the law of gravity. But not even so elemental and critical an idea as the "fact" that the earth revolves around the sun is induced directly from nature. It is something we are taught through a social process; to the extent that it is induced from natural observations, it draws from the accumulated observations of a collective historical experience preserved and passed from one generation to the next through society.

Because, in all of these ways, our cognitive structures are anchored in a social setting, our attachment to social groups can be interpreted as an attempt to preserve the space in which these structures are relevant and we are "operational." Because the structures derive from these groups, the attachment is also part of a process of alienation, the effort to overcome contingency by attaching these structures to a stable and enduring anchor outside ourselves. It is like our belief in God or in nature. We have an overwhelming need to preserve the social settings in which we feel at home, because without them the world degenerates into chaos.

But if our cognitive structures are socially derived and their range of applicability socially circumscribed, one can nonetheless see how societies might be constructed so that the individual's actual experience hides these social limits and the *felt* experience is one of individual autonomy, leaving each person with the impression that his or her cognitive structures are natural and immutable. This would be the case, for example, if the individual always operated within the boundaries of a single society. But it might also be the case if social units were arranged so that interactions between them were limited and governed by a set of "meta-rules" that they shared with one another. A federal system could be constructed in this way.

The Marbles of Neuchatel

The way in which such a system would operate and its governing principles come to be perceived by its members is suggested by the Swiss psychologist Jean Piaget in *The Moral Judgement of the Child,* a study of how children understand the rules of the games they play.[12] The first chapter of this book is about the game of marbles played by boys in Neuchatel, Switzerland. The basic structure of the game is the same throughout the city, but the rules vary somewhat from one neighborhood to another, and when it is played by children who come from different neighborhoods they have to decide which rules will govern before the game begins.

Children, Piaget reports, go through stages in their understanding of these rules. Very young children vaguely perceive that the game has a structure but do not understand what it is, and hence they make believe, imitating the motions and emotions of their older brothers without actually playing a game. Older children understand the rules of the game and actually do play it, but they think the rules are fixed and immutable. At a third stage the children understand that the rules change as one moves from neighborhood to neighborhood; they have mastered a formula invoked at the beginning of the game to determine which rules will prevail. In a final stage the children have a sense that, although the particular rules may be determined by the formula, there is also a distinction between *better* rules and *worse* rules: therefore you need not select among the possible rules in terms of some arbitrary formula; you can pick the better rules. The better rules are those which make the outcome of the game more dependent on the relative skills of the players and less on luck. Skill thus comes to be seen as the *natural* metric for judging the rules of the game.

Piaget himself had a complex (and not uncontroversial) theory of what produced this progression. But for our purposes, the critical element in the process is the *range of experience*. Children's understanding of the rules of marbles depends upon the range of variation they encounter in how the game is played. They form their initial understanding by memorizing a routine, first a simple sequence of things they do to play marbles, then a repertoire of responses to the situations that the unfolding game creates, and ultimately a repertoire of responses associated not only with the situations within the game but also with the particular neighborhoods in which the game might be played. Finally they induce out of the collection of memorized experiences the notion that skill governs the shifting rules of the game. But if they do not encounter sufficient variation in experience, they will never arrive at the abstraction, and the rules will remain a memorized collection. And a sense of the social contingency of the rules can only emerge if the children actually move across neighborhoods and experience alternative ways of playing the game. Otherwise, the rules will seem natural and objective.

In these childhood games, objectivity—the perception of the rules as embedded in nature—is not only associated with the child confined to a single neighborhood. It is paradoxically also the perception of the child who moves across many neighborhoods and learns (through that experience) that the rules are judged by a common metric of skill. Piaget, and even more so his disciple Lawrence Kohlberg, interpreted this kind of abstract metric that reconciles otherwise contingent social norms as if it were truly objective.[13] But anthropological studies suggest that the abstract norms through which games like marbles are ultimately judged are not universal. In some situations, even in Switzerland, pure chance—in other words, luck—is the norm sought in the design of games. In other societies, games are designed to validate a preestablished social hierarchy, or to maintain equity between social forces, and the outcomes are preordained.[14]

Thus, the principle of skill that the child discovers by playing marbles in the different neighborhoods of Neuchatel is not a truly universal norm, but a norm of Swiss, or perhaps only Neuchatel, culture, a norm that is shared by all of the different neighborhoods of the city and that binds them together into a single community. Skill is a contingent norm in the way that neighborhood rules are contingent; the range over which it prevails is simply much wider. The existence of norms of this kind is what enables Neuchatel to exist as a single community despite the variation in rules across its neighborhoods. This is not the only way in which different neighborhoods could conceivably combine to form a larger whole, but it does provide an important clue as to how the American experience might generate the perception of the objectivity of knowledge.

The Federal Structure of the American Experience

American society is formed, like the marbles game in Neuchatel, from the ground up. It is composed of many "neighborhoods," distinct communities, each with its own parochial set of rules and norms. These communities are grouped, or federated, to form larger units, and those units are grouped, in turn, to form still larger jurisdictions, counties to form a state, states to form the nation. Or to take a completely different example, manufacturing shops are federated to form a local union, locals to form the national union, national unions to form the AFL-CIO. At each level of federation, a set of more universal procedures and standards is created for reconciling conflicts among norms, but always in a way that preserves the autonomy of the norms of each constituent community within its own boundaries.

We term this structure *contractual,* but it is really a hierarchy of contracts. And it is contractual not so much in the sense that it is voluntary, which it often is not. It is contractual in the sense that the jurisdiction of each set of norms and procedures is limited, preserving the space for the rule of the norms at the levels below it. The construction, moreover, is actually even more complex than the term *contract* suggests. It does not simply involve limits upon the jurisdiction of the rules at any level; it involves a partitioning of *activity* as well, so that we place activities at the lowest level of the hierarchy where they can be performed without reference to other jurisdictions and hence can be governed by their own rules or norms without reference to a more universal standard. This partitioning of activity generates two extreme experiences of objectivity at the same time. The social contingency of one range of experience is hidden from us by the fact that it is always dealt with through local norms and we never encounter variation at all. And the contingency of another range of experience is hidden by the fact that conflicts of norms are always resolved by reference to apparently universal standards.

Another aspect of the architecture of American society that obscures the contingency of knowledge is the distinction we draw between the public and private spheres. This distinction replicates in the most personal aspects of our lives the structure that hierarchical federalism creates in the political sphere. In the public realm we encounter universal rules; in the private realm the rules of behavior are viewed as a matter of "taste," by which we

mean purely subjective criteria in judgment. Civil liberties, the great free-
doms of the Constitution, of the press, of religion, the newly emerging
rights of privacy, are all ways of personalizing and individualizing what
might otherwise be perceived as social knowledge. The very term *lifestyle*
suggests this element of subjectivity or personal choice and is itself a way
of denying or effacing the social implications of ethnicity or sexual orientation or even sex-based differences in experience, by relegating them to a
personal realm.

The national ethos reinforces this notion of the objectivity of knowledge
and the strong sense of individuality that seems to accompany it. The dominance of Protestant religions with their emphasis on the direct and unmediated relationship between the individual and God works in this direction. The salience of the frontier in American iconography also works
in this way. The frontier experience—where the individual grew up relatively isolated from other people in close contact with nature—must have
powerfully reinforced, if it did not actually originate, the sense of the objectivity of experience and of the individual as separate from, distinct from,
and prior to society. Of course, the interpretation of the experience in
nature on the frontier was every bit as dependent upon inherited culture
as the interpretations we give to nature in a more densely populated world.
But the isolation of the frontier served both to obscure the social origins
of the interpretations we get from those around us and, at the same time,
to insulate us from other, alternative, and possibly conflicting, ways of
living and of understanding.[15]

Urbanization and industrialization worked in many ways to preserve the
sense of objectivity and individuality generated on the frontier. These processes involved an enormous social turnover and physical mobility so that
people ended up moving constantly across social settings, experiencing
their existence as separate and distinct from any particular setting. Much
of that mobility, it seems, was such that people never stayed long enough
in one place to absorb the deeper social norms prevailing there, and cooperative endeavors were built around a simpler, stripped-down set of rules
and procedures analogous to what linguists call a pidgin (as opposed to a
true language).

And in the twentieth century, with the advent of mass consumption, we
have come to share a completely homogeneous national culture. We share
a common language and a common set of consumption goods and enter-

tainment experiences. As we travel around the country, we see the same fast food restaurants, watch the same television soap operas and sitcoms, follow the same major sports events, and share national politics. Below this national culture there are innumerable separate, particularistic cultures associated with various religious sects, ethnic groups, and special interests. All of us participate in some of these local cultures, but we have learned to think of them as part of our private experience.

Even the immigration experience, which we now associate with cohesive ethnic communities, seems to have lent itself to this construction. The great waves of immigration in the late nineteenth and early twentieth centuries came from parts of Europe that did not yet have a strong national identity; in many cases, the immigrants spoke local dialects rather than national languages.[16] The ethnicity with which they came to associate in the United States was thus something constructed here, not brought with them from abroad. It had the plasticity to conform to the American models.

The immigrant experience placed people in completely novel situations, situations with which their cultures of origin had no experience. They were therefore predisposed to adopt American norms and the English language, in a way that they were not prepared to adopt the national norms and language in their country of origin, where they already had an operating model of long standing which was perfectly adequate to deal with their life experiences.

The relationship between the immigrant and the national culture thus mirrored the relationship between the individual and nature on the frontier. The particular experience of the immigrants was privatized and relegated to an individualistic realm or to a newly created ethnic subculture that they might share with others coming from the same general region but that, since it was formed in the United States and had no prior existence as such, was always subordinated to the more universal, national standards.

Parallels in Economic Theory

Many of the divisions that underlie the American social structure are reflected in the structure of competitive economic theory, and this undoubtedly reinforces the theory's appeal in the American context. The theory, for example, draws a distinction among three types of economic activity: consumption, production, and exchange. The distinction between exchange and consumption parallels the distinction in American life between the public and private spheres. Exchange is public. It requires a common set of understandings and interpretative frames. Consumption is private, governed by individual preferences that are peculiar and personalistic. The theory is carefully constructed so that the preferences of individual consumers need not even be commensurate. Within this realm, the individual is completely autonomous. Production is autonomous in a different sense. Within each productive enterprise a common set of understandings is required, but these understandings need not extend across enterprises. The different spheres of understanding need only be compatible, and that compatibility is achieved through the market. Thus the relationship among the different productive enterprises is federal and the relationship between them and the market is hierarchical.

All of this, of course, is very much a construction. It may or may not be realized in the actual operation of society. Consumption and production are not in fact wholly separate and independent realms; much of our consumption—our clothing, our transportation, even what and where we eat—is determined by our productive roles. The theory, as we stressed earlier, does not specify the process through which the common understandings that are required for the market to operate are produced, and it is not clear that such a process could function without having an impact upon the realms of consumption and production. And this is before the issue of technological change—the Achilles' heel of competitive economic theory—ever arises.

But here the division of labor within the social sciences reinforces the construction of economics itself. These issues are referred elsewhere in scholarly territory. If the most extreme rational choice theorists complete their theory through biology, the other members of the discipline escape the puzzles by parceling out its assumptions to psychology, sociology, or politics in a way that enables them forever to avoid coming to terms with the consistency or plausibility of the whole.[17] .

Mass Production

The structures of a mass production economy, although very different from those of the competitive system upon which economic theory is focused, tend to foster a similar sense of individual autonomy. Mass production preserves the distinction between consumption and exchange. It leaves consumption within the private sphere.[18] It differs from a competitive economy in the realms of production and exchange. Many of the exchanges that in a competitive economy are made through the market are in mass production internalized within the corporation. The corporation is organized as a large bureaucracy, and the bureaucratic organization becomes the characteristic institution of a mass production economy.

The hallmark of such organizations is the rules that define the various positions within them, assign tasks, and delimit responsibilities. From one perspective, these rules severely limit the autonomy of the individuals within the organization. But, as noted in the preceding chapter, they also limit the claims that the organization can make upon the individual, and outside the roles and responsibilities that the rules define the individual remains free and autonomous.[19] The productive enterprise in mass production is, moreover, organized, like other American institutions, in a federal, hierarchical structure. At lower levels of the hierarchy, the individual need not pay any attention to the rules governing other units of the enterprises, need not even be aware of what those rules are.

Interactions among administrative units are governed by an explicit set of common rules; the experience of moving across the organizational structure is thus comparable to that of the marble players moving across neighborhoods in Neuchatel. The problems of technological change, and more broadly of creating and changing products, production processes, and the rules that define organizational roles and govern interactions, are relegated to a separate administrative unit.

Joseph Schumpeter argues that even the work of these innovative units is reduced to a set of routines that could be invoked by individual members of the organization without direct social interaction.[20] Perhaps one could understand this proposition through an analogy to the role that skill plays in developing new rules for the game of marbles. I shall argue below, however, that Schumpeter is wrong: that innovation involves a direct social interaction that cognitive psychology as we have developed it thus far cannot capture and that must of necessity compromise the autonomy of the individuals involved in the process. But mass production is driven by economies of scale in the production of a single standardized product, and innovation in a mass production economy is limited. Liberal notions of individual autonomy capture the felt experience of the broad mass of people who inhabit the corporate world.

As mass production developed in the United States, moreover, a significant portion of the labor force were never asked to "think" about their work at all. So long as the product line was confined to a limited set of standardized items produced in volume, each job in the organization could be reduced to the particular operations that that set of products required. This led to the stereotypical production jobs at the bottom of the organizational hierarchy consisting of a few operations repeated in a cycle again and again throughout the workday.

The job under these circumstances is understood *concretely,* that is, the cycle is memorized and performed by rote. The operator's span of control represents such a small part of the overall process that it would be virtually impossible for workers to grasp the underlying principles that govern the job directly from what they themselves are doing, and since the jobs are in any case quickly memorized, it does not pay for the employer to try to teach the governing principles. Indeed, the economies of rote learning are presumably one of the advantages of organizing work in this way. When something out of the ordinary occurs—when, for example, a machine breaks down—skilled repair people and managers who have a broader understanding of the product and the production process are called upon. But even these people encounter so many of the problems they handle repeatedly that they tend to invoke routine solutions as well.

We can see both the power and the limits of cognitive theory in addressing the dilemmas of economic policy by turning to look at how these bureaucratic structures absorbed the oil shock of 1974 and adjusted to the increasing instability of the economic environment that followed. There were three adjustment strategies. One was conceived within the framework of mass production itself. It was to develop a new product each time environmental conditions changed. In effect, the companies assumed that each change was permanent, although as they lived through a series of such changes they developed a collection of different products. For each new product, they retrained the labor force in essentially the same way it had been trained when only a simple product was being produced. The workers learned their jobs concretely; they memorized a sequence of tasks.

The second strategy was to anticipate the range of environmental conditions and to develop a series of different products, spread out over that range, in advance. In some of these cases the workers were also trained concretely. But in other cases they were taught the more general abstract principles governing their work; they were given, in effect, broad-based general education that enabled them to figure out how to do the jobs associated with each new product as it was introduced in response to a shift in demand.

The two strategies look similar and the terms used to describe them are often the same. Management thinks of the human resources policies associated with both strategies as skill upgrading and uses the terms *cross-training* and *education* interchangeably. But the policies are in fact very different. Concrete training is more efficient if the number of products is very limited and predictable. General education that focuses on abstract principles is better adapted to a wide and highly variable product range. General education also facilitates other practices associated with what has been termed high-performance human resources management. It permits workers to operate with less supervision and to take over planning and quality control, which have historically been performed by management or separate specialists. It permits worker participation in managerial decisions through, for example, quality circles. It makes it possible to eliminate in-process inventories, a reform that is essentially an in-house version of the Kan-Ban system and often introduced as an adjunct to it, but that requires very close cooperation and active problem-solving on the part of workers doing adjacent jobs.

When workers have essentially memorized their jobs they cannot absorb these other functions and are not in a position to discuss the work process in an analytical way. The distinction that cognitive theory makes between abstract and concrete learning makes this obvious. But because that distinction is not generally recognized by American management, the differences between the two adjustment strategies are not understood and the interrelationships among various reforms in the organizational and work design are not appreciated. The confusion between the two strategies has made it very difficult to prove conclusively that one or the other approach is effective and has aggravated the problems of gaining closure in the debates among managerial factions discussed in the last chapter.

The two approaches that emerge in cognitive theory do not, however, exhaust the ways in which the organization might adjust to the new environment. The first is essentially an extension of mass production. The second is what one analyst has termed *mass customization*.[21] But the firm might also pursue a strategy of true customization: it could develop the product to fit specific customer needs, adjusting to a "market" it had never foreseen. This third strategy calls upon workers to do things for which they have not been prepared in advance. Neither the repetition of memorized routines nor the application of abstract principles to concrete situations will suffice. The workforce is required to *improvise,* to *invent.* Cognitive theory does not have categories for these capacities. The third strategy of adjustment is not readily captured in its vocabulary.

Cognitive Theory

This problem is symptomatic of the limits of cognitive science more generally. Cognitive science goes a long way toward enlarging the liberal conceptual framework to provide a richer and more nuanced understanding of the relationship between social structures and individual behavior, but it does not go quite far enough to enable us to address the economic and social dilemmas discussed in earlier chapters. It is most helpful in suggesting that competitive economic theory presumes a base of knowledge, a framework of analysis, that is in fact quite problematic. It forces us to recognize processes through which that framework of analysis is generated, processes that precede the decisions upon which conventional economic theory focuses. It teaches us that these processes are preeminently social and must necessarily compromise the autonomy of individual actors, which conventional economic theory has made the overriding norm of economic organization and which constitutes the principal attraction of that theory for American social thought.

Cognitive psychology also helps us to understand that attraction. It points toward the structures in American social organization that hide the social contingency of knowledge from those within it, making the world seem natural and objective. It suggests how those structures also generate a sense of individuality and autonomy that belies the way in which we are dependent upon society for the knowledge that enables us to operate in the world and the way in which this dependence in turn circumscribes our ability to operate outside the society from which that knowledge derives.

In all of this, cognitive psychology underscores the profound way in which both the new identity groups that are disturbing American politics and the forms of economic organization that we are facing in international competition challenge the basic structures of American society and the underlying beliefs about nature associated with them. The new identity groups do this by asserting the validity of a set of norms and a concept of individuality that is centered in the group itself, quite separate and distinct from whatever relationship that group might have to a broader American society. And the new forms of economic organization do so by playing upon changes in the very framework of understanding that economic theory and American epistemology take as natural and unchanging. Explicit recognition of those frameworks of understanding and the processes through which they are generated thus enables us to see through the conflicts and confusions that plague the pursuit of organizational reform.

Ultimately, in fact, the social mechanisms through which cognitive psychology suggests we acquire our understandings of the world merge fairly readily with economic theory. They suggest that the behavioral foundations of theory can be neatly divided into two parts. One part is concerned with how individuals acquire the fundamentals of behavior, the causal models that optimization requires, and possibly the disposition to optimize in the first place. The second part focuses on how the individual acts once these dispositions and models are in place.

The first is a social process: the individual must necessarily be part of a society. The capacities may also be socially delimited in the sense that they may not be effective outside the boundaries of the society that generates them in the first place. But once the society has done its work, once the capacities have been generated, and so long as the person remains within the relevant social bounds, he or she is an autonomous actor, more or less as liberal theory suggests and as we in America would like to believe. It actually fits rather nicely with some of the more enduring puzzles of economic theory: for example, how do commodity markets arise in a competitive market economy? Where do the rules come from that govern the bureaucratic structures of mass production? All of these issues can be relegated to a social sphere that is prior to economic activity and in which the economy is embedded.

But this theoretical construction does not really solve our problem. It is, in terms of the issues with which we are concerned in this book, too static a view of social and cognitive structures. It seems to explain how individuals within a *given* social configuration might develop a *given* set of cognitive structures. And yet both economic growth and the new identity

5

An Interpretative Approach to Cognition

The understanding of social organization and group attachment to which cognitive psychology—at least as it has developed so far—gives rise has an extremely mechanical flavor. That flavor contrasts with the politics of the new identity groups, which is often expressive, exuberant, spontaneous, and creative. The appeal of such groups to their members is frequently cast in these terms. Oliver Sacks builds his case for separate institutions for the deaf, for example, around the claim that the sign language that develops within such institutions is associated with the capacity of deaf persons to express themselves in spontaneous ways, a capacity that uniquely liberates their humanity.[1] The same theme of spontaneous expression is reflected in the gay pride parades, in Hasidic Jewish dancing, and in African-American jazz.

Ethnographic studies of business organizations reveal similar attributes. They imply that parts of even the most structured companies—research and development, advertising, marketing, even strategy—involve a kind of creativity that sits uneasily within the bureaucratic structures of modern organizations. The very capacity of mechanical theories of cognitive structure to capture the nature of such organizations limits their capacity to capture these deviant forms. The notion of *creativity* is alien to a conception of thought in which the range of possible ideas is anticipated in advance and encoded in memorized routines or in abstract principles that are evoked by cues from the external environment.

To return to the problem of how a mass production firm adopts to the instability and uncertainty of a business environment, the solutions suggested by cognitive theory all require that one cast the problem of the business environment in terms analogous to forecasting the weather. There are distinct series of possibilities, a series of specific market circumstances or a range of weather conditions, which we can imagine in advance. What we do not know is what conditions will actually obtain. We can design products in advance that will be appropriate for each of the possible conditions that may arise, but we cannot know in advance which to produce. The production strategy is a way of hedging against uncertainty comparable to the diversification of a financial portfolio.

But there is such a thing as *radical uncertainty,*[2] in which we cannot even imagine the possible states of the world. Radical uncertainty allows for the completely unexpected, the twist that distinguishes a great jazz performance, the surprise product discovery that was the Sony Walkman. These are events to which we do not know what probabilities to attach—we do not know what they are. To handle this kind of uncertainty we need the capacity to invent. That is the capacity required for a strategy of true customization, and that capacity is what the cognitive theory we have explored so far cannot capture.

The underlying problem for cognitive theory in dealing with *radical uncertainty* is that the structures of thought that it contemplates are closed and bounded. This problem has also emerged in the attempt to use cognitive psychology as the basis for information technology. In that field it has led to a different way of looking at cognitive structure: one that is more open and dynamic. It suggests a more open and dynamic approach to understanding group attachment and technological change as well, one that is *interpretative* or *hermeneutic.*

This chapter develops that approach as an alternative to liberalism and rational choice theory, drawing upon three bodies of scholarship and research. The first of these is research in information technology and machine language translation. It clarifies what it means to call language open and unbounded. Second, the chapter turns to hermeneutics, particularly the hermeneutic theories of Martin Heidegger. Heidegger proposes that we abandon the liberal notion of human behavior as a set of deliberate acts and conceptualize it instead as a process ongoing in time, and he provides a set of categories for thinking about it in these terms.

Heidegger's categories do not, however, translate directly into politics and economics. To make that bridge, I shall turn to Hannah Arendt and a typology of human activity she draws from ancient Greek society. Of particular interest here is the activity of action and its role in the Greek conception of political life.

Finally, this chapter looks at the way this alternative conceptual framework alters our thinking about new social groups and networked economic organizations and about how politics and public policy might affect their evolution. Both economic networks and the new social groups can be thought of as communities of action in the Greek sense. They emerge and evolve in a process that can be likened to a conversation among their members. That process can be directed by political leadership conceived, in terms of the conversational metaphor, as orchestrating the conversation, influencing who talks to whom, what they talk about, and how they interpret what has been said.

Language and Language Translation

Translation Problems

The limits of cognitive psychology, and the outlines of an alternative approach, have emerged most prominently in the attempt to develop programs for machine translation between two languages. In cognitive psychology a language is a kind of cognitive structure. It plays the role in communication that a causal model plays in rational choice. A language enables us to translate our thoughts into a message in the way that a causal model enables us to translate means into ends. The analogy suggests that the distinction I made earlier with respect to causal models—between cognitive development, which is social, and rational choice, which is individual—can be applied to language and communication. We acquire language through a social process, but communication is an individual act.

In this view, language is basically a sophisticated Morse code; a linguistic communication is essentially a set of signals. A language is thus independent of the message being sent, and a communication is separate from the sender and the receiver. For communication to work, however, the sender and receiver must be *compatible:* they must both share the same language. When they do not, a "translation problem" arises. The solution to the translation problem is a set of algorithms, a transformation, for converting from the rules of one language to the rules of another. A program for machine translation would be like a converter.

Translation programs that convert effectively from one language to another have, however, proved extremely elusive. Machines can translate simple messages, but complex texts, literary works, even business reports they invariably garble. Communication apparently cannot be reduced to a set of rules; at least, it has not been reduced to a set of rules as yet. Some analysts have come to believe that it never will be, that it involves something more.

Categories

The clues as to what that something more might be are suggested by recent research on the way we use categories in common speech.[3] A vocabulary is, in many respects, like a set of categories that we use for classifying our experience. The classic view of categories—the view most consistent with the approach to machine translation I have just sketched—is that a category is a well-defined, closed, and self-contained set. Something either is a member of a category or is not. An object either is a chair or is not a chair. A creature is a bird, or it is not a bird.

If this view were valid, a category could be exemplified by any one of its members: one example would be as good as another. But the way we use categories in speech is very different. There are *good* examples of most categories, and there are less good examples. A robin is a good example of a bird. An ostrich is also a bird, but it is not a good example. When we think of "chair," we think of a straight-backed dining room chair. Modern living rooms are sometimes furnished with gigantic bean bags. These are also chairs, but they are not at all what the word brings to mind. Evidently, categories are more like the patterns generated by a handful of rocks thrown into a still pond. Each has a core that fades gradually as you move out from the center. At their edges, categories overlap and are ambiguous.

The ambiguity of the categories we use in daily life suggests that it should be very difficult for people to communicate with one another, even if they speak the same language. But, in practice, communication is not that difficult. Somehow we manage the ambiguity; we resolve it, or at least limit its impact upon understanding. One view of how this happens is that the sender and receiver are not separate and independent of the communication process. Linguistic communication cannot be reduced to a set of rules. Something that is left out of the rules happens in the process of speech. Some kind of interaction occurs between speakers that clarifies the meaning of the signals that are exchanged. And the signals, the formal content of the exchange, might convey different meanings if the sender were changed, or the receiver, or both, even if all the parties interchanged were members of the same linguistic community. The content of the communication cannot, in other words, be separated from the actors in the process of communication.

This, of course, is not a general characterization of the nature of communication. Not all messages involve the kind of ambiguity that makes communication dependent on the specifics of a particular exchange. It should be possible, the research on categories suggests, to communicate in a relatively straightforward and unambiguous way about robins, but communications about ostriches will necessarily involve discussion and clarification. They require, one can say, *interpretation*. This cannot be done at arm's length; direct interaction between the communicants is required. Communication then becomes a social process, not easily distinguishable, indeed perhaps not actually different, from the process of language acquisition.

The general implications of this are very disturbing to the attempt to distinguish between the social process through which cognitive structure is generated and the individual process of choice that generates behavior. If language is insufficient for communication and communication itself involves direct social interaction, then perhaps social interaction is required for other kinds of behavior as well. If language is analogous to a causal model in rational choice theory, this implies that the process through which we acquire causal models cannot always be separated from the process through which we apply those models to make choices. It implies, more generally, that understanding and behavior cannot necessarily be distinguished from each other; the two are intertwined. The proposal for combining cognitive psychology and rational choice theory by postulating two distinct processes, one social and the other individual, is not viable. A much more fundamental departure from the rational choice view of behavior is required.

Hermeneutics

The apparent need to understand language and speech (cognitive structure and concerted action) as a single process has led psychologists to turn to hermeneutics, a field of study originally concerned with the interpretation of the Bible, which has since developed as a general science of interpretation. The relevance of biblical interpretation to language translation is obvious; it poses not only the problem of translation across societies of very different linguistic traditions but also the problem of translating moral lessons abstracted from a distant historical context and applied in a radically different social setting. But modern linguistics sees the translation of a text from one written language to another as one instance of a broader class of *interpretative* problems.[4]

The canonical problem in modern hermeneutic theory is the oral presentation of a written text. The speaker gives the text a particular meaning when he or she reads it. The meaning is derived from the text in the sense that the speaker gets the clues for how to read it from the written words, but the words do not determine the reading. Once having heard them read out loud, a subsequent reader will understand the words in a different way. If the text is passed around a circle of people, each reading it out loud in his or her turn, the meaning will evolve continuously in the process.

The key issue here is how one understands the relationship between the parts and the whole. Does the whole take its meaning from the parts? Or do the parts determine the meaning of the whole? The hermeneutic answer is that neither is the case. The meaning emerges in the movement back and forth *between* the parts and whole in what is known as the *hermeneutic circle*. The interpretation that emerges as the text is spoken is a whole that grows out of the parts. But the meaning of the individual words comes out of that interpretation. And both the meaning of the words and the interpretation of the text change as the text moves around the circle and the readers cycle back and forth between them. Again, this makes interpretation a social process. It is not a matter of the autonomous reader and an inanimate text, but something that occurs among people.

The conceptual framework of rational choice theory does not lend itself to a process of this kind. It is not just that cognitive structure and behavior are interdependent. The way the words and the text (or rather its interpretation) are intertwined makes it very difficult for even an outside analyst to explain what is going on in terms of cause and effect. At best, one could say that the words and the text are alternately cause and effect, but even this does not really capture the process. At the same time, the words and the text cannot be understood as part of a broader structure that might be generating both; the meaning of the words and of the text changes perpetually as one moves from one to the other so that there is no stable relationship between them.

Heidegger

The solution to this dilemma is suggested by Martin Heidegger.[5] It is to abandon the distinction between cause and effect altogether and to characterize human behavior as an ongoing process that takes place in time. This approach breaks sharply with that of conventional economic theory and rational choice theory in a way that cognitive psychology itself does not and, as we shall see, offers a very different perspective on economic and social processes.

Conventional economics attempts to understand human activity as a series of deliberate acts, each of which needs to be explained. Heidegger proposes instead to understand human behavior as a continuous stream: people exist "always and already in the world, coping." Think, he suggests, of a man building a house, engaged in the process of hammering a nail. He is not unaware of what he is doing: he knows that he is hammering in order to drive the nail into the wood, and that he is putting the nail in the wood in order to build the house. His activity is thus purposeful. But it is not self-conscious or reflective. The hammer, the nail, the wood are *instruments* for the project. They are, in the language of rational choice theory, *means,* and the house is the *end.* But the process dominates the instruments of the activity. The instruments are typically already at hand; we are hardly conscious of their separate existence; they appear to us as so much a part of the process that they are *transparent.*

It is only in the case of a *breakdown* that we become self-conscious about what we are doing and we may be forced into the analytical stance that rational choice theory takes as prototypical. If, for example, the head were to fly off the hammer, we would suddenly focus upon the elements of what we are doing. We might consider how to replace the head on the hammer, get a new hammer, go on to a different operation, or even give up building the house altogether. Under these circumstances, but *only* under these circumstances, would we worry about how a hammer is built, what a hammer costs on the market, why we are hammering now instead of later, why indeed we are building the house at all.

Short of such a breakdown—in most circumstances, in other words—Heidegger argues, we should conceptualize behavior in terms of a process that takes place in time. We should think, he suggests, in terms of past, present, and future. The thrust of his work is to develop an apparatus for describing these components of time. The details of that apparatus need not concern us here. Essentially he argues that we enter the present moment with a series of predispositions that we bring with us from the past, which he calls a *fore-structure,* and with a perception of where we are going that gives direction to our activity, which he calls *projection.* We encounter a set of circumstances in the present and deal with them in terms of the fore-structure and projection, moving on into the future. The encounter changes our fore-structure and may alter the projection, but often in subtle ways. Fore-structure and projection are, in this way of looking at human activity, like means and causal models on the one hand and goals and ends on the other. But they are generally much vaguer and less well-defined. They determine behavior only in the sense in which words determine the meaning of a conversation.

Indeed, conversation is the underlying analogy; the basic thrust is to think of human activity as an ongoing conversation. In conversation, people generally share a common language. That language is an *instrument* of conversation, but it is transparent to the speakers in the sense that they are virtually unaware that it exists. Conversations are generally about something, but the subject is not generally well-defined and easily migrates as the conversation proceeds. Language as an instrument is not fully adequate to the task at hand; it is ambiguous. But the ambiguity is generally dealt with and resolved without a breakdown.

If the ambiguity becomes intense, however, a breakdown occurs. In that breakdown, the parties focus on the ambiguity in a deliberate and self-conscious way, seeking clarification. That effort at clarification may lead the situation gradually to conform to the mold of economic analysis. The parties will eventually be forced to decide what precisely the conversation is about. This will provide a precise context in which the ambiguity can be resolved. It will also enable them to focus explicitly and self-consciously upon the question of whether the conversation is worth continuing. In this way, the purpose becomes an end and the conversation a means.

Thus, finally, the Heideggerian and the rational choice approaches appear to converge. But even here the convergence is incomplete: for Heidegger, the purpose of the conversation is only an *interpretation* of what the conversation is about. It is not what the conversation is really about. There is no ultimate reality in this sense.

Interpretation and Politics

It is difficult to go directly from this way of looking at human activity to concerns of politics and public policy. That relationship is easier to see through the work of Hannah Arendt, a student and colleague of Heidegger's but also a philosopher much more concerned with economics and politics. In a typology that she draws from the ancient Greek city-state, Arendt distinguishes three human activities: labor, work, and action.[6]

Labor is an activity associated with the reproduction of life, with agriculture and the birth and nurturing of children. This original meaning survives in the modern usage of *labor* to refer to women in the act of giving birth. In ancient Greece, labor was conducted in the private sphere of the household and was the responsibility of women and slaves. Its products were ephemeral; they were consumed almost as soon as they were produced, sometimes even in the act of production itself, and were reabsorbed into nature. The activity of labor was structured by nature and cyclical in character, governed by the progression of the seasons and the passage of life from birth to death. To labor, individuals were called upon to align themselves with the rhythm of nature, yielding a sense of the separateness of self and merging with the process in which they were engaged, forgoing individuality. Arendt likens labor in ancient Greece to the jobs of mass production, and the accommodation to, and immersion in, a repeated cycle of activity corresponds to the intense commitment to routine of workers who understand their jobs in terms of concrete structures of thought.

Work in ancient Greece was the activity of the craftsman and artist. Like labor, it was conducted in the privacy of the household, but the products of work were not ephemeral. They were durable objects that emerged from the household to be sold in the public sphere of the marketplace. Work required individuals to distance themselves from nature and to mobilize their instruments to order and control nature's materials. The durability of the products conferred a kind of immortality, surmounting nature in this sense as well.

This conception of work resembles human activity as modeled by economists. The object and its sale in the marketplace constitute well-defined ends. The craftsman's instruments are a set of identifiable means. Craftsmanship is a set of understandings that enable the instruments to be directed at the creation of the object, a repertoire of causal models. The craftsman, organizing all of this alone in his shop, is the independent agent of a competitive economy, the autonomous individual idealized in liberal theory. But the work of the craftsman was not the ideal activity for the ancient Greeks. The preferred activity in the Greek city-state was politics. And while politics shared characteristics with both labor and work, it was also distinctly different from these. The activity of politics was characterized by *action*.

Politics was an activity reserved for the Greek citizen. It took place in the public sphere, but was supported by the labor of the household in private and was possible only for those who were freed by such support from a preoccupation with the mere reproduction of life. Through politics, the citizens directed and defined the state. But in the process they also defined themselves as individuals.

It is the nature of action, Arendt asserts, that its consequences cannot be foreseen. Each act provokes responses from other actors, and these in turn provoke further acts, until the original actor is led to act again. But the chain is so complex and involved that it cannot be anticipated. Each action is like the product of labor in that it is ephemeral. But labor is cyclical and action is sequential. Through the sequence of acts in which an individual engages in his life, he creates a story. That story, if it attracts the attention of his fellow citizens, is told and repeated from one generation to the next, defining the individual and giving him a kind of immortality.

Arendt draws an analogy between the politics of the Greek city-state and a theater in which the actors play to one another, a theater in which the actors are their own audience. It requires a community of equals, a set of people who are so much alike, who share so much of the same material of life, that they and they alone are able to appreciate the uniqueness of what any one of them can make out of his or her life. If they were less alike, they would be less able to appreciate their differences.

The structure resembles academic communities of research scholars and theoreticians. The members of such communities compete fiercely with one another but ultimately depend upon their competitors to appreciate their accomplishments. They are dependent upon their competitors in this way because only people working in the same domain have the expertise to understand fully what they have done and to comprehend the hurdles they have overcome to do it. It resembles even more closely a team sport in which a member can achieve individual recognition only through the team and in which the team's reputation grows out of its members' pursuit of personal glory. It is the kind of construction that would render fully comprehensible the commitment of the Gallaudet student to remain deaf even if it meant poking out his eardrums.

Arendt's characterization of Greek politics is hermeneutic. The way the action of one individual leads to the action of the next in a sequence that eventually returns to the first actor is analogous to the way the meaning of a text emerges in a circle of readers. It lends itself to a conceptualization in Heidegger's terms as a process ongoing in time. It is a hermeneutic circle.

This is most apparent in the narrative toward which Arendt argues political action is directed. The narrative links together the actions of an individual's life in a time sequence. The sequence makes the actions seem to be related as cause and effect, but what appears to be a cause is really an interpretation that can change depending on how particular actions in the sequence are emphasized in the telling. The actions are the parts that emerge as a whole through the story of an individual's life. The story comes to an end in the "breakdown" of death. When told, the story is interpreted and the life given meaning as we would give purpose to a conversation that was interrupted by a misunderstanding.

Greek politics was like a conversation in other senses as well. It was, one could say, a debate about the nature and direction of the State. The actions of the individuals in debate led to actions of the State. And those actions too constituted the history of the State, also a story that was continually told and interpreted.

This hermeneutic notion of politics yields a conception of individuality, but one that is very different from liberal individualism. The hermeneutic notion of individuality breaks the opposition that liberalism draws between the individual and community and binds the two inextricably together. For the Greeks, individuality was achieved through the story of one's life, and that story was dependent on the community in at least three distinct ways. It was dependent first because it was made up of actions undertaken in the attempt to define and direct the community. It was dependent second because the actions that composed the story occurred in the community; they were, in fact, *interactions* with fellow citizens. And the story was dependent upon community finally because those actions achieved the meaning and significance that conferred individuality only through the recognition of the community in the retelling of the story by its citizens.

The Interpretative Approach to Social Groups and Economic Networks

Rational Choice vs. Interpretation

For our purposes the most important characteristic of the interpretative approach is that it breaks down the opposition between individuality and community set up by rational choice theory. But this is actually a manifestation of the more general contrast between the two approaches, a tendency for the interpretative approach to see as intertwined aspects of a single process what rational choice theory views as a sharp dichotomy. Thus in the interpretative approach not only the differentiation between individuality and community is lost, but also those between means and ends, learning and behavior, structure and content, and the whole and its parts. The distinction between wholes and parts is submerged in the *hermeneutic circle,* and that circle really stands for the way the other distinctions are submerged as well; the parts and the whole grow out of each other through a continual cycling back and forth in which meaning gradually emerges and evolves over time.

It is because meaning emerges and evolves in this way and is not carried by the grammar and the vocabulary of the language alone that structure and content cannot be completely separated, or the message fully distinguished from the messenger or, for that matter, the message. Similarly, what appear as ends and means in the rational choice view are in the interpretative view simply elements (objects, events, persons, and tools) strung out in a sequence over time as words are strung out in a sentence. For the people actually engaged in the process of which these elements are a part, the elements lose their separate identities and become, as Heidegger would say, transparent. When that same process is reviewed in retrospect or interrupted in a breakdown, the elements become part of a story or a narrative. The relationship among the different elements in the narrative is an interpretation. The interpretation is conveyed by the way one or another is given emphasis by the narrator in the telling of the historical sequence.

Communities of Action and the Politics of Identity

Arendt's notion of politics as action is easily extended to the new identity groups in American political life. These groups are clearly engaged in defining themselves as a community in the larger context of American life, just as the ancient Greek city-states were engaged in defining themselves in the broader context of their civilization. And that process of community definition is driven by a process within the groups themselves in which the individual members, like the citizens of ancient Greece, achieve their own personal identity and self-definition through their actions; through, in other words, the roles they play in the internal life of the group.

In the process of talking to and acting for each other, the members define what it means to be deaf, or gay, or handicapped, to be a woman or an African American. As they define themselves, they also define deafness, handicap, or femininity. The deaf student at Gallaudet would have been prepared to poke out his eardrums if he could hear, this implies, because hearing would cut him off from the deaf community. Hearing would make him so different from its other members that they would no longer be able to appreciate him as an individual. He would lose his ability to participate in deaf life as an equal and, in so doing, he would lose not only his community attachment but also the possibility of defining and realizing himself as a separate person. The horror at what he is prepared to do felt by those of us who are not deaf is understandable in exactly the same terms: attached as we are to non-deaf communities, the capacity to hear is fundamental to our ability to speak and to be understood; deafness would cut us off from the process through which we achieve self-definition. Because we interpret the meaning of hearing in the context of our own communities of self-definition, we *mis*interpret its meaning in the deaf community.

Understood in this way, Gallaudet becomes symptomatic of the way the politics of the new identity groups is creating a set of self-absorbed worlds in which citizens speak increasingly to others like themselves and there is less and less conversation across group boundaries. We are losing interest in speaking to one another and are, as a result, gradually losing the capacity to do so. This might not matter if each group were actually isolated and self-contained, but it becomes a problem when the groups share the same physical space and economic resources. As we lose ourselves in a politics increasingly centered on our own identities, we lose the capacity to engage in the political process required to resolve the problems of living together in the same domain.

Action in Economic Life

Arendt saw the modern economy as a system of mass production.[7] The business enterprise faced a choice of what to produce and how to produce it. The choice was driven by a technical logic that lent itself to a rational calculus more or less as characterized in conventional economic theory. To the extent that decisionmaking resembled any of the activities of ancient Greece, it resembled work (although she was unable to bring herself to dignify it with that term). As suggested earlier, she likened the semi-skilled production jobs in mass production to the labor of ancient Greece. Mass production in manufacturing grew out of a craft economy that Arendt seems to have thought of as part of a competitive economic system. Productive activity in that system was equivalent to production in the craft economy of ancient Greece, characterized, like Greek craftsmanship, by work.

The networked economic structures that seem most effective in the current economic environment have emerged to address economic problems that Arendt did not recognize. They draw upon the capacity of the different and administratively autonomous components of a complex productive system to evolve over time in synergy with one another and with their clients and customers. The way this happens looks very much like politics in Arendt's communities of action. It lends itself to characterization in Heidegger's terms as a process ongoing in time.

Think of the New York City garment district as a center of high fashion. It is embedded in various ethnic communities, originally the Jewish and Italian communities, now increasingly the Chinese and Hispanic communities as well. It is linked to a world of high-fashion designers that spills over into the theatrical and gay and black subcultures but draws many of its members from the same ethnic communities that provide the entrepreneurs and the labor force of the industry's productive structure. The garment district has a direction of evolution. That direction is understood and shared by all of its members but too vague and ill-defined to be thought of as a goal. At any particular time, we call it the "New York look." It emerges through a process in which designers, in association with competing manufacturers and a network of subcontractors, try to outdo each other in the creation of collections of new designs.

That process is very much a series of interconnected conversations about the identity of the productive community in which each of its component members is, at the same time, talking about and attempting to establish an individual identity based on his or her unique capabilities. Everybody is trying, of course, to earn a living. But their more fundamental goal is to establish a reputation within their ethnic community or in the demimonde of theater and design. Fashion in New York is, moreover, like action in ancient Greece, ephemeral: any given success is quickly forgotten; the contest is repeated every season. Reputation is built over many seasons in a lifetime.

This process and the community structures in which it occurs are characteristic of all high-fashion centers, Milan, London, and Paris as well as New York. Indeed, it is characteristic more generally of industrial districts like those of Northern Italy or like Silicon Valley in the United States. It has, as I have already suggested, essentially the same character as the process that occurs within a community of research scholars or a team of professional athletes. In all of these configurations, the process goes on without central direction although the community tends to have a sense of itself as a productive entity in much the same way the Greek city-state or the deaf at Gallaudet have a sense of themselves as a defined political entity.

The operation of the network structures that are emerging out of large corporate enterprises can be characterized in very much the same way. Where the components of these networks are the administrative units of a single company and a complex of suppliers, subcontractors, consultants, clients, and customers who are generally smaller and have less economic autonomy, identity and direction appear to be the product of a more conscious decisionmaking process and managerial directives. But much of that appearance is the vestige of the system of mass production out of which these networked corporations evolved. Success actually seems dependent upon the ability to move away from rational decisionmaking to a more hermeneutic process.

Leadership and Management

The difference between the two approaches, in politics as well as economics, can be seen in the roles they would ascribe to leadership. In rational choice theory the leader, in business or politics, plays a twofold role. The leader is first a technical decisionmaker; his or her ultimate responsibility is to select the optimal policies and to convince his or her constituency of their efficacy. The leader's second role is to manage and resolve conflicts among competing goals. Here, the leader is a negotiator, a mediator, a deal-maker.

In a hermeneutic process, the leader is orchestrating a series of conversations. He or she is attempting to control and direct who talks to whom and what they talk about. The major problem in American life, both economic and political, is, in these terms, that those conversations are too narrowly focused within self-contained groups. To develop networks that will be effective in the current business environment, we need to promote an interchange across the functional boundaries of our economic organizations. We need to promote exactly the same kinds of interchange among political groups in order to manage the political process.

That problem, hermeneutic theory suggests, cannot be solved simply by direction. A solution requires the initiation of a process that is like the opening of a conversation between two separate and distinct linguistic groups. Communication will initially be fraught with ambiguity and misunderstanding. It will be like a discussion of birds focused on ostriches. But if it continues, the ambiguities will gradually be resolved, and in the process a vocabulary will emerge, a new set of categories, around which an increasingly refined communication can be built. The leader's role is to cultivate this process, to be a mediator less in the sense of resolving conflicts among goals than in the sense of translating and interpreting between languages, helping the parties to work through the misunderstandings in a way that avoids a breakdown and prevents each from withdrawing, in the face of ambiguity, into his or her own separate conversational world.

Just as the leadership functions differ, the prospects for an endeavor of this kind also look very different from the hermeneutic and rational choice perspectives. In the former, human behavior is an ongoing process. Once started, it is natural for it to continue. We are in this sense social animals. In rational choice theory, action is never natural. It has always to be motivated and explained.

But the problem of motivation does not completely disappear in the hermeneutic perspective, especially in a complex modern society such as ours. It arises because, however self-involved communities like those constituted by the new identity groups may become, the fact that they are organized independently of the structure of the productive system places each member in two communities simultaneously. As the production system becomes more and more organized in networks as communities of action, the two become competitive as the locus of identity and self-realization. Our commitment to the productive system as a setting for self-realization is always in danger of being undermined by the instrumental role that system plays in generating the income to support our social selves in the identity groups to which we are also attached.

This problem seems particularly acute in the early phases of interactions when ambiguity is substantial, the potential for misunderstanding high, and hence the danger of breakdown great. The capacity to circumvent this danger then depends heavily on trust, the belief that the other side is not exploiting the relationship for personal gain. The managerial problem in an economic system is thus clearly one of defining a distribution of the material rewards that prevents a breakdown from happening.

The problem, however, is not limited to the economic sphere. It comes to the fore in the political sphere as soon as the conversation across groups comes to focus on the distribution of material resources. And this creates an incentive for political leadership to engage in symbolic politics, for that politics channels the discussion in other directions, especially in its initial stages. Clearly, the ways in which American political leadership has relied on symbolic politics in recent years is a not inconsiderable factor in the fact the new identity groups seem to lack a language that recognizes economic constraints.

Breakdowns and Narrative

The problem of leadership is compounded by the fact that politics and economics may not operate consistently in either a rational or an interpretative mode. Behavior may shift back and forth in complex ways. Some messages are machine translatable and others are not. When we talk about birds, we sometimes mean ostriches but we often actually do mean robins.

In Arendt's typology of activity, only politics is hermeneutic. Labor involves memorized routines that one may not want to characterize as truly rational behavior. But her characterization of work clearly lends itself to understanding in terms of rational choice theory. Even Heidegger suggests that when ongoing activity is interrupted by a breakdown, the actors are thrown into an analytical mode and led to distinguish the instruments they are using and think about their relationship to outcomes in causal terms. He uses the example of the broken hammer of a man building a house to illustrate how this change in perspective might occur in a breakdown. War and depression are breakdowns in the ongoing life of a nation that lead political action to shift in a similar way. Revolutionary new products or the sudden collapse of a market may play a similar role in the lives of economic enterprises. Much lesser perturbations could presumably throw politics and business into an analytical mode.

If the breakdown provides an occasion for a shift from hermeneutic process to rational calculus, the bridge back in the opposite direction is the narrative.[8] A narrative is a story told about an interruption in a sequence of historical events. In the Greek city-state, it was occasioned by the death of a citizen and was the story of the actions of his political life. In the affairs of state, the wars and depressions that are breakdowns in political life are the occasions for equivalent stories. New products and great deals give rise to such stories in the life of the firm.

The role of narratives in modern political life is confusing. The story they tell is a chain of historical events. Because one event follows another, they appear to be connected in a causal chain. This appearance is reinforced when the story is built around a scholarly theory. But a narrative is not an explanation in a scientific sense. It is an interpretation. Its meaning is generated by the way certain events are accented in the telling and others are pushed to the background. A narrative is not so much an explanation of the past as a way of giving direction to the future. The heroic narratives of ancient Greece were the templates around which subsequent generations of citizens modeled their political action. The narratives that companies tell about important products mold the evolution of the organization. And the course of a country's politics is channeled by the stories that are told about the crises in national life.

No single person can control a narrative; the stories that grab our attention are told too often by too many people. It is this constant repetition on all sides, in fact, that gives them their power. As with all stories, moreover, the interpretation evolves continually as they are retold; that is the lesson of the reading aloud in the canonical hermeneutic circle. But a leader is a most prominent narrator. He or she gets to talk first, to tell the story most often, and it is the leader's voice that is heard above all others and by the most people. This makes the narrative the most powerful instrument in the direction of a hermeneutic process, the most selective political instrument in contemporary economic and political life.

Conclusion

We emerge from this epistemological excursion with four key ideas. The first, and most important of these, is a reinterpretation of individualism. That reinterpretation breaks down the liberal opposition between the individual and society and replaces it with a conception of individualism as realized through community. Following Arendt, the communities in terms of which individuals realize themselves are called *communities of action*. But they can as well be called *communities of meaning*. Both the new productive systems that American business is trying to create through the transformation of mass production and the identity groups that are emerging in national politics are communities of action and meaning.

Such communities are not created through the aggregation of individuals. They are created through the *interaction* among individuals. That interaction is the process through which individuals define themselves, create their identities, and simultaneously define the community and create its identity in the broader social context in which it exists. In the case of productive units that compose the economy, that context is the surrounding universe of collaborators and competitors, what one might call in a loose sense "the market" (although it is definitely not the market as that term is used in competitive economic theory). In the case of the identity groups, the context is the larger social and political process in which people of different backgrounds with diverse physical and biological traits interact.

This leads to the second general lesson: the national society and economy are to be thought of as constituted through the interaction of communities of meaning. Politics and economics are then conceived of as the processes through which that interaction occurs. This contrasts sharply with the notion of a federation in which a hierarchical set of rules preserves the autonomy of the constituent units and govern the interactions among them. The constitution of the nation is not a structure but an ongoing process. And because the process through which individuals define themselves and create their identities within groups is bound up with the process through which groups define and create themselves in relation to one another, the groups themselves evolve and the boundaries separating them change over time. By the same token, the economy is constituted through the interaction of productive systems in a process that again is not one of arm's-length adjustments to impersonal price signals but one of direct interaction that leads to an evolution within and between productive systems whose boundaries are in continuous evolution.

The third lesson concerns the relationship between the economy, on the one hand, and politics and society, on the other. It is an extension of the lesson that each is constituted through the interaction of communities. The relationship between the economy and society must also be understood in terms of process. It may be a single process in which the communities of productive activity are closely aligned with the communities of political identity and the two evolve together. It may involve distinct communities evolving through separate processes. Most probably, it involves relatively distinct communities that interact in multiple ways.

This view is to be sharply distinguished from the analytical perspective in which the economy provides the resources that the society consumes and is thus conceived as a constraint on the political process. The analytical perspective leads to efforts to address the relationship between economics and politics in terms of structure, as if the problems it poses could be *solved* once and for all through institutions that separate the two and *make* the economy a constraint upon political outcomes. Whether such a solution is consistent with a politics and an economy composed of communities of meaning is an open question. It is certainly not the way political and economic activity are related to each other in the United States today.

The final lesson concerns how the processes that constitute politics, economics, and the relationship between them can be managed and directed through public policy. Here there are two key ideas. One is that the processes are like conversations. Their evolution is governed by who talks to whom and what they talk about. The role of public policy and political leadership is to orchestrate those conversations, initiating discussions among previously isolated groups, guiding them through disagreements and misunderstandings that might otherwise lead conversation to break off, introducing new topics for discussion and debate.

The second aspect of these processes that is important for policy is the role of storytelling and of the narrative. The narrative is a way in which we organize the events of the past and interpret them to ourselves. It serves not as an explanation in a scientific sense but as a template for future action. The direction of our economic and political conversations, whom we talk to and what we talk about, are thus guided by the stories we tell about our past, and those stories thus become instruments of policy and leadership.

How can this view of individualism and the ideas about politics and economics to which it leads be made meaningful in a society apparently so wedded to liberalism? What, concretely, would it mean for American leadership today? If political and economic processes are to be thought of as so many conversations, what kind of conversations need to be encouraged? Who should be talking to whom? What should they be talking about? What kinds of narratives, what sorts of interpretations of our national life are likely to bring these conversations about? These questions are the focus of the next two chapters.

6

The American Repertoire

American society has trouble recognizing and coming to terms with cohesive social groups. But we do not ignore them. The reality of everyday life is such that we must recognize and deal with cohesive social groups all the time. And we have accumulated a not inconsiderable collection of practical experience in doing so. Some of that experience has crystallized in institutions and intellectual constructs; much is merely latent in practice that goes unrecognized in the high rhetoric of politics and social theory. If culture is a repertoire of patterns out of which a society fashions its response to changing historical circumstance, it is toward these practical experiences that we must turn to operationalize the insights drawn from cognitive theory and Hannah Arendt's interpretation of communities of action.

This chapter reviews four bodies of such cultural material: the tradition of civic republicanism and its embodiment in yeoman democracy and small town life; ethnic communities and the interpretation of ethnicity in the formation of American society; the efforts of the new identity groups to interpret themselves; and the legal recognition accorded to cohesive groups. This is not meant to be an exhaustive review of our cultural repertoire, but it should be enough to suggest that the abstract ideas developed in the preceding chapter can be grounded in American experience.

Civic Republicanism

We saw in the preceding chapter that both the new identity groups and the emerging forms of business organization can be likened to what Hannah Arendt, drawing upon an understanding of ancient Greek political life, calls communities of action. At first glance, this does not appear to be a very promising way to approach the problems of American politics and economics. What could possibly be more remote from contemporary American life than the ancient Greek city-state? But in fact recent historiography suggests that our basic political institutions were initially conceived not in terms of the liberal individualism through which we understand them today but rather in terms of *civic republicanism,* a tradition of thought that draws heavily upon the model of the Greek city-state from which Arendt derives the notion of action.

The influence of civic republicanism is most evident in the writings of Thomas Jefferson, but it is prominent also in the work of James Madison, Benjamin Franklin, indeed most of the founding fathers. In that tradition, as in Greek thought, the political community does not constrain the individual; it provides the context through which the individual realizes himself or herself as a person. Public policy is not a science, the application of technical principles to arrive at efficient solutions; it is a process of discussion and debate. Jefferson's ideal of yeoman democracy, a political community of equals, is essentially comparable to the community of citizens in the Greek city-state.[1]

One can well understand the attraction of this construction. It captured the experience of men in the relatively egalitarian world of the American colonies, a world the colonists saw as quite distinct from England and continental Europe, with their extremes of wealth and social status. It had an especially strong resonance in the New England townships, which were religious communities grounded in a Protestant theology that gave all members of the community equal and direct access to God. But it captured the experience even of the more dispersed settlements in the South and on the western frontier. Economic life in these regions, before the spread of the cotton culture and the rise of the great plantations, may have generated a sense of direct and unmediated relationship to nature, an experience comparable to Arendt's notion of labor. But in political life, in working out their relationship to England and to the other colonies, even the frontiersmen could easily see themselves as comparable to the citizens of the Greek city-state.

The analogy was not accidental. The roots of eighteenth-century American social thought ran to England and Scotland and from there to the Italian political theory that developed to support the Florentine republic in the fourteenth and fifteenth centuries. And the Italian philosophers, seeking to escape the limits of medieval scholasticism and its hierarchical models of social organization, into which their own political experience would not fit, drew heavily upon the Greek texts from which Arendt, five hundred years later, abstracted the notion of action.[2]

Understood in civic republican terms, the United States, as constructed first through the Articles of Confederation and subsequently through the Constitution, was not actually a single political unit but a federation of democracies similar to those of the Greeks. The important issues of political life were meant to be resolved at the local level. National politics dealt with relations among these local communities and with the external world, issues very remote from the felt experience of everyday life. But as the nation became more and more integrated economically and the population became increasingly mobile across geographic regions, the correspondence between communities of action and the political experience within these formal structures diminished. The decisions important in everyday life were increasingly made at the national level, where the citizens participated only through an elector. A representative in Washington may have been able to realize himself as an individual through political discussion and debate in a small circle of fellow legislators, but the citizen could no longer do so. And the federal structure came to obscure the social contingency of knowledge, creating a sense of autonomous individualism in place of an individualism realized through community. To maintain the political structure as it was envisaged by the founding fathers, this implies, the country would have had to replace geographic representation with representation based upon the new communities of action that emerged as the country developed.

To some extent, the structures of our business organization, and even more so the neocorporatist structure of labor organization, were an effort to do precisely this. The disintegration of the country's original social structure was driven by the economic forces that these new institutions were designed to accommodate. But the emergence of the new identity groups suggests that the effort to revise the structure of representation to keep up with the evolution of the social structure is a doomed endeavor. That evolution is simply too rapid and too unpredictable. We would do better to capture the spirit of civic republicanism than to reproduce its institutional recipes, even reinterpreted to fit our own times.

A number of contemporary American social theorists have advocated this approach. A group of legal scholars have sought to reinterpret the Constitution in these terms, in part precisely in order to make it more responsive to the demands of racial and sexual minorities. Charles Sabel and I suggested in 1984 that we might find in yeoman democracy an indigenous model for our business institutions comparable to the networked organizations of the Italian industrial districts and Japanese corporations. Later in that decade a team of sociologists offered civic republicanism as a way for mainstream middle-class Americans to come to terms with feelings of connectedness they had difficulty expressing in the limited vocabulary of liberal individualism, through which they had been taught to understand themselves. No less a contemporary political figure than Ronald Reagan employed a theatrical metaphor similar to the one Arendt uses in her characterization of ancient Greek politics to describe his experience of small-town life, in which his own political philosophy was rooted.[3]

The difficulty is that the changes in the economic and social structure that make our present-day institutions operate so differently from the terms in which they were originally conceived also make it very difficult for us to perceive and understand the original conception. Too little of the tradition of yeoman democracy, or even of its subsequent transposition in the politics of small-town life, remain for us to understand communities of meaning in those terms. Very few of today's Americans actually grew up in such a community. Most of us, in fact, do not even *know* somebody who did.

The problems with that image become readily apparent if we look more closely at the way Reagan invoked it and compare that to the role of the small-town community in the life of Eugene V. Debs, who grew up—years earlier—in Terre Haute, Indiana. At first blush the comparison is unlikely: Reagan the conservative Republican President of the late twentieth century, and Debs the perennial socialist candidate of the late nineteenth. But the parallels between them are actually quite strong. For many years, in fact,

Reagan was, like Debs, a fringe candidate, more a political preacher than a legislator or executive, for whom political life was an endless series of banquets and rallies removed from either power or responsibility. Both grew up in small midwestern towns, and both evoke that experience as pivotal in forming them as men and in shaping the vision they expounded from the platform. For both men, too, the experience of individualism rooted in their small-town communities infuses their political idealism.

Debs, however, was actually born in Terre Haute and in a certain sense never left there. Much of his life was lived on the road, but he kept his family at home in Indiana. His parents and brothers and sisters, to whom he remained close throughout his life, continued to live there, and his wife maintained their home there. The constant core of Debs's political program was the restoration of the fusion between individualism and community in American life and the social equality among men that had sustained it in the Terre Haute of his youth.

But Debs developed during his political career an increasingly profound and complex understanding of how the structures of his youth had come apart and what would be required to restore them. The culprit was the historical process of industrialization; that same historical process precluded a retreat to the past and made a newly constructed socialist society the only viable solution. This vision, moreover, was an integral part of the debate in his times. While he was perceived as standing at one end of the political spectrum, his socialism was for many a compromise between the Wilsonian rhetoric of agrarian democracy and Roosevelt's vision of the inevitability of monopoly capitalism.[4]

Reagan's ideal of small-town life is the Dixon, Illinois, of his boyhood, but in his own description he himself is something of a stranger to that town. His family moves among a number of small midwestern towns in his early youth and settles in Dixon only when he is nine years old.[5] He himself leaves town after college to pursue his career in Hollywood and moves his parents to California as soon as he can afford it. His marriage has nothing to do with Dixon. And in reality the community of Dixon, as Reagan describes it, is not a community of equal individuals. Indeed, the community of his memories contains no individuals in Arendt's sense at all.

The theater is not just a metaphor for the structure of life in Dixon. In

Reagan's telling, it *is* that structure. The major experiences he recounts are of being an actor in the school plays. The townspeople are an audience, and Reagan himself plays a written part that, in stark contrast to the public life in a community of action, hides the self rather than reveals it. His boyhood comes across less as a creation of the self than as an enactment of a part written by others. The other seminal experiences Reagan recounts from his childhood are of being on the football team, and these have a similar flavor. The team is the background for Reagan's play; the audience is in the stands. And there is little more to the image of small-town life that Reagan preached in politics. That image was more fantasy than lost reality. If Americans bought the image, it was probably because the political tradition with which it is associated had become largely fantasy for us too, not something to draw upon to understand and interpret our real life.

But if we have lost the tradition of yeoman democracy, there are other ways of fusing community and individualism, ways more grounded in continuing experience. One of these is the athletic experience that Reagan evokes in his memories. Reagan's picture of the individual playing to the stands does not, however, do justice to that experience. The experience as characterized by most athletes is one in which they are dependent upon the team to realize their individual prowess as athletes; the team provides the context in which they are able to excel as individuals, but it is also the audience to which they turn for a judgment of their accomplishments, the audience whose recognition they really value. A central conflict in professional sports is indeed between the athletes who play for the team and the Reagans who play for the stands. But it is not presented in most characterizations as one in which the individual sacrifices for the team but rather as one in which he realizes his identity as a player through the team. In many ways the other teams on the field play a role similar to that of the members of a player's own team: they are the referent against which the individual defines his identity and to which he turns to gain recognition for it. The audience in the stands is in these accounts analogous to the private realm of ancient Greece, necessary for the support of the game but not what the game is all about.

Paradoxically, in terms of the vision of the founding fathers, political representatives in the Congress or in the state legislatures constitute similar communities of action. They work for the respect and recognition of other legislators, a recognition based upon the way they play the legislative game irrespective of the substance of their political positions. The task of winning elections is something performed outside of the legislative process, like labor in the private life of ancient Greece, a precondition for participation but not a part of that process or the recognition it affords. The electors are like the paying customers in a sports arena.

Still another arena of action in modern American life is the community of scholars in elite academic communities. Here again individuals work for recognition from their colleagues. They may compete with one another to prove a critical theorem or find a cure for a major disease, but at the same time they rely upon their competitors to judge and appreciate the results. If they win fame and fortune in the process, those rewards are not allowed to separate them from the scholarly community.[6]

These examples show that the ancient Greek experience is certainly not irrelevant to modern American life, but their value in translating the notion of communities of action into contemporary terms is limited. With the possible exception of team sports, which many Americans participate in in school and appreciate as spectators, none of them represents a widely shared experience.

Ethnicity: From Melting Pots to Borderlands

A broader model for community in American life, more directly linked to the current debate and also more grounded in continuing experience, is the model of ethnicity. Racial and ethnic affinity groups have provided the structure for the organization of political life in many—one is tempted to say most—of the nation's large cities. And they have, as already noted, been used to structure economic activities in which trust and cooperation are critical to efficiency in industries ranging from garments and construction stretching back into the nineteenth century to the Korean greengroceries in contemporary New York City and the Cuban enclave economy of Miami.[7]

Of course, such affinities are not always used in ways as conducive to the welfare of the members of the groups as these examples suggest. In mass production industries, the racial and ethnic distribution of jobs and organization of tasks was used as a deliberate managerial tactic to divide the labor force and forestall class identification and union organization.[8] In the American South, the racial division of labor was not efficient even from a managerial point of view: when I first went to Mississippi in 1964, gas meters were read by a black and white team; the black man bent down and took the cover off the meter, which was buried in the ground, the white man read the meter and recorded the reading, and the black man replaced the cover. Soft-drink deliveries also involved a black man who did the heavy lifting and a white one to do the paperwork.

How and why the relationships between ethnic community and economic organization took these various forms has never been fully explored, but what the American experience suggests is that when the economic organization requires institutional structures that marry competition and community, ethnic communities have proved capable of generating them. And the way this operates also seems well characterized by Arendt's version of the Greek city-state.

What has been explored, most recently in the multicultural debate, is the way the groups themselves form and evolve in the larger American society. Fresh insight into this phenomenon is provided by the anthropologist Renaldo Rosaldo in a recent book, *Culture and Truth*. Rosaldo's views gain added significance from the fact that he is Hispanic and teaches at Stanford University, where the movement for multicultural education first began, or at any rate first attracted the attention of the popular press and became a focus of national political debate. In a sense, this book may be taken as an insider's view of what ethnic studies is all about.[9]

Somewhat surprisingly, if one wants to read the book in this way, Rosaldo's focus is not on ethnicity per se but on anthropology as an intellectual discipline and the concept of culture that it promulgates. It is an *autocritique,* a critique of his own work as an anthropologist. The concept of culture in classical anthropology, Rosaldo argues, is too holistic, too all-encompassing. It reduces human beings to a repertoire preordained by the culture to which they belong; it has no room for novelty, spontaneity, or change, or for the personal or individual aspects of experience.

He makes his point through two specific examples of the way this view of culture distorts the nature of human experience. The first is the convention for the characterization of funeral rites, a characterization in which grief and mourning are reduced to ritual and the anthropological observer writes that at certain moments in the ceremony the mourners are *supposed* to shed tears and hence they cry, as if their grief and sorrow were somehow ritualistic and the tears merely *represented* feeling rather than expressing feeling itself.

Rosaldo's second example focuses on contemporary Hispanic culture in the United States. The traditional machismo of that culture, he argues, is being moderated at present, under the influence of the women's movement, through work of Hispanic women novelists that reinterprets Hispanic experience through feminist eyes. This is a phenomenon of what Rosaldo terms *borderland* cultures, in which people are led to reflect on their experience in ways that ultimately alter the interpretative framework of the culture itself. Such reflections have no place in the conceptual apparatus of classic anthropology. Rosaldo argues for a research agenda that focuses on the borderland cultures and highlights the realm of spontaneity in human experience in order to develop a more open and fluid concept of culture itself.

If economics provides the framework for constructing an understanding of society out of autonomous individual actors, anthropology is its obverse, a framework in which society is holistic and all-embracing and its constituent parts have no autonomy at all. Understood in these terms, Rosaldo's critique of anthropology is the obverse of the critique I have been making of economics. Just as I accused economics of reducing society to the individuals who compose it, he accuses anthropology of reducing individuals to their culture. But his critique of anthropology is also a critique of mechanical theories of cognition, and points toward communities of action and the hermeneutic view of knowledge. It reveals the limits of the notions of society and individuality that are generated by attempts to correct the social vision that emerges from competitive economic theory by building beneath it a foundation based on a model of human interaction as basically an exchange of unambiguous signals.

The melting-pot metaphor that has structured the debate about ethnicity in American life has a parallel construction. What melts in the metaphor is individuals, not cultures. Each individual, it is imagined, is faced with a choice between two cultures, an ethnic culture on the one hand and the national culture on the other. National unity is achieved when the individuals abandon their ethnic cultures and adopt the national one. The schools are particularly important in this process because it is in them that the national culture is presented and the conversion—or "integration," to use the preferred term—occurs. The cultures in this view are classically anthropological, holistic, fully integrated, and complete. In the more open view of culture that Rosaldo proposes, there is another possibility: the cultures themselves could evolve and change and the individuals might not simply reflect the culture but also be agents in its creation.

American society could be defined as a collection of cultures of this kind, *borderland* cultures, to use Rosaldo's term. What defines the nation, then, would not be a national culture in the classic anthropological sense of the term. Instead it would be a *process* in which all the cultures that coexist on the national territory are engaged. Alternatively, or additionally, one could argue that in the United States the nation is defined by a set of common themes to which all the communities that coexist on the national territory must respond.

In our time, communities—and cultures—are constituted in two cross-cutting ways, one through the experience of ethnicity, the other through the experience of socially limiting physical and biological traits that some members of every ethnic group share: gender, physical "handicap," sexual orientation, age, and the like. It is this structure of cross-cutting cultures that produces Rosaldo's example of the Hispanic feminist novelists. The themes this structure generates are feminism, abortion, homosexuality, affirmative action. For the preceding political generation, the key themes were the civil rights movement and the war in Vietnam. Enduring themes in the United States include industrialization, immigration, the opposition between our lives in America and those in some distant foreign place from which we, or our families, originate.

Individuals are, in this view, not separate and autonomous from the culture but active agents in the process through which it is generated. This is particularly true of individuals who, for one reason or another, move in the borderlands where cultures intersect or where they are forced to confront the important national themes. Those individuals include not only people like Rosaldo's Hispanic women writers but also ethnic soldiers in the national army and ethnic students at national universities.

In this view of the relationship between the nation and the cultures within it, institutions like schools and universities play a role different from the one they play in the melting pot. These institutions are "borderlands" where the students are exposed to these broader national themes. But they are also places where the several cultures are changed through reflection, debate, and discussion. They are places where, to continue with Rosaldo's example, the writings that introduce the feminist influence into Hispanic culture are produced and where they are assimilated through the classroom and through discussion, debate, and criticism by other writers and scholars. For all of this, of course, it is important that the Hispanic women writers have the visibility that forces them to the attention of one another and, particularly, of the other Hispanics whose culture they are in the process of transforming.

What should concern us in evaluating the educational system, then, is not whether the schools are integrated or segregated but whether the system as a whole contributes to an evolutionary process that is conducive to national unity. The problem, from this point of view, with the dual system in the old South was not that the schools were segregated but that the old colored system was isolated and self-contained. The issue is not whether blacks or women choose to go to all-black or all-women colleges, but whether the faculties of these schools are also the product of exclusively black or exclusively female educational institutions, whether the schools are isolated from the themes and debates that confront students in other educational institutions, whether, when the students leave these institutions and move out into the larger society, they will meet only women and blacks who have had educational experiences like their own.

This emphasis on *process* should not be allowed to obscure the issue of content. It is not enough that the various cultures evolve through interaction with one another. They must also evolve in a way that is conducive to national unity, that preserves enough mutual tolerance for them to share the same territory and resource base. For this, the broader national context in which that evolution is occurring would seem to be critically important. The evolution will probably be very different if citizenship in a broader society is being reinforced by the evolution of the medical insurance system, or the delivery system for social services, or the patterns of employment than if these institutions are being increasingly defined in narrow, exclusive terms. Tolerance, this same logic would seem to imply, is likely to be aided at the present time by the fact that the social structure is increasingly defined by groups, like women or the deaf, which cut across ethnic divisions.

Rosaldo's message about how societies are constructed is just as relevant to our economic dilemma as it is to our social and political dilemmas. The interdependencies of the economy have always provided the universalizing themes for a discussion of macroeconomic policy. But comparable interdependencies in production have not been recognized. The networked organizations fostered by the new competitive environment involve enlarging the borderlands between traditional business firms and would seem to require borderland economic institutions comparable to the multicultural schools that facilitate social cohesion.

The divorce between economic and social structures created by the emergence of the new social groups can also be conceived as a borderlands problem. This suggests that we might think about trade unions not as competitors with identity groups to represent social claims but as a borderland institution that bridges such groups and might introduce economic constraints into their internal discussions in much the same way that Hispanic women writers introduce feminist concerns into internal discussions of Hispanic communities. I shall return to this point shortly.

The primary implication that emerges from Rosaldo's perspective, then, is that in all of these areas we need themes of discussion and institutional structures of interaction that reinforce the borderlands. The remainder of this chapter will examine some of these.

The Internal Debates of the New Groups

One set of universalizing themes coming out of these debates was already alluded to in the discussion of Rosaldo's notion of borderland cultures: the challenge to the conception and structure of one group posed by the campaigns for liberation and independence of another. The challenge the feminist movement poses for Hispanics, which Rosaldo himself explores, is only one of a number that have provoked discussion and debate within particular groups. Others include the challenge the congenitally handicapped pose to feminist views on abortion rights; the challenge the Nazis' extermination of gays in the Holocaust poses for Jews; the challenge lesbians pose to the cultural norms of gay men; the challenge the epidemiology of AIDS in the black community poses to the structures that gays have created to handle AIDS among gay men.[10]

These, however, are all particular issues. Rosaldo's notion of borderland cultures links them all together, but it has not emerged explicitly within the groups themselves and remains to be developed. A second set of universalizing themes, and one that is explicit in the literature the groups are generating, has crystallized in the debate about essentialism and social construction.

Essentialism vs. Social Construction

Virtually all of the stigmatized groups have been led, more or less independently of one another, to a singular internal debate about their origins and the nature of their existence. The debate is sparked by the physical and biological traits through which the groups are defined. Are those traits, despite their protestations to the contrary, actually the reasons for their economic and social inferiority? Is there, in the end, a real foundation for stereotypes and prejudice? And if not, why do some physical traits get singled out and become the fulcrum for social and economic oppression while other physical traits, which seem equally salient, are socially irrelevant? Are blacks inherently less intelligent and more athletic than whites? Are women by nature better caretakers and worse leaders than men? Are Jews and Asians better mathematicians? Are gays more artistic?

In these concrete terms, the questions are so threatening that they have been largely repressed in public debate. But within the groups themselves, they are the subject of lingering doubts and deep-seated guilt, the locus of nagging insecurities. The debates internal to the groups are a response to these insecurities. In each of the groups, moreover, they tend to take a similar form, one defined in terms of the dichotomy between essentialism and social construction.

Simply put, the essentialist's position in the debate is that at root the groups are physically, or biologically, constituted and hence that they are an enduring feature of human cultures in general. The constructionist position is that, on the contrary, the very definition of a group is a social product. A debate of this form is taking place in virtually all of the identity groups, but the issues at stake are perhaps best exemplified by the debate opened in the gay community by the publication of, on the one hand, *Christianity, Social Tolerance and Homosexuality* by the Yale historian John Boswell, and on the other, of Michel Foucault's *History of Sexuality* and his American interpreter David Halperin's *One Hundred Years of Homosexuality*.[11]

Boswell is the essentialist.[12] For him, homosexuality is an enduring, naturally rooted category; his book is an attempt to show that homosexuals have always existed, in all times and in all human societies. What differs across time and space is the value that is placed upon homosexuals. Boswell seeks to demonstrate that in Western society that value has shifted radically from a benign tolerance, even a certain celebration, of homosexuality that prevailed in the middle ages to the negative, censorial view that came to characterize social attitudes in the nineteenth and twentieth centuries. Boswell's main focus is on homosexuality in Christian civilization, but his work is complemented by studies that demonstrate the existence and the variety of attitudes toward homosexuality in a much wider range of cultures and civilizations.

Foucault and Halperin focus on the contrast between Western industrial society in the twentieth century and the culture of classical Greece. Their argument is that the very category of homosexuality is a social creation, reflecting the structure of power, authority, and political control in modern times. The essentialists have read that category into the literature of classical Greece, in which authority and control were exerted in a very different way, through a different construction of sexuality, one that did not recognize the existence of homosexuals, as such, at all.

What might be biologically rooted, Halperin argues, are differences among individuals in the tastes for various types of people and/or particular acts as the focus of sexual desire. But that would not explain why such differences in taste become the fulcrum around which we judge individuals, create social categories, and define the rules of social relations. We recognize that some people prefer chicken and others red meat, but, in American society, we would never think of dividing the world into chicken lovers and red meat lovers; we do not place relative values on their tastes or behavior, let alone censure one and encourage the other.

Homosexuals, a category of people who prefer sexual relations with members of their own sex, are a wholly modern creation, a category that has existed, as the title of Halperin's book suggests, only for the past hundred years. It was not a relevant category in classical Greece. Social categories there were structured differently. The Greeks were not basically concerned with the object of one's sexual desire; tastes for women, or boys, or other men, were viewed as we view a preference for chicken, meat, or fish. But Greek society was very concerned with certain categories of sexual acts, particularly the act of sexual penetration. The distinction between the active and the passive partner played an important role in the definition of social status and authority; it was basic to the distinction between citizen and noncitizen of the Greek city-state.

We think of the category of homosexual as universal because we read Greek literature through contemporary eyes; we read into it our own way of thinking. Halperin shows that the Greeks made equivalent mistakes in interpreting ancient literature, attributing sexual roles and identifying patterns of dominance and subordination in relationships that the authors conceived of as essentially ones of parity involving no necessary sexual relations at all. Boswell, this argument seems to imply, has made an analogous mistake in reading early Christian texts.

Clearly, Foucault and Halperin have a radically different view of homosexuality from that of Boswell. But for the larger debate about the legitimacy of homosexuality in modern society, it is not clear what difference that makes. In a world where identity is bound up with a social category— as it was for the Gallaudet student protesting the search for a cure for deafness—it probably makes very little difference whether the category is ultimately social or biological. Both Boswell and Foucault hold out the promise of a world where the category would be valued in a very different way. Ultimately, perhaps, they imply differing agendas for political action. They probably imply differing agendas for research, social and scientific, which would support that action as well. But in the current state of the debate, what those differences will be is not at all clear.

The importance of the essentialist/constructionist debate is not the contrast between the two positions but the way in which, in combination, they define the terms of a particular discourse, to use a term drawn from the literature that has grown up around the debate. The distinctiveness of that discourse is seen by the contrast with sociobiology, a discipline that focuses upon the biological evolution of socially significant physical traits, thus short-circuiting altogether an analysis of processes that give some traits their social significance.

Somewhat independently of one another, pushed by the common stance they have assumed vis-à-vis the larger society, virtually all of the new identity groups are being drawn into this same debate. And the debate thus has a unifying effect among them, breaking down barriers between them by providing them with a shared vocabulary, a set of intersecting interests, a common way, not so much of thinking about the world as of talking about it, a consensus not about answers but about what constitutes an interesting and significant question.

The danger in this development is that, however much it serves to break down barriers among the stigmatized groups themselves, it will increasingly isolate them from the rest of society. The distinctive nature of this new discourse could, in other words, close them off in a set of parochial debates among themselves, rendering them less and less able to communicate with, and justify their existence within, the larger society. In a certain sense, this is what happened to the American labor movement as it split with the left in the Vietnam war. But in the case of the new identity groups this seems an unlikely outcome. The break with older notions about the interpretation of reality that this new perspective represents is also evident in other areas of national concern and in a very different, and diverse, set of groups and institutions.

Cognitive Technologies

As suggested earlier, the ideas that emerge in the essentialist/constructionist debate parallel developments in the domain of cognitive science. Applied scientists, engineers, and managers are being increasingly drawn into discussions about the social foundations of understanding by the *cognitive technologies,* the technologies emerging out of the attempt to automate, through the extension of information technology, a wider and wider range of human activities.

The focus is shifting in this process from computerizing mechanical choices toward activities that call upon the engineer to have a progressively greater understanding of how people think and make judgments. The task of simulating, for example, how doctors diagnose disease or how interpreters translate from one spoken language to another has revealed the importance of socially contingent models and has led to debates among scientists and engineers about how these models are constructed and what the relationship is between them and biologically and physically rooted phenomena. We saw in the preceding chapter that this also moves the engineer and computer scientist out of the discourse of sociobiology and Lockean epistemology into the realm of ideas in which the essentialist/constructionist debate is grounded.

The growing concern of an important faction of management with the social structure of the enterprise operates to similar effect within the business community and in management science and economics. This concern is premised on the idea that effective business organization depends upon the enterprise as a social institution and the way it translates and interprets its environment. It underscores the task of managing this process, of creating and maintaining organizational "cultures" that are effective "interpreters" of their surroundings.

What managers need to understand for this purpose is exactly what the

·essentialist/constructionist debate is concerned with understanding: how the social interpretation of environmental characteristics emerges and evolves over time. This concern increasingly separates the progressive faction in management from their colleagues who remain focused upon how to identify a given set of constraints and how to optimize a response to it, conceived as separate and distinct from the constraints themselves.[13] It joins them in a common vocabulary and way of thinking about the world with the new identity groups.[14]

Environmentalism

In the short run, and for politics, the most important avenue through which the essentialist/constructionist discourse universalizes the politics of the new identity groups is environmentalism. On the surface, the politics of the environmental movement would appear to be totally different from that of the new identity groups. It is universalistic precisely because it highlights what we share with one another rather than the peculiarities that distinguish us and give us our separate identities. It makes additional demands upon economic resources that are likely to compete with those of particular groups. Its strongest link to the politics of identity, one might presume, is the refuge it provides for the white middle class, which has been excluded in the reorganization of political life around minority identities.

But environmentalism raises in the most straightforward and insistent way the question of the relationship between the physical and the social worlds. The management of that relationship is the central issue of environmental policy. And this places the environmentalists squarely within the essentialist/constructionist discourse. And because environmentalism is a universal concern, it tends to universalize the discourse.

Of course, this is not the only way the environmental issues can be conceptualized. Indeed, the split within the business community in thinking about American competitiveness is reproduced in thinking about environmental policy. The analogue to the view that competitiveness depends upon lowering production costs is the view that social and economic processes are separate and distinct from the physical environment in which they operate; that environmental protection is a price that must be paid to preserve the physical world from the intrusion of social and economic processes, a price we may or may not be able to afford or willing to pay, a cost that must somehow be distributed. This is the view that leads George Bush to argue that the American economy is too weak or the budget deficit too large to admit environmental concerns, to contend that environmental protection and employment are competitive goals. Conceived in this way, the environment is clearly competitive with the demands being made by the new identity groups as well, for medical care, for access to public facilities, even for equal employment opportunity, for all these too impose costs.

But once one abrogates the distinction between the social and physical world and recognizes that nature is always defined and understood through socially created categories, environmentalism becomes less a question of constraining social activity than of reconceptualizing what we are doing in the world. Our impact upon the environment is buried in the way we distinguish between production and consumption, in the distinctions we make between input and output, between product and waste, between means and ends.[15]

The solution to "environmental" problems involves a reconceptualization of social processes, a solution similar in character to the solutions to the problems of worker safety in nineteenth-century American industry.[16] And environmentalism becomes the key to the new politics not simply because our sharing of the environment makes it capable of universalizing a political movement that would otherwise consist of many discrete groups. It becomes the key because it is symbolic of the underlying intellectual problem of the social interpretation of the physical world, and because the resolution of our environmental problems, like the resolution of our economic problems and the political problems posed by the new identity groups, lies in the realignment of our structures of thought.

Class Action

The essentialist-constructionist debate thus promises a vocabulary in terms of which the conversations of the borderlands might be thought about and conducted. But how might such borderlands be realized? The only form in which the new identity groups have achieved anything approaching institutional recognition is the class action suit in the law. Could this legal category constitute an instrument through which borderland cultures might be promoted or an institutional structure in which they might be housed?

At first blush, class action does not appear very promising in this regard. It is basically a legal instrument for circumventing the rules through which access to the judicial process has traditionally been limited and the courts have controlled their case load. Under these rules only individuals and well-established institutions with a significant interest—generally a significant financial interest—in the outcome of a case are granted recognition. The interest of a single black child excluded from a white school is not considered substantial in these terms, and the collectivity of black children has no institutional existence. Similarly, the stake of a single consumer defrauded by a false advertising for a cheap product is too small, and the collectivity of all such consumers too vaguely defined, to let the one or the other bring its case to court. The class action suit opens the courts to these groups and others like them.

The class action suit is, however, a troublesome legal category. It contrasts sharply with the legal recognition granted other institutions. The contrast is particularly marked to the way our major economic institutions, the business enterprise and the trade union, are constituted. It raises issues about representativeness and about the protection of individuals. Since the class is not constituted through a clearly defined process, there is no obvious way of ensuring that the individuals who initiate the suit represent the class or that the members of the class accept the remedy those individuals propose. When financial damages are awarded, it is not clear how the settlement should be distributed.

Legal scholars offer three distinct models to address these problems. One of these models would define the class in essentially economic terms. It is built around the figure of the entrepreneurial lawyer motivated by contingent legal fees, who seeks out and puts together financial claimants. The *classes* that the law is led to recognize are thus regulated by the market. A class is a group that because of either its size or the size of its financial claims is able to reward a lawyer for his or her efforts. The need to compensate the lawyer in this way serves to limit the number of such suits. The issue of representativeness is resolved by the requirement that the lawyer, if he or she wins the case, actually find the members of the class and distribute the financial award among them. This requirement also translates into a financial constraint upon would-be class representatives.[17]

This interpretation grows out of the pluralistic tradition of liberal thought. It seeks to define the class in terms of a series of common but also limited and particular interests. One never knows how far a clever lawyer might stretch the case law that it generates, but the approach itself is fundamentally antagonistic to the nature of the groups we are seeking to accommodate in the borderlands. These groups, as stressed in Chapter 1, are corporatist in nature.

A second model is one of public interest litigation. Here the class action is mainly an excuse to bring before the courts issues of general public policy, and the courts decide the cases on the basis of broad policy principles rather than in terms of the class interest. The issue of representativeness no longer arises because it is not class interest but general public policy that is being litigated. And the probable outcomes concern prescriptions for future conduct and behavior (the integration of the schools, the provision of services for the handicapped) rather than financial damages to compensate for past wrongs.[18]

The public interest model is flexible enough to accommodate almost anything that can be construed as a public purpose, but since the suits are basically an occasion for the courts to make social policy, they do not really provide institutional recognition for the classes in whose name they are brought. The policies the courts have actually pursued through the vehicle of class action have, moreover, been generally conceived in terms of the liberal individualistic ideal, and they reflect all of the contradictions I reviewed earlier under the headings of education, health insurance, and employment.

Nonetheless, the public interest model would certainly permit the courts to use class action to reinforce communities of meaning and to enlarge the borderlands among those communities were they ever to conceive of the public interest in these terms. The model would then imply that the courts should use class action suits not as an occasion to impose particular remedies but rather to orchestrate the relations among groups and between them and the larger society. In school cases, for example, the court might be less concerned with actually integrating the schools than with encouraging debates within them and exchanges among them that would serve to enhance the borderlands. It might recognize, to take another example, the concerns the handicapped, the deaf, and gays and lesbians are bound to develop about abortion as genetic research into the origins of the characteristics that define them progresses, not by reviewing provisions for individual counseling, but by insisting that groups whose characteristics are likely to be screened out in abortion decisions have a voice in the community debates that surround this issue.

A third, and in the context of this book, most telling, model is offered by Stephen Yeazell. For him, class action is a vestige of medieval law in which cohesive social groups were central to the organization of the society, a period in which the social and economic organization was corporatist in the generic sense of the term. The classes the law was called upon to recognize were so internally cohesive that the issue of representativeness did not arise. In the individualistic terms in which we have come to understand modern society, he argues, such groups are viewed as exceptional. They are allowed to exist only for particular and limited purposes and require special legislative recognition. The class action suit has come to serve as a temporary legal halfway house in the process through which that recognition is granted.[19]

For Yeazell, the two most important groups associated with class action are the joint stock company and the friendly society. The former was the precursor of the limited liability corporation. The latter provided the fulcrum for early trade union activity but also is an antecedent of the social security system and the modern welfare state. Yeazell sees no prospect that the new social groups currently recognized through class action will be institutionalized in this way and implies that, since they will not, class action will atrophy and the recognition it currently affords will gradually be withdrawn.

But the borderland concept suggests that Yeazell is wrong. He is wrong not simply about class action as a vehicle for the new social groups but also about the appropriateness and durability of the legal structures in which the business enterprise and the trade union are presently housed: given the current evolution of our productive structures, class action may be a better model for these institutions in the future than the permanent legal structures that emerged in the past to replace it. In terms of the problems upon which this book focuses, the implications of this argument for trade unions are most important. But before turning to these, I shall examine its implications for corporate reform.

The Corporation

The clearest case for Yeazell's view of the class action suit as a halfway house on the road to permanent legal status is the joint stock company. The institutional form that the joint stock company ultimately took was the modern corporation with "freely transferable shares, entity status open to all complying with the formalities of registration and disclosure." The corporation achieved the status of a person and came to be accorded the same rights as real individuals. At the same time, the new legal status limited the liability of the individual shareholders and "a fiduciary management controlled in theory by a democracy of shareholders" but increasingly by government regulation and criminal statutes as well.

The modern corporation is basically an economic organization, and the problem of the relationship between the group (that is, the institution) and its members has been resolved in a very specific way. The individual members are presumed to be associated with the institution *only* for economic gain, and the rights are thus secured by the ability to exit from one such institution and enter another.[20] The stockholders (who were the principal litigants in the nineteenth century) can sell out and liquidate their holdings, suppliers can find other customers, customers can find other suppliers, and so on. This way of looking at the problem transforms all the issues of internal representativeness into issues of external options and makes the question of the competitiveness of the markets in which the corporation operates central. In a sense, therefore, the issue of representativeness has been transformed in the case of the corporation into antitrust policy. Our first instinct in the case of abuse of power has been to break up the corporation into competing units. The one individual right that was not granted the corporation in the process of making it a person is that of freedom of association.

This solution, however, has had two important consequences, both of which make it ill-adapted to present circumstances. First, it is predicated upon a radical separation of economic and social activity. Such a separation is fostered both by a competitive market economy and by the structures of mass production, but the new productive processes and organizational forms, as we have seen, place a premium on the reintegration of the economic and social realms. Second, antitrust policy as it has developed in the United States forecloses intermediate forms of business organization.

And the new productive forms are generating associations among enterprises that abridge the competitive forces upon which the protection of the individual within the organization is predicated; such associations are becoming increasingly prevalent.

U.S. practice is evolving to accommodate these changes, although perhaps not fast enough to preserve our competitive position in the international marketplace. But one wonders where the evolution is likely to take us. So far, the laws governing competition have been relaxed primarily to meet the needs of business in international competition. Virtually no attention has been paid to the effect of these changes upon the relationship between the organization and the individuals who are involved with it in one way or another. But as competition among enterprises in the United States declines, the issue of the protection of these individuals is bound to come increasingly to the fore. And in the absence of legislative efforts to address this problem, the class action suit could once again become a factor in corporate governance.[21]

The Trade Union

Yeazell's second example of an institutional form that has emerged from the penumbra of class action and achieved statutory recognition is the trade union. This section on trade unions provides an occasion to consolidate the insights that have emerged in the discussion thus far and to consider the ways in which they shift the perspective on the social deficit with which the book began.

The discussion of the country's social and economic dilemmas in the initial chapters was organized around two competing notions of social groups. One was the pluralist model, basically an extension of liberal individualism, in which the group is a coalition of diverse individuals coming together to achieve a limited objective. The individual remains the basic unit of analysis. The second was the corporatist model, in which public policy operates through cohesive groups and institutions. This might be a reflection of the underlying social structure, as were the group structures in medieval Europe. Or, as in *neo*corporatism, the cohesive groups and institutions might be a product of state interventions in a society that would otherwise be composed of autonomous individuals and pluralistic groups.

The evolution of American labor law reflects the ambivalence of a liberal society toward neocorporatist solutions to its social problems. The basic legislative framework as it emerged in the early postwar period is neocorporatist, but the cohesiveness of the institutions it created has been progressively weakened in the last several decades by Congress and the courts solicitous of the rights of workers and employers as individuals in the liberal sense. Yeazell's view of class action has a similar flavor, an unstable compromise between the coherent alternatives offered by corporatism on the one hand and liberalism on the other.

The conceptual framework that emerged in the last chapter suggests a third way of thinking about social groups. Two additional conceptual categories grow out of that framework, both distinct from pluralist and corporatist groups but also different from each other. One of these is Arendt's notion of communities of action. These are groups that provide the context in which the individual realizes himself or herself. They are much more cohesive than the groups of pluralism, but they are fluid in a way that corporatist groups are not. I have interpreted both the new identity groups and the networked economic organizations as communities of this kind.

The second concept is Rosaldo's notion of borderlands. It recognizes that particular individuals may be attached to more than one group. That attachment is distinguished from the multiple attachments of pluralism by the facts, first, that most individuals belong primarily to one group and, second, that the attachments of those who do not are still quite limited. The several attachments of the few nonetheless have a disproportionate impact on the many, because the borderland individuals carry the themes they encounter in each of the communities to which they are attached into the discussions and debates of the others, changing the content and character of the conversations through which these communities are defined and evolve over time and making them more cognizant of and able to talk to one another. It seems natural to think in terms of borderland individuals who perform this function but also of borderland institutions where those individuals encounter the themes they import into the communities to which they belong. (The leading example of such an institution that I have discussed is the schools, but churches and community organizations play a similar role.)

The recognition of communities of action and borderland institutions does not change the underlying nature of our political and economic dilemmas. The fundamental political problem remains the relative isolation of the new identity groups and the resulting tendency for them to formulate their demands independently of one another and of the underlying economic constraints. The weakness of networked organizations continues to be central to the problems in the economy. But if the underlying problems remain, their transposition into the new conceptual framework does greatly enlarge the range of available solutions. We now have a different way of thinking about networked organizations in the economy. And we can imagine solutions to our political problems through borderland institutions.

How, in this context, might one think about trade unions? Unions could be viewed as communities of action. The analogy is suggested by the literature on working-class culture and its expression through the labor movement. The parallels are strongest, however, in Europe. In the United States, the union organizations that lend themselves to characterization as communities of action could as well be interpreted as extensions of ethnic subcultures rather than as representative of labor unions more broadly. In any case, the evolution of the job structure and of the technology is greatly compromising the cohesiveness of the working class as it is understood in the literature on class culture.

Alternatively, however, one might think of trade unions in the United States as borderland institutions, precisely the kind of borderland institutions that seem to be required to overcome the isolation of the groups from one another and from the economy. In the relations among the various groups, unions would seem to supplement the role played by schools, churches, and local government.[22] But in the relationship between the groups and the economy, the unions would seem play a unique borderland role, one that introduces an awareness of economic constraints and a vocabulary for discussing them into groups that are constituted in such a way that otherwise they would have neither.

American unions have actually functioned in the past as borderlands. As noted earlier, the unions have often encompassed various ethnically defined organizational components that have been integrated with one another through a series of intersecting conversations and social interactions. The garment unions in the days when the industry was composed largely of Jewish and Italian immigrants were the most vivid examples of this phenomenon. Behind the interaction within the union itself were an endless series of "functions" and events in which the members of one ethnic group attended the charity benefits and the religious rites of passage (bar mitzvahs, christenings, confirmations, weddings, funerals) of the other. In more recent times, several of the more dynamic national unions have made great efforts to reach out and encompass the new ethnic and identity groups within their membership. The most prominent example is the Service Employees International Union, which has caucuses of blacks, Hispanics, gays, and women, and in which members of these groups interact at political and cultural events in ways reminiscent of the ethnic interactions surrounding the garment unions.

The garment unions, along with the construction unions, provide a model of an organization that constitutes not only a borderland among social groups or between those groups and the economy but also a borderland within the economy itself. In this, their roles have been even more extensive. These unions have been exactly the kind of networked institution into which the originally closed mass production corporation has been trying remake itself through new relationships with its suppliers, customers, and employees. They have created and maintained training institutions, sponsored research and development institutes, even plotted industrial strategies and engaged in trade negotiations for the industry as a whole. They have constituted, in other words, the glue that holds together productive networks.

The notion of unions as borderland institutions points to a very different set of issues in labor law from the issues highlighted earlier. The earlier discussion focused on the ability of unions to help manage conflict in a period of social mobilization. The concern was that the introduction of the individual rights of workers and employers into an essentially neocorporatist legislative structure had undermined the willingness and ability of union leaders to confront their members with the realities of economic life. A retreat toward the neocorporatist model might help manage conflict in the short run, especially if the social claims were to be expressed through trade unions, but it will not serve in the long run to diffuse a consciousness of those economic constraints throughout the society. Furthermore, if the new social groups emerge as the primarily representative of the grievances generated by the social deficit, it will serve little purpose even in the short run.

Most of the amendments that undermine the neocorporatist character of the structure set up by the National Labor Relations Act (NLRA) actually work to strengthen the union as a borderland institution. They do so by generating internal institutional pressure for conversations. They enhance the ability of individuals within the organization to place new topics of conversation on the agenda and to force the leaders to engage in a contin- uous internal dialogue with the members. From a borderland perspective that dialogue internal to the organization is more important than the po- sitions the organization actually endorses at any given time. The amend- ments coming out of liberalism have also enhanced management's ability to thrust itself into the midst of the internal discussions of the workforce and inject a set of topics and perspectives coming out of the economy.

But the borderland functions of the trade union have been inhibited by a very different dynamic in the evolution of the law, one that worked out in practice the notion of the union as a self-contained organization with definite boundaries and a strictly delimited set of functions. These were not present in the initial act but introduced by congressional amendments and court interpretations. The boundaries of the union were defined, for example, by provisions prohibiting secondary boycotts. Specific exemp- tions were written into the law for networked industries like garments and construction; the exemptions serve to underscore the way the law now limits the ability of the unions to expand their borderland functions as other industries begin to dissolve into networks.[23]

Another frontier that was sharpened by amendments was the line be- tween workers and managers; the important change here was the exclusion of the foreman from the bargaining unit. This is another distinction the construction and garment unions have not drawn in the past (although in this case the law recognized no exceptions). The courts also introduced a distinction between mandatory and voluntary subjects of bargaining and a concept of management prerogatives that created a sharp boundary around the subjects discussed between labor and management, a particular im- pediment for an organization that is supposed to be the locus of a con- stantly evolving and shifting set of conversations.

Indeed, the NLRA gives the National Labor Relations Board a degree of discretion in defining the jurisdiction of particular unions and the role of collective bargaining comparable to the discretion the courts have to rec- ognize groups in class action.[24] Much of that discretion remains in the hands of the NLRB even today. To this extent, the NLRB could realize the borderland potential of trade unions without repealing the sharp bound- aries that have emerged in the postwar period simply by thinking about how to use the discretion in a creative way. It is in this sense that class action suits form a model for labor law.

Conclusion

This chapter has sought to translate the theoretical categories of interpretative politics and communities of action that emerged at the end of the last chapter into forms recognizable in terms of American experience. This endeavor suggests that those categories are neither as abstract nor as remote as they at first appear. They are linked through civic republicanism to the country's historic past. Ethnic communities and the borderland cultures that grow up around them through interaction with other socially stigmatized groups provide a real and meaningful image of communities of action and interpretative politics today. The garment and construction unions provide examples of borderlands linking ethnic communities to the economy and within the economy itself. The discussions already occurring within the new identity groups provide a vocabulary in which interpretative politics might be thought about and conducted.

The debate over essentialism and social construction seems particularly rich in this regard; it is being conducted within the vocabulary of the interpretative framework out of which the concept of communities of action arises. And the themes it highlights are also emerging in the discussions within economic institutions about new organizational forms and new informational technologies, and are central to the pervasive debate about the environment. Finally, class action constitutes a model for the institutional forms through which communities of action could be realized, and might itself serve to accommodate some of these groups and/or the borderlands between them.

The reexamination of the issue of trade unions suggests that the exploration of the interpretative framework within the American context yields an unexpected dividend. Rosaldo's concept of borderlands is not simply an application of the interpretative framework; it is itself a separate and powerful conceptual category. It yields new insight into how a society composed of communities of action might be integrated socially, into how networked organizations might emerge in the economy, and into processes that might reconcile the conflicts among the claims of such communities and between those claims and the constraints imposed by the economy.

7

Toward a Politics of Common Understanding

It remains in this final chapter to close the argument, to bring to bear the conceptual framework that emerged in the later chapters upon the range of particular problems with which the book began. The intent in doing so is not to formulate a series of specific policy proposals. The direct implications of the preceding discussion for public policy, at least as policy is conventionally understood, are limited. Despite their seeming intractability, moreover, our current policy problems will not last forever; the capacity to address those particular problems will not sustain the general argument. But the focus upon policy nonetheless grounds the abstract theoretical argument in concrete experience. In this way, it illustrates and amplifies the underlying ideas and opens a path of escape not simply from the immediate impasse at which American policy has arrived but also from the cycles that seem to throw us periodically into crises of this kind.

From this perspective, the most important insight to emerge from this book is the view of the political process that it suggests. Politics in that view operates at two levels. The current impasse in the United States is in high politics. But it is politics at the second, deeper level that explains how we got into the impasse and how we are likely to work our way out.

Two Levels of Politics

High politics readily fits the analytical framework offered by liberal theory in its model of rational choice. The problems as they are understood and addressed at this level lend themselves to the distinctions rational choice draws among means, ends, and the causal models that connect them. The tasks of leadership divide neatly between the politician and the technician. The politician is the negotiator working out compromises among conflicting goals and agreements among the various groups and individuals who are parties to the political process. The technician is concerned with the means, devising alternative policies designed to stretch available resources and minimize the conflicts that the politician must resolve. Behind the technician stands the social scientist, identifying the underlying relationships that govern economic and social processes, resolving conflicts among alternative theories, and estimating the parameters of the constraints upon policy.

At a deep level, however, politics is a process through which both the goals and the understandings of the political actors emerge and evolve over time. Politics at this level can be likened to a series of intersecting conversations. As those conversations proceed, the people involved in them develop a shared vocabulary and common ways of thinking about the world. They also develop their identities and the identities of the groups and communities with which they are associated. These constitute the background for, and the preconditions of, the focused negotiations of politics understood as rational choice.

The politician and policymaker also play roles in deep politics, but those roles do not lend themselves to the neat division of labor among negotiator, technician, and social scientist. The role of political leadership in deep politics is one of directing and interpreting conversations so as to mold the understandings that emerge from them. In politics at this level, the leader is more like an orchestra conductor or, in a less elegant but more apt metaphor, a hostess at a cocktail party, directing who talks to whom, what they talk about, and how those conversations are understood and interpreted by the people involved in them and by the eavesdroppers on the periphery.

Deep politics, because it involves the evolution of meaning, needs to be understood broadly to include everyday life. But in understanding how it operates it is useful to make a distinction within it between idle conversation on the one hand and purposive discussions of the kind that occur in political and economic decisionmaking on the other. The distinction is important because of differences in response to ambiguity and misunderstanding. Ambiguity and misunderstanding are inevitable in any human interchange. It is by working through them that we generate common vocabularies and shared visions of how the world operates. To the extent that these determine what is possible in high politics, this is a critical dimension of the deep political process.

In idle conversation we tend to resolve ambiguities and work through misunderstandings automatically, often without being fully conscious that we have done so. But in purposeful conversations ambiguity and misunderstanding are often interpreted as willful and malicious, and lead to breakdowns in the process through which common meanings and understandings evolve. Thus identity and meaning often become frozen when political actors are drawn into formal decisionmaking processes and the alternatives are narrowly circumscribed. The same people, if left to talk with one another in a context where nothing particular is at stake, may over time develop the understandings requisite for agreement.

Contemporary Politics as Rational Choice

The origins of the current impasse in American politics and the potential avenues of escape look very different depending upon whether one is thinking about high politics or deep politics. Understood in rational choice terms—at the level of high politics, in other words—the impasse in contemporary American politics results from a failure to think clearly about our problems and to face up to hard choices. It grows out of a focus in politics and policy upon individual programs rather than broad social visions, a preoccupation with tactics rather than strategy, a confusion of means and ends. It represents a failure of politicians as negotiators: they have built compromises around particular programs, leaving unresolved the conflicts over the ends the programs are designed to serve.

Thus, as we have seen, business firms have prematurely sought closure in internal debates around organizational reform by agreeing, for example, upon the Kan-Ban system of on-time delivery of parts while leaving unresolved the question of whether Kan-Ban is part of a new strategy of cooperation with parts suppliers built on trust or one of intensified competition for profits in which inventory costs are shifted to the suppliers. The economics profession, which has coalesced around a policy of deregulation, is actually divided between one school that sees this as a way of promoting efficiency through enhanced competition and another that views it as a way of promoting entrepreneurial activities, activities that would also be aided by competitive restraints imposed by businesses upon one another. The federal budget, which was compromised around limitations on aggregate spending without any agreement on program and content, reflects a tendency to substitute an agreement on means for a consensus that we cannot achieve on the ends.

But the failure of leadership is also technical and scientific: the broad conceptual understandings about how economic and social policies would work that prevailed in the past have been called into question by the developments of the last two decades, but we have not developed widely accepted alternatives to replace them and thus we cling to anachronistic visions, drawn from periods of our history remote from current reality. The Democratic vision is the product of the 1930s and attuned to the requirements of a closed, virtually self-contained economy that has little to do with the exigencies of business in the international marketplace in which American enterprises find themselves enmeshed today. Ronald Reagan's vision went back still further to mid-nineteenth-century small-town American life, which, as we saw, had very little to do with his own experience, let alone the experience of the much younger electorate that voted him into office.

Both visions, moreover, have become so closely associated with the programs originally derived from them, on the one hand, and with the values they were designed to achieve, on the other, that we are no longer able to think in a creative and constructive way about alternative policies. In this process we have lost the ability to distinguish means from ends and to think in an instrumental way about policy. We have become attached to school integration as a goal separate from the end of white supremacy; we confuse abortion with the role of women in the society or with human life itself.

Given these confusions, a solution to the impasse in politics understood as rational choice would be to require a combination of two unlikely events. It would require first a breakthrough in the social sciences that would clarify the underlying constraints upon policy. We would then need an especially skilled and persuasive political leader who could develop a consensus around these newly generated theories about the constraints upon policy and negotiate a stable compromise among the various political actors and social claimants. It is hardly surprising that this favorable combination has failed to emerge. It seems almost inevitable that economic and social policy will drift and that the best we can hope for is more or less to muddle through.

Contemporary Problems and Deep Politics

But at a deeper level the confusion takes on a very different appearance. While high politics remains at an impasse, the conversations and interactions that constitute the deep political process continue to evolve, and it is this evolution that determines whether we will be able, over time, to work ourselves out of the impasses of ungovernability and gridlock.

Unfortunately, from this point of view, the direction of evolution in the 1980s aggravated the impasse rather than alleviating it. The country may not have been able to agree upon policy during this period but it was not because it ignored the issues at hand. On the contrary, policy alternatives were continually discussed and debated. But the way that debate was orchestrated and conducted by the political leadership served to inhibit dialogue among the various groups within the society, increasing the divergence in vocabularies and understandings and hence progressively limiting the foundations upon which compromises could be constructed. This was true in social policy, where the way both Reagan and Bush baited the women's movement, blacks, and homosexuals served to turn each of these groups in upon itself and reinforce among its members the felt sense of kinship with one another and difference from those on the outside. It was also true in the choice of business strategy at the level of the firm: the progressive removal of regulation and restraint within the labor market enhanced the attraction of simple cost reduction and made it increasingly difficult to work out new organizational structures based upon trust and cooperation.

These effects were intensified by the interpretative dimension of the political process, a dimension that is not readily encompassed by the framework of rational choice but that was central to deep politics in the 1980s. The interpretative dimension involves an interaction between events, the "experiences" of our public lives, the speeches that explicitly interpret those events and highlight the relations among them, and the policies that assign normative values to these events and promise to enhance or diminish their weight in our lives. This politics can be orchestrated by politicians. They determine what experiences are salient in our cognitive maps through the audiences to whom they speak, the individuals they pick out from the crowd for their "photo opportunities," the historical events they commemorate; the families, communities, factories, and government programs they visit, the different aspects of their own lives they choose to emphasize in their public presentations of themselves. The process is interpretative in that it is like the reading of a written text out loud. The politician accents certain parts of social experience the way a reader accents certain words in a text.[1]

But politicians do not alone provide the material that politics is called upon to interpret. History, if only in the form of the daily news, disturbs these rituals, introducing new experiences into the public consciousness and rearranging old ones. Extra-electoral politics, the politics of marches, protests, and rebellion, is a way of making the protesters and their problems salient as a feature of the national reality that the ritualistic visions do not take into account or accommodate. The fact that the body politic may come to resent and despise the protesters is in this context irrelevant. The protesters are not trying to be liked; they are trying to force their way onto our cognitive maps. It is left to political leaders to weave the protesters, along with the events associated with them, into mainstream politics by trying out various visions of American reality that take them into account and link them to everyday experiences.

The past master of this kind of politics was Franklin Roosevelt. He did with economic events in the 1930s what one might have hoped our political leaders could have done with the socially stigmatized groups in the 1980s. His appeal to the electorate was that he recognized and talked about the economic calamities of the Great Depression at a time when his Republican adversaries claimed that the central experiences of people's lives either were not there at all or would go away. He sought a set of policies that would reconcile those events with the rest of the American experience. The programs and policies Roosevelt tried, the social visions he articulated along the way, took numerous, even contradictory forms. Americans tolerated the apparent vacillation, perhaps because his recognition of the experiences that others had pretended did not exist was more important than the particular interpretations he gave to them. Ultimately, a package of policies and meanings emerged that seemed not only to recognize the problem but also to resolve it, restoring direction and coherence to national life.

A comparable leader in the 1980s might have sought to link the new

identity groups into the fabric of American politics. This, as argued in
Chapter 2, was what Jesse Jackson in fact sought to do. But the mainstream
politicians, in both Democratic and Republican parties, picked these "experiences," wrote their speeches, and designed their policies in ritualistic
ways. The result was to reinforce a vision of reality in which those groups
had no place. And because the groups were bringing onto the public stage
issues like condoms and hypodermic needles, drugs and street crime, sex
and abortion, physical deformity—things that were completely foreign to
the experience of many Americans and conventionally hidden by those to
whom they were not—the effect of the events with which they were associated was to underscore the theme of difference and separation that
Reagan and Bush were already developing in other ways.

The role played by interpretative politics is a role that rational choice
basically assigns to the policymaker and the social scientist. But the operation of politics at this deep level serves to undermine, and in a sense even
to invert, the distinction between policy and social science envisaged in
the rational choice model. To appreciate what it means to exercise some
influence over the evolution of deep politics, it is important to see why
this occurs. It occurs because the relationships the social scientist is trying
to capture are social rather than "natural"; they are products of the political
process at its deepest level. As that process evolves, those relationships,
and with them what it is possible to achieve through policy, change as well.
For current policy concerns, the most important example of this phenomenon discussed earlier in this book is the impact of training and other labor
market interventions on the employment experience of black youth.

We have been trying to improve the employment experience of black
youth through these kinds of interventions since the late 1960s, and there
is a debate within the policymaking community as to whether or not such
interventions are effective. The dominant policymaking model suggests that
this question can be answered through properly designed evaluation procedures, and that the basic defect of past programs has been their lack of
such procedures.[2]

The discussion of black employment problems in Chapter 3, however,
implied that the programs were working against the underlying structure
of the labor market and the changing attitudes within the black community.
The structure of the labor market has now changed in a way that should
lower resistance to programs designed to move blacks into higher-level

jobs. The changed attitude of the black labor force was catalyzed by the civil rights movement and reflected the disappointments of a second generation reacting against the experience of their parents, who had migrated from the South. The new politics of race and identity could well produce changes in the attitudes of the present black labor force, now several generations removed from the South, as sudden and complete as the changes produced by the politics of the civil rights movement in the 1960s. The potential for change could never be inferred from an experimental evaluation of the training programs themselves, and such an evaluation would be a poor guide to the effectiveness of the programs once that change had taken place.[3]

Comparable effects are involved in the policies through which enterprises adjust to the new competitive environment, which were also discussed in Chapter 3. These policies can be divided into a series of specific managerial reforms (the Kan-Ban system, parallel engineering, quality circles, matrix management, and so on), and we can in principle evaluate the efficacy of those reforms by measuring their impact, separately and in combination, upon the productivity of the productive unit. But when the impact of the reforms varies with the interpretation of those who are administering the program, and when that interpretation itself is changing with time, the data are being generated by an unstable process and provide little guidance as to how the same program components would affect productivity in other times and places. The results of scientific evaluations that are collected in an attempt to resolve the managerial debates are, in other words, products of the debates themselves and tell us little about the effectiveness of the reforms where one or the other of the managerial factions comes to control the administration of the new programs.

Under these circumstances, social science is not very different from interpretation. It is basically the telling of stories.[4] The stories give meaning to the actions of the individuals who subscribe to them, and if everybody shared the same meaning the theories might actually describe the functioning of the system as a whole. But when people subscribe to divergent theories, the theories have to be understood as shaping behavior, not as predicting it. What the social scientist can contribute to the policymaker is then better seen as a series of alternative scenarios than as the kind of understanding of natural processes offered by the physical sciences.[5]

The program evaluations that technicians produce under these circumstances are also a kind of story. In the specific case of employment programs for the disadvantaged, the stories are too pessimistic about the possibilities of changing labor market outcomes through public policy. The stories of managerial reforms similarly underestimate the potential of this competitive strategy relative to cost reduction through wage cuts. And in this sense the techniques of formal policy evaluation are another example of the general point: that the policies and practices conceived, at the level of high politics, in terms of rational choice operated in the 1980s, at the level of deep politics, to reinforce the dilemmas from which they were ostensibly trying to help us escape.

Resolving Policy Dilemmas

But if the conceptual framework and theoretical ideas developed in earlier chapters suggest deep politics has operated to reinforce our current dilemmas, they also suggest that politics at that level can be managed and directed in a more constructive way. A framework for doing so emerged in Chapter 5. The framework, it will be recalled, is built around a conception of human behavior generally, and economic and political behavior in particular, as a process ongoing in time. It introduces two concepts, forestructure and projection, which are designed to help us to think about behavior in this way. We act in the present by drawing material from our forestructure in the light of our projection. Our actions move us forward in history.

Policymaking and political leadership affect this process in two ways, through interpretation and orchestration. Interpretation includes the ceremonial politics of "commemoration" and "baby kissing" in which professional politicians are continually engaged as well as the processes of scenario building, theoretical storytelling, and policy evaluations that preoccupy the technician and the social scientist. Orchestration involves the conduct of the interchange among various economic agents and political actors, which I likened to the direction of a series of intersecting conversations. This last dimension of the process has, in turn, two distinct dimensions: who talks to whom and what they talk about.

Earlier chapters discussed the country's difficulties in managing the interplay between the reorganization of the economic structure around new identity groups and an economy plagued by deficits in trade and in the federal budget and struggling to succeed in the international marketplace. This is the forestructure of today's politics and economics. The next section summarizes the principal implications of these discussions first for social and then for economic policy. That summary provides a projection, a set of directions in which political and economic policy ought to move. The concluding section then turns to specific examples of how the country could be led to move in these directions through narration on the one hand and orchestration on the other.

Moving to Deep Politics

In both social and economic policy, the task is partly one of changing the way we think about the issues, partly one of specific policies that implement and reinforce these new modes of thought. For the social groups the requisite changes in our mode of thought may be summarized in five points, which are closely related and intertwined.

First we need to move away from thinking about groups as in opposition to individuals; we need to recognize that some groups provide a necessary context in which people can realize themselves as individuals, and that the new identity groups are of this kind. Second, this implies that we need to move away from thinking in terms of the old pluralism, in which an individual's concerns are dispersed over, and represented by, a virtually infinite number of different "interest" groups. The new groups do not represent interests, they represent people. But they are plural in the sense that there are many of them, and, although overlapping membership is not pervasive, there are specific points at which the groups do overlap: women, gays, the aged, the physically handicapped, the deaf, all share members with one another and with racial and ethnic groups as well. We need to learn to exploit these points of intersection—what Rosaldo calls the *borderlands*—in order to foster recognition and respect among the groups for one another and for the larger society.

Third, to use the borderlands in this way we need to give up the notion of a melting pot in which cohesive groups simply dissolve into a mass of individuals who share a universal American culture. We need to recognize instead that the critical evolution will occur *within* the groups themselves, in how they think about themselves in relation to one another and to the society—in how, for example, Spanish-American culture absorbs the lessons of feminism or Jewish culture absorbs the lessons of the suffering of gays in the Holocaust. Politics and policy are very much an attempt to influence this evolution.

Fourth, to exert this influence, we need to abandon the notion that society is a reflection of nature, to see through the physical traits and biological proclivities that *seem* to define the members of the groups to the processes that interpret those traits and give them their social meaning and significance. Finally, we need to stop denying our peculiarities and move, instead, to emphasize in our discourse, and to build institutions that make salient, the world that we do share.

This last point feeds directly into concrete policy. In policy, the issue of universalism and particularity is raised most immediately in the area of medical insurance. As we saw in Chapter 2, the private insurance system not only is increasingly inadequate to cover medical needs, aggravating individual economic insecurity and the federal budgetary crisis; it is also evolving in a way that makes cost and availability dependent on the traits that define the new identity groups and thus augments their sense of separateness as well as their anger and insecurity. A single national health policy built around a system of universal health insurance in which charges are not tied to the defining characteristics that divide us into separate groups is thus the first opportunity in public policy to reverse the slide of society toward particularism.

A similar logic suggests that we should resolve issues in other areas— education and employment opportunity, for example—in favor of universalistic institutions. This need not imply restricting the rights of particular groups to create their own institutions, and in education it certainly does not mean restricting the capacity of these groups to explore their own histories and work out their group identities in teaching and research. On the contrary, it means encouraging them to do so. But it also means that public funds should be devoted to universal institutions, open to all, in which, to extend Rosaldo's metaphor, the borders between these groups are open. The idea is to encourage, as much as possible, the groups to have their separate debates in an environment in which they will be exposed to themes generated by other groups and problems common to the society as a whole.

But to manage a society organized into separate groups, we probably need not only to preserve and expand existing borderlands but also to create new borderlands. Two ways this can be done were suggested earlier. One is to strengthen geographic groupings by delivering public services, in education, health, custodial care, and the like, which span a number of identity groups, in geographically based centers also tied, where possible, to the economy as a geographic unit. The second is to encourage and reinforce trade union organizations, which have been weakened in the last decade by federal policy and by the tendency for individuals to secure substantive employment rights through federal protection for particular groups. We shall return to both these issues in the discussion of economic policy below.

After the economy, the most salient of the universalizing issues in public policy are environmental. The environment is important not only in itself but, as emphasized in the previous chapter, because it raises the issue of the social interpretation of nature, which is so central in the debates of the new identity groups about themselves. This is hardly the place to enter into a detailed discussion of environmental policy. But the point made earlier bears repeating: its value in resolving the dilemmas of economic and social policy lies not in interpretations of environmental issues that stress the conflicts with economic goals, seeing environmental concerns as a constraint upon economic policy, but rather in examinations of the impact of the economy upon the natural environment in terms of the way we think about and structure the economy itself.[6] The difference is captured by the contrast between, on the one hand, policies that create polluters' rights that companies can then buy and sell, and on the other, policies that require business organizations to reformulate their thinking so that pollution becomes virtually inconceivable. The contrast is mainly illustrative; it is probably not possible to completely reconceptualize our way out of pollution. Nonetheless, it is striking that we never talk about selling rights to employment discrimination or sexual harassment.

Since virtually all measures of social policy absorb economic resources, they appear to conflict with national economic performance and competitiveness, but in fact, this impression too is a product of a structure of thought from which we need to escape. The success of the American economy in the past, both of policies of national economic management and of the strategies of particular business enterprises—to recapitulate the argument— depended upon a relatively self-contained domestic economy operating in an environment in which the basic parameters of business decisions were stable and predictable. The background conditions of our earlier success have long since disappeared, and it is hard to see how they could possibly be restored. American businesses have been struggling, quite consciously since the early 1980s but in a less deliberate and self-conscious way since the oil crisis in 1974, to find a new competitive strategy.

A somewhat stylized view of that struggle, but one that nonetheless captures the essence of what is involved, is that the managerial community has split between two alternative approaches. One approach would maintain the traditional industrial strategy, producing long runs of standardized products, preserving the bulk of the institutional structure and standard business practices, but enhancing their viability in the international marketplace by progressively reducing costs, lowering wages, reducing the margins of domestic parts suppliers, drawing more heavily upon low-cost foreign producers for labor-intensive inputs, reducing business contributions to social overhead, possibly even narrowing profit margins. The alternative would revise traditional practices and institutions and compete in the international marketplace on the basis of specialized goods that might cost more to produce but would appeal to customers because they were better adapted to specific needs than the standardized, off-the-rack products in which the country has historically excelled. This approach involves high value-added, high quality, high skill, and high wages. The choice, in short, is between the *high* road and the *low* road to international competitiveness.

These terms are, of course, loaded, but they do effectively capture the social implications of the managerial debate. The low road places the country in competition with developing countries in labor-surplus parts of the world who seem nonetheless able to adopt the technologies and institutional structures that have given the United States its competitive advantage in the past. Countries like Korea and Taiwan appear in fact to have significantly *improved* upon the borrowed structures. The United States can hold its own against these new competitors in this strategy only by progressively lowering wages, business taxes, and the like over time. It is thus not a one-shot adjustment, but a prescription for a continuous decline in the standard of living, if not of the nation as a whole then definitely, and even more precipitously, for a sizable portion of the lower end of the income distribution. In such a situation the social tensions that are the focus of this book would be only the beginning of a series of upheavals that would eventually lead to revolt and rebellion, if it were not forestalled by legislative restrictions.

But the high road alternative has been difficult to work out because, as we have seen, we do not have a set of ready-made and widely understood business models for implementing this strategy. We have social structures within our cultural repertoire—in sports, in high-level research communities, in ethnic enclaves, somewhat more problematically in small-town life—upon which we could draw in building such models. But unlike the situation in many other industrial countries, Japan, for instance, or Germany or Italy, these arrangements are not reflected in our economic institutions, and hence to adopt this strategy any individual business firm has to embark on an uncertain process of institutional learning, innovation, and experimentation, borrowing from corners of the culture and national life seemingly remote from traditional business experience.

Two major obstacles have discouraged firms from making this choice. Given the social implications of the low-road alternative, it seems clear that the principal goal of economic policy must be to overcome them. One of these obstacles is the continuing presence of the low-road strategy. For an individual business enterprise, it is the easier, more obvious, more accessible alternative. Its costs are borne by the society, not by the firm that pursues it, and it entails very little that is new or different, especially for the managers who make strategic choices. As I have emphasized at several points, it continues to hold the allegiance of an important faction of management even in firms where it is not the dominant strategy, serving to prolong the debate, distracting management from the task of working out the new alternative, and in many cases undermining and sabotaging the effort to do so.

Nothing would serve to develop new institutional arrangements faster than a policy that made clear that the old arrangements could not be preserved. The policies and pronouncements of Reagan and Bush, beginning with the firing of the striking air traffic controllers and continuing to the free trade treaty with Mexico and the promise it offered of continual downward pressure on U.S. wage rates, obviously had quite the opposite effect, and a consistent rhetorical commitment to a different approach would by itself have an important impact. But the kind of business changes involved in a national health insurance program, the limits upon continual wage cuts implicit in a revival of trade unionism, the social overhead charges entailed by a geographically based delivery system for social services, and the pressures for organizational reform implicit in strong environmental standards would all serve to drive home the necessity of working out the mechanics of the high-road strategic response.

The second obstacle to the high-road strategy is the preoccupation with individualism in the national debate on economic policy. It reinforces the individualism of the American national ethos, and makes it difficult to recognize, let alone think through in a systematic, analytical way, institutional models that emphasize the enterprise as a community and draw upon the social processes within the enterprise for their competitive advantage. A change in the national debate about social policy away from individualism and away from efforts to deny the legitimacy of social groups would have a salutary effect on the climate in which management is trying to develop the high-road model. But a new economics in which the role of cognitive structures and the place of social structure in their evolution were explicitly recognized would be even more beneficial.

Finally, in a summary of the public policy implications of the argument of this book, two developments deserve to be highlighted. One is the change in the social structure away from the single-dominant-wage-earner family; the second is the increasing porousness, in the institutional arrangements associated with the high-road competitive strategy, of the boundaries of business enterprises. A striking implication of this second development is that employment continuity will be associated less and less with a single firm and more and more with a community of firms consisting of suppliers, customers, clients, and even erstwhile competitors of what used to be a stand-alone enterprise, and that workers must expect to move, in the course of their careers, across the different enterprises belonging to this constellation.

The country needs to experiment with other institutional arrangements for providing the training and employment continuity and security that used to be provided by individual enterprises. This is not simply a matter of social policy. It is also critical to economic policy: as the firm becomes more and more integrated in a larger network, it loses incentives to provide workers with training and to conserve trained labor through job security. Unless we create new institutions to play these roles, we will under-train new workers and fail to conserve our existing reservoir of skills at the very time in which we are moving to a development strategy that requires a more highly educated and broadly skilled labor force.

The demise of the dominant-earner family and the stand-alone business enterprise also has more general implications, both for our thinking about public policy and for the implementation of the specific policies I have proposed. As the country moves once again to the kind of activist public policy it pursued in earlier periods—through Johnson's Great Society or Roosevelt's New Deal—we cannot simply interpret this shift as another swing of some kind of perpetual pendulum that characterizes American politics. The new political climate may resemble the social mobilizations of the 1930s or the 1960s, but history has forward movement as well as recurrent themes. The context in which we are resurrecting social policy today is new and different from the context in which it was pursued in the past, and the institutions through which it is implemented must be different as well, even if we call them by names borrowed from the past and charge them with functionally equivalent missions. (To say this is basically to repeat the point made earlier about the relationship between wholes and parts, between particular institutions and the broader system in which they are embedded, between the separate elements of reality and the larger cognitive model in terms of which they are perceived and understood.)

The changes in the nature of the family and in the business enterprise require particularly sharp adjustments for trade unions. Since the 1930s unions have thought of themselves—and have been encouraged by public policy to do so—as representing workers who were the primary wage earners in their families and whose economic fate was, or could be, tied to a single business enterprise. If, as I have just argued, they will be driven in the future by the need to address the tensions associated with multi-earner families in an economy in which single enterprises no longer function as independent economic units and cannot provide continuity of employment over time, then structures of worker organization, to be effective, will have to span many enterprises and focus less on a person's fate within any one of them than on the capacity of a family of earners to maintain its income through the movement of its members among a larger constellation of interdependent units in a single geographic area. To argue for a revival of unionism today is not necessarily to argue for any particular amendment of the National Labor Relations Act. What is called for may well be a policy that allows new worker organizations greater freedom to develop outside the framework of existing legislation in forms that are less constrained by a law that embodies the models worked out in terms of the realities of the past.

policy, drug smuggling. And both immigration and drugs link the treaty directly to the quality of urban life. Whether NAFTA is understood in the broader context of these other issues, and if so which ones, is central to the interpretative politics of the treaty.

The Bush administration presented the agreement as an extension of a policy of free trade. It was part of the broader effort to deregulate economic activity and extend the role of the market. It was one dimension of a trade policy that would progressively expand world markets and open national economies to one another. The preferred instruments of this policy were multinational negotiations conducted through the General Agreement on Tariffs and Trade (GATT); NAFTA opened a second front, one that could be extended over time to the rest of Latin America, especially if, as seemed likely in the waning years of the Bush administration, multinational negotiations were to falter. The ideological groundings of Bush's case for the treaty were reinforced by secondary arguments emphasizing the agreement as a way of securing "liberalization" within Mexico itself, the "privatization" of the Mexican economy, increased internal competition, and greater internal democracy and civil rights and liberties.

The case for democracy and civil liberties was a stretch, but the Mexicans had indeed proposed the agreement as a way of securing the economic liberalization that it had been pursuing on its own, and it was understood in this way by the Bush administration and in the policymaking community, especially among economists. But in terms of the debate about competitive strategy within the American business community, the primary impact of an agreement interpreted in this way is to signal continuing pressure on the wage level of the less-skilled portion of the U.S. workforce. Its effect in this regard is not linked to the number of jobs that actually move to Mexico. Indeed, the effect is achieved primarily by threatening to move, not by actually doing so.

The agreement thus seemed essentially a promise to re-create a labor reserve analogous to the one that in earlier decades had existed in the rural South, and to re-create it just when the South itself had industrialized to the point where its own reserves had ceased to act as a drag upon the national wage structure. The notion that the treaty might serve as a model for economic relations with the rest of Latin America and would eventually be extended to other countries was in this context a promise to replenish those reserves and reinforce the threat of movement periodically in the future. The message of the agreement was then very much the message of Reagan's handling of the air traffic controllers' strike: a signal to the managerial and labor communities about their relative strengths not only at that time but in the future as well.

The same agreement was, however, subject to virtually the opposite interpretation, as part of a broader strategy of reorienting the U.S. economy toward high-skilled, high-wage jobs. The argument that it would have this effect is that the low-skilled jobs that are likely to move to Mexico are complementary to a set of managerial and professional jobs. Absent the agreement, the two sets of jobs would move as a package to Asia and Eastern Europe, but the geographic proximity of Mexico would permit companies to preserve the high-wage component in the continental United States. The net effect of the treaty would thus be to tilt the U.S. job distribution toward the high end.

This interpretation becomes more credible if the treaty is combined with other measures that are part of a high-wage strategy: an increase in the minimum wage, renewed protection for union organizations, the elimination of subsidies to low-wage jobs implicit in our health and training policies, and an expanded program of education and training designed to facilitate upward mobility of low-wage workers. These complementary measures would also provide the kinds of signals to the black community that are most likely to foster a change in the attitudes toward and behavior in low-wage work. And both the message to employers and the message to low-wage workers become more plausible still if the case for the treaty is linked to immigration and drug policy.

As we saw in Chapter 3, the tenor of Clinton's campaign and many of the specific proposals he put forth there lent themselves to this interpretation, but once he took office the complementary proposals were quietly dropped, and the terms on which he promoted the agreement were essentially the same as those on which Bush had promoted it. In the prevailing political climate, admittedly, none of the complementary proposals had a realistic hope of passage. But from the perspective of an interpretative politics and in terms of the direction of American economic development, the central issue is not the passage of specific programmatic components. What is at stake is the coherence of the vision and its credibility among American managers selecting among alternative competitive strategies and among low-income workers seeking a stance vis-à-vis the labor market that will preserve their dignity and identity as individuals within their own communities. This does not preclude legislative compromises. But the way in which those compromises are made is critical. And the point where the high-wage interpretation was lost and Clinton's vision of the agreement, if not of economic policy more broadly, blurred into that of Bush, was when he claimed as a principled victory what could have been presented as a necessary but unfortunate compromise.

The NAFTA debate was like a Heideggerian breakdown in the evolution of the several social and economic processes with which the agreement was bound up. It was not of course a literal breakdown. But it was an interruption in those processes. It led us to reflect upon what we were doing in a way analogous that in which Heidegger suggests we might be led to rethink the project of building a house were the head to fall off the hammer we were using to nail the roof. Those reflections were conducted in an analytical vocabulary. But the analysis also generated two basically different stories about what the social and economic processes were and where they were going. The stories gave very different projections, providing very different directions to the economy and the society. The debate provided Clinton with an opportunity to tell a story of his own and thereby to change that direction. He lost that opportunity when he began to view NAFTA itself as the battle to be won and adopted the story that Bush had been telling to win it.

The opportunity missed in the NAFTA debate is particularly great because it is relatively rare that a single issue offers an opportunity to develop such sharply contrasting visions and to so radically reorient political and economic processes. More often what is available for the politician to manage are the structures of interaction through which visions develop and meaning emerges. Here too a very stark example of the what this might mean in an interpretative approach to politics and how that contrasts with other conceptions of the politician's role is offered by the early years of the Clinton administration. The example is the town meeting that Clinton perfected in his campaign and continued to use to win public acceptance once in office.

The Town Meeting

The town meeting derives its name from the meetings of the citizens through which New England towns were governed in the eighteenth and nineteenth centuries. (Some are still governed in this way.) The original town meetings were thus the locus of communities of meaning, or in Arendt's vocabulary, communities of action; they were, like the politics of ancient Greece, the occasions for a conversation *among* the citizens, a place where people talked and interacted with one another and where policies were actually developed and implemented. One could imagine analogous meetings in which the different identity groups would talk to one another. There are, as we have seen, plenty of things they might talk about, ranging from the issues of education, health care, and employment opportunity to abortion and its implications for groups defined by traits that are genetically determined or the participation of gays and women in the military service.

But Clinton's town meetings are not forums where the citizens talk with one another; they are rather occasions for the citizens to talk *at* the President. They might, as we saw earlier, provide the occasion for the President to enhance the visibility of one or another group, one or another problem, or even particular policies and programs; they constitute in that sense an instrument of interpretation. But they do not create the kind of conversations among groups or within them that would open frontiers, expand the borderlands, and make American politics more tractable over the long run.

One could imagine a different type of town meetings, in which the President would meet periodically with the same group of people and encourage those people to debate the issues not so much with him as with one another. Televised nationally, such debates might diffuse to other communities. The President might encourage the diffusion by visiting cities where debates had begun and injecting ideas from one community into the debates of another. These town meetings would have the potential for opening up exactly the kinds of conversations out of which an acceptable reconciliation between social claims and economic constraints might emerge.

Following the original New England model, these forums might be encouraged to design actual programs, even to collaborate in their implementation. This would involve, however, a redefinition of the policymaking process in a way that would break down the distinction between problem and solution and force policymakers to cede to the town meetings the power to craft technical solutions to political problems. In a certain sense, the conduct of the town meetings becomes the policy; the programs, even their implementation, grow out of the debate.

To say this is to suggest a much broader policy of fostering geographically centered networks of debate and discussion. And indeed the whole logic of interpretative politics in the context of the economic and political dilemmas we face points toward this as a critical direction for public policy both in economic organization and in the organization of social services.

Geographic Networks

Geographic networks of business firms appear in many ways to be the most natural structures in which to house the new productive forms emerging as alternatives to mass production. Henry Ford built an integrated automobile production system in a single gigantic plant in River Rouge, Michigan, but in mass production that geographic concentration turned out in practice to be irrelevant. There was no need for the pieces of the integrated production process to be geographically contiguous. The integration was inherent in the design; once the system had been properly engineered, the pieces could fit together no matter where they were produced. By the end of the mass production era, River Rouge had been broken up; the components of automobile production were being dispersed all over the world and brought together in assembly plants adjacent to the markets in which they were sold. General Motors was talking about the world car.

The new production forms may, however, require that the components be geographically contiguous. Their coherence is, as we have seen, dependent not on design and engineering but on the direct communication and intense cooperation of people sharing something akin to language and culture. Language and culture are generally locally specific and geographically bounded. To the extent that they are present in the large corporation at all, they are an unlooked-for by-product of placing so many people in regular communication with one another, and their effects under mass production were generally considered counterproductive.

In fact, although it does possess a kind of extra-geographic culture, even the larger corporation tends to be realizing the new forms of productive organization in localized clusters, building production (as well as assembly) facilities in small units, close to the markets they serve, and encouraging (even commanding) suppliers to locate around the plants they provision. Such organizational innovations as the Kan-Ban system and the participation of parts producers in product design and engineering almost require that this be the case, and the breaking up of mass markets and efforts to adapt to local tastes clearly encourage it.[7]

Insofar as Italy and Germany—as opposed to Japan—are the models of success, moreover, localized networks are clearly indicated. The economic prowess of central Italy in particular is dependent upon communities of differentiated small firms with distinctive but overlapping specialties and expertise, which interact with one another in patterns that Charles Sabel and I have termed flexible specialization. The firms in this community network share a common culture and language, a kind of dialect of production. They also share a variety of common institutional supports ranging from canteens and medical facilities to marketing mechanisms and to schools, training facilities, hiring halls, and, of course, a common labor force. The worker loyalty that the large corporation tries to attach to itself is in central Italy attached to the local community and the collectivity of enterprises embedded in it.[8]

The geographically local industrial districts of central Italy are very similar in the way they work and the cultural and supplementary institutional supports within them to the structures of the ethnically embedded garment and construction industries in the United States. Perhaps more to the point, the same social and institutional patterns can be found in the high tech districts of Route 128 in Massachusetts and Silicon Valley in California.

In Silicon Valley, in particular, the workforce—managers, professionals, craft, and production workers alike—seem to have virtually no company loyalty. They conceive of themselves as attached only provisionally to any given firm and maintain and cultivate vast networks of personal contacts in the region that enable them to pursue an upwardly mobile career through a progression from one company to another. The pattern presents something of a contrast even with that around Route 128, where there are more relatively large companies and attachment tends to be more permanent. The exaggeration of the pattern of interfirm mobility in California is given credit by one analyst for the recent success of that region over its Massachusetts rival in the battle to maintain their positions in the computer market.[9]

Such networks resolve many of the contradictions inherent in the attempt to realize the new models through a transformation of the corporate structure that is now spread out across the national, or in fact international, territory. They should, for example, be able to provide the portfolio of employment opportunities that would create the employment security that single business units, even relatively large corporations, no longer seem able to provide. A diversified portfolio of employment opportunities should also address the tensions associated with dual-career households. Geographic concentration would permit the creation of labor market institutions in the form of employment services and hiring halls to realize the new job security potential. Education and training structures to replace the training that stand-alone businesses once had an incentive to provide on their own could also be organized on a geographic basis and the businesses that drew upon the local labor pool taxed to finance the training.

The Social Structure

An increased emphasis upon geographic unity would also serve to enlarge the borderlands and diffuse the tensions associated with the emerging social structure. Their impact in this regard could be enhanced by a greater emphasis upon geographically defined units in the delivery of existing social services and in the design of new programs to meet the demands of the emerging identity groups. Ultimately, the geographic organization of social services could provide a way of bridging the gap between the social and economic structures and making economic constraints more salient to those demanding social services.

Virtually all of the new identity groups, for example, need places to meet and to stage communal activities. The older ethnic communities used church facilities for this purpose, but few of the newer ethnic groups and virtually none of the lifestyle groups are held together by a common religious affiliation. (In one study in San Jose, California, they seemed to be using shopping malls and flea markets for this purpose.)[10] A number of the identity groups also need special services—daycare, elder care, ambulatory medical attention, and the like. When these are provided to each group separately or occur in proprietary public spaces (like flea markets and malls), the groups' sense of separateness is reinforced. But many of the groups could easily share the same facilities, and this would serve to break down barriers among groups and reduce the sense of exclusivity.

That effect would be strengthened if the facilities were controlled by public bodies in which the members of the different groups were represented as individuals rather than through group affiliation. In most local communities it would be natural to provide these services in public school facilities, which are underutilized. And one could easily imagine staffing them in ways that further served to break down barriers and exclusivity.

Retirees—even the handicapped—might be drawn, as they already are in some places, into daycare, for example. In fact, there is no reason why the aged and the handicapped could not be organized to serve one another. AIDS organizations have operated support networks where the more well provide services to the less well. In their current form, these networks reinforce the sense of separateness of Persons-with-AIDS from the larger gay community. But essentially the same services that they provide are also required by the handicapped, the aged and, to some extent, even small children in daycare. And there is no reason why they could not be provided to all of these groups by a single organization with a mixed staff drawn from the same groups as the client population.

The crisis in medical insurance costs provides an occasion to reinforce local community structures in both the productive and the social realms. Tying medical care to HMOs would reinforce the local orientation. (The HMOs might also be located in the vicinity of local schools.) Financial responsibility could be shifted from the employer to larger groups of employers or even to a community tax base, which, with a local payroll tax, would in effect make the local business community a single employer group.

As the example of medical insurance suggests, once economic activity and social services have been reorganized on a geographic basis, it is a small step to merge the two so that the economic base is made to support the services. Social services need not be made completely dependent on local economic activity. It would be possible to temper the relationship through federal grants-in-aid, for which there are a variety of precedents in existing federal programs, and through various forms of national reinsurance for local funds (the current unemployment insurance system works in this way). The important point is that the two be sufficiently linked so that organized client groups are forced to recognize the constraints imposed by the productive system and are led to conceive of their demands with those constraints in mind.

Most of the public policies that would lead to this result are already in existence. The actions that would bring it about depend upon how these policies evolve and how the instruments they create are deployed over time in response to economic exigencies, on the one hand, and political demands and social pressures, on the other. It is a matter of making a very large variety of different and often minute policies, each a response to a particular set of pressures, work in harmony and press toward the same end.

This is hardly something that can be planned out in advance. It requires that a vision of the direction in which the society ought to be moving be widely shared among the diverse actors who make the small decisions that in the aggregate determine the trajectory of social and economic organization. In particular, it requires a vision shared by economic policymakers, the makers of social policy, and the practitioners who make and implement business strategy.

We lack a single occasion to articulate such a vision. But the list of directions for the political process outlined earlier constitutes a kind of story about our economic and social problems. And each of the debates about particular policies, health insurance, education, trade, and so on constitutes not only an occasion to introduce policies that will move the country toward geographically coherent economic or social structures but also an occasion to tell the story, to outline the vision, in which these particular policies fit.

Conclusion

That a discussion about contemporary American social and economic policy should conclude by advocating approaches that promote geographic cohesion is ironic, for as we have seen the Republic was founded upon a vision of society organized in this way. And the country has risen to its current economic and political prominence in the world by moving progressively away from that form of organization. But the way in which a policy of geographic concentration seems to follow from the analysis is emblematic of the underlying argument of this book.

That argument is built around the contrast between two individualistic norms, a norm of individual autonomy in classical liberalism and a norm of individuality realized in a community of equals that is associated with the civic republican tradition. Those norms are linked to alternative ways of understanding human behavior: liberalism to behavior as a series of deliberate acts, civic republicanism to behavior as a continuous process. The transition that we underwent in this country from one set of norms and understandings to the other was not the outcome of a conscious choice; it was the outgrowth of a course of economic development that made autonomous individuality increasingly consistent with our social experience and made economic success more and more dependent upon the exercise of rational choice. But the old individuality embedded in community has reemerged within the new identity groups, and economic organization increasingly requires the management of an ongoing process of social interaction. To manage the dilemmas of the contemporary world we need to recover the structures in which the original notion of individuality makes sense.

I have argued for recovering these structures as a way of maintaining political stability and economic prosperity. But it is hard to imagine how the United States, given the juncture at which we have arrived, could survive as a moral society on any other terms. The new identity groups whose claims must be addressed if stability and prosperity are to be achieved are composed of people who grew up in a world in which their personal characteristics—their physical handicaps, their race, their ethnicity, their sex, their sexual orientation—isolated them from society and make them acutely conscious of their individuality, sometimes quite literally, sometimes in terms of the images that society projected around them in media representations of daily life and in role models it offered for success.

The early life experiences of the members of these groups led them to think of themselves as separate and autonomous in the liberal sense of these terms, but in ways that provided none of the freedom or liberty promised by liberalism. That which seemed to mark them most as individuals denied them access to benefits that society offered those who were less distinctive. They sought protection as what the novelist Ralph Ellison called "invisible men"; they were led to hide their distinctiveness in the closet if they could and to evoke the constitutional protections for this private space out of fear. They found the liberty that the Constitution was supposed to afford only by breaking open those protected spaces, reclaiming their defining characteristics from other people's dirty jokes, sick jokes, Polish and Italian jokes. They brought the stereotypical out into a public space and made out of it material with which to create their individual selves. To understand these groups as "special-interest groups" is to reduce them once again to their defining characteristics, to conceive of solutions to the dilemmas they create for society by reimposing the very structures of oppression from which they so recently escaped.

The promise of the interpretative perspective is that it offers an alternative, not only an alternative concept of individuality but an alternative way of managing the politics that such groups create. It implies that by entering into the process through which these communities are defined, by participating in a reflective way in the continuing conversations within and between them, politicians and policymakers will be able to direct their evolution in ways that will bring those communities into a more harmonious relationship with one another and with the structures of the economy.

Notes

Introduction

1. James Miller, *"Democracy Is in the Streets": From Port Huron to the Siege of Chicago* (New York: Simon and Schuster, 1987; Cambridge, Mass.: Harvard University Press, 1994). Milton Viorst, *Fire in the Streets: America in the 1960s* (New York: Simon and Schuster, 1979). Paul Potter, *A Name for Ourselves* (Boston, 1971). Allen J. Matusow, *Unraveling of America: A History of Liberalism in the 1960s* (New York, Harper and Row, 1989).

1. The Social Deficit and the New Identity Groups

1. Wayne Vroman, *The Decline in Unemployment Insurance Claims Activity in the 1980s,* Unemployment Insurance Occupational Paper 91-2 (Washington: U.S. Department of Labor, Employment and Training Administration, 1991), p. 2.

2. U.S. Department of Labor, Employment Standards Administration, *Employment and Earnings,* January 1993.

3. Lawrence Katz and Kevin Murphy, "Changes in Relative Wages, 1963–1987: Supply and Demand Factors," *Quarterly Journal of Economics* (Feb. 1992): 35–78; Kevin M. Murphy and Finis Welsh, "The Structure of Wages," *Quarterly Journal of Economics* (Feb. 1992): 285ff.

4. David Cutler and Lawrence Katz, "Macro-economic Performance and the Disadvantaged," Brookings Papers on Economic Activity, 1991, no. 2, pp. 1–74. Maria Hanratty and Rebecca Blank, "Down and Out in North America: Recent Trends in Poverty Rates in the United States and Canada," *Quarterly Journal of Economics* (Feb. 1992): 233–254. William J. Wilson, *The Truly Disadvantaged* (Chicago: University of Chicago Press, 1987).

5. McKinley L. Blackburn, David E. Bloom, and Richard B. Freeman, "The Declining Economic Position of Less Skilled American Men," in Gary Burtless, ed., *The Future of Lousy Jobs: The Changing Structure of U.S. Wages* (Washington: Brookings Institution, 1990), pp. 31–67. Curiously enough, I have been unable to find unambiguous statistics on the economic position of low-wage women workers, who are the other important potential source of union growth. However, the var-

197

iance in the distribution of working wives clearly increased: Maria Cancian, Sheldon Danziger and Peter Gottschalk, "Working Wives and Family Income Inequality among Married Couples," in Danziger and Gottschalk, eds., *Uneven Tides: Rising Inequality in America* (New York: Russell Sage Foundation, 1992), p. 208. See also Francine D. Blau, "Gender Earnings Gap: Some International Evidence," National Bureau of Economic Research Working Paper Series, no. 4224.

6. Katz and Murphy, "Changes in Relative Wages," pp. 43–46.

7. Michael J. Piore, ed., *Unemployment and Inflation: Institutionalist and Structuralist Views* (White Plains, N.Y.: Sharpe Press, 1979).

8. Jack Stieber, *The Steel Industry Wage Structure: A Study of the Joint Union-Management Job Evaluation Program in the Basic Steel Industry* (Cambridge, Mass.: Harvard University Press, 1959). Daniel Quinn Mills, *Government, Labor, and Inflation: Wage Stabilization in the United States* (Chicago: Chicago University Press, 1975). See also Hugh Rockoff, *Drastic Measures: A History of Wage-Price Controls in the United States* (New York: Cambridge University Press, 1984).

9. Michael G. Hadjimichalakis, *The Federal Reserve, Money and Interest Rates: The Volcker Years and Beyond* (New York: Praeger, 1984). William Greider, *Secrets of the Temple: How the Federal Reserve Runs the Country* (New York: Simon and Schuster, 1987). John Woolley, *Monetary Politics: The Federal Reserve and the Politics of Monetary Policy* (New York: Cambridge University Press, 1984).

10. U.S. Bureau of Statistics, *Statistical Abstract of the United States* (Washington: U.S. Government Printing Office, 1988 and 1991).

11. *New York Times,* June 8, 1991, p. 46. Albert H. Karr, "Teamsters Leadership under New Rule for Elections Is Experiencing Disarray," *Wall Street Journal,* March 25, 1991, p. A5A.

12. *Business Week,* no. 3275, March 23, 1993, pp. 82, 84.

13. Katherine Van Wezel Stone, "The Legacy of Industrial Pluralism: The Tension between Individual Employment Rights and the New Deal Collective Bargaining System," *University of Chicago Law Review* 59, no. 2 (Spring 1992): 575–644.

14. George Kannar, "Making the Teamsters Safe for Democracy," *Yale Law Review* 102, no. 7 (May 1993): 1645–1718.

15. See, for example, Robert Allen Dahl, *Who Governs? Democracy and Power in an American City* (New Haven: Yale University Press, 1962), and *Pluralistic Democracy in the United States: Conflict and Consent* (Chicago: Rand McNally, 1967).

16. Suzanne D. Berger, ed., *Organizing Interests in Western Europe: Pluralism, Corporatism and the Transformation of Politics* (Cambridge: Cambridge University Press, 1981).

17. The nature of U.S. labor law in this regard is well described in Katherine Stone, "The Post-War Paradigm in American Labor Law," *Yale Law Journal* 90, no. 7 (June 1991): 1509–1580. Stone, however, uses the term *pluralism* to characterize U.S. arrangements. As I have defined the term in the text above, this is a misnomer. Stone seems to use pluralism nonetheless because she wants to make the point

that the law fails to recognize the imbalance in power between labor and business and that this is because it thinks of them as simply two among a multitude of groups in the society.

18. Felix Rohatyn, *The Twenty-Year Century: Essays on Economics and Public Finance* (New York: Random House, 1983).

19. Marc Bloch, *Land and Work in Medieval Europe* (London: Routledge and Kegan Paul, 1967).

20. Edward Shorter, *The Making of the Modern Family* (New York: Basic Books, 1975). Jacques Donselot, *The Policing of Families* (New York: Pantheon, 1979). See also Philippe Ariès, *Centuries of Children: A Social History of the Family* (New York: Knopf, 1962).

21. Paul Osterman, *Getting Started: The Youth Labor Market* (Cambridge, Mass.: MIT Press, 1980), pp. 51–75, 150.

22. Maureen Honey, *Creating Rosie the Riveter: Class, Gender and Propaganda During World War II* (Amherst: University of Massachusetts Press, 1984).

23. H. Hoetink, *Slavery and Race Relations in America: Comparative Notes on Their Nature and Nexus* (New York: Harper and Row, 1973). Also David W. Cohen and Jack P. Greene, eds., *Neither Slave nor Free: The Freedmen of African Descent in the Slave Societies of the New World* (Baltimore: Johns Hopkins University Press, 1972).

24. Gunnar Myrdal, *The American Dilemma: The Negro Problem and Modern Democracy* (New York, Harper and Row, 1962), esp. pp. 83–112.

25. Dennis Altman, *The Homosexualization of America: The Americanization of the Homosexual* (New York: St. Martin's Press, 1982). See also Dennis Altman et al., *Homosexuality, Which Homosexuality?* (London: GMP Publications, 1989).

26. U.S. Congress Immigration Commission (Dillingham Commission, *Reports,* 42 vols. (Washington: U.S. Government Printing Office, 1911). Steven Fraser, *Labor Will Rule: Sidney Hillman and the Rise of American Labor* (New York: Free Press, 1991). Gerald Rosenbaum, *Immigrant Workers* (New York: Basic Books, 1973). Stanley Feldstein and Lawrence Costello, eds., *The Ordeal of Assimilation* (Garden City, N.Y.: Anchor Books, 1974), pp. 319–356.

2. Politics and Policy

1. Toni Morrison, ed., *Race-ing Justice, En-gendering Power: Essays on Anita Hill, Clarence Thomas and the Construction of Social Reality* (New York: Pantheon, 1992). Timothy M. Phelps, *Capitol Games: Clarence Thomas, Anita Hill and the Story of the Supreme Court Nomination* (New York: Hyperion, 1992).

2. Townsend Davis, "Hearing Aid: The New Politics of Deafness," *New Republic* 199, no.2 (Sept. 12, 1988): 20.

3. For other views in the debate about the interpretation of deafness see Oliver Sacks, *Seeing Voices: A Journey into the World of the Deaf* (New York: Harper Collins, 1990); and the highly critical review of Sacks's book by David M. Perlmutter in the *New York Review of Books* 38, no. 6 (March 25, 1991): 65–72.

4. Joan Nestle, *A Restricted Country* (Ithaca, N.Y.: Firebrand Books, 1987), pp. 9, 178.

5. Elie Wiesel, *Souls on Fire: Portraits and Legends of the Hasidic Masters* (New York: Random House, 1972.)

6. Kenji Hakuta, *Mirror of Language: The Debate on Bilingualism* (New York, Basic Books, 1985).

7. Arthur Schlesinger, *Wall Street Journal,* June 25, 1991, sec. A, p. 14. These views are developed at greater length in Arthur Schlesinger Jr., *The Disuniting of America* (Knoxville, Tenn.: Whittle Direct Books, 1991).

8. Quotes from Schlesinger, *Wall Street Journal.*

9. Ibid. Kenneth Jackson, "Dissention on Multicultural Education," *New York Times,* June 23, 1991, sec. 4, p. 14.

10. M. Spencer, G. Brooking and W. Allen, eds., *Beginnings: The Social and Affective Development of Black Children* (Hillsdale, N.J.: Lawrence Erlbaum Associates, 1985). M. G. Willis. "Learning Styles of African-American Children: A Review of the Literature," *Journal of Black Psychology* 16, no. 1 (1989): 47–65.

11. Derrick Bell, ed., *Shades of Brown: New Perspectives on School Desegregation* (New York: Teachers College Press, Columbia University, 1980).

12. *New York Times,* Aug. 11, 1991, sec. 1, pt. 1, p. 1. Schlesinger, *Wall Street Journal.*

13. U.S. Congress, Congressional Budget Office, *Rising Health Care Costs: Causes, Implications and Strategies* (Washington: U.S. Government Printing Office, 1991).

14. Calculated on assumption that the "Canadian System" in the U.S. would be financed by a payroll tax, uniform across all industry, and equal to the current average cost of employer financed medical insurance.

15. *New York Times,* March 24, 1991, pp. 1, 28.

16. For the background and history of equal employment opportunity legislation, see Michael I. Sovern, *Legal Restraints on Racial Discrimination in Employment* (New York: Twentieth Century Fund, 1966); Ruth G. Schaeffer, *Nondiscrimination in Employment: Changing Perspectives, 1963–1972* (New York: Conference Board, 1973); Charles W. Whalen, *The Longest Debate: A Legislative History of the 1964 Civil Rights Act* (Washington: Seven Locks Press, 1985); U.S. Congress, Senate Committee on Labor and Public Welfare, Subcommittee on Labor, *Equal Employment Opportunities Enforcement Act Hearings,* 91st Congress, 1st sess. on S. 2453 (Washington: U.S. Government Printing Office, 1969); Peter C. Reid, *The Employer's Guide to Avoiding Job Bias Litigation: How to Prevent and Remedy Discrimination before You're Sued* (New York: Random House Business Division, 1986); Barbara Lindeman Schlei and Paul Grossman, *Employment Discrimination Law* (Washington: Bureau of National Affairs, 1983); Herbert Hill, *Black Labor and the American Legal System* (Washington: Bureau of National Affairs, 1977).

17. Peter B. Doeringer and Michael J. Piore, *Internal Labor Markets and Manpower Adjustment* (New York: D. C. Heath, 1971).

18. Shelby Steele, *The Content of Our Character: A New Vision of Race in America* (New York: St. Martin's Press, 1990), pp. 111–126.

3. Economic Constraints and Social Demands

1. John L. Palmer and Isabel V. Sawhill, *The Reagan Experiment: An Examination of Economic and Social Policies under the Reagan Administration* (Washington: Urban Institute Press, 1982), and *The Reagan Record; An Assessment of America's Changing Domestic Priorities* (Cambridge, Mass.: Ballinger, 1984). William A. Niskanen, *Reaganomics: An Insider's Account of the Policies and the People* (New York: Oxford University Press, 1988). Michael J. Boskin, *Reagan and the Economy: The Successes, Failures, and the Unfinished Agenda* (San Francisco: ICS Press, 1987).

2. George Gilder, *Wealth and Poverty* (New York: Basic Books, 1981).

3. Alfred D. Chandler, Jr., *The Visible Hand: The Managerial Revolution in American Business* (Cambridge, Mass.: Harvard University Press, 1977).

4. Michael J. Piore and Charles F. Sabel, *The Second Industrial Divide: Possibilities for Prosperity* (New York: Basic Books, 1984), pp. 19–49.

5. Ibid. Also Suzanne Berger and Michael J. Piore, *Dualism and Discontinuity in Industrial Societies* (Cambridge and New York: Cambridge University Press, 1980), pp. 55–82.

6. Piore and Sabel, *Second Industrial Divide*. See also John Kenneth Galbraith, *The New Industrial State* (Boston: Houghton Mifflin, 1967), and Robert Averitt, *The Dual Economy* (New York: Norton, 1968).

7. This point is developed in Karl Marx, *Capital* (Moscow: Foreign Languages Publishing Houses, 1961), vol. 1, p. 355 (ch. 14, sec. 4).

8. Michel Crozier, *The Bureaucratic Phenomenon* (Chicago: University of Chicago Press, 1964). But for an essentially opposite interpretation of these structures see Shoshanna Zuboff, *In the Age of the Smart Machine: The Future of Work and Power* (New York: Basic Books, 1984), pp. 319–320, and Michel Foucault, *Discipline and Punish: the Birth of the Prison* (New York: Vintage, 1979).

9. John Kenneth Galbraith, *The Affluent Society* (Boston: Houghton Mifflin, 1958).

10. Piore and Sabel, *Second Industrial Divide*, pp. 73–104.

11. Thomas J. Peters, *Thriving on Chaos* (New York: Random House, 1988). Rosabeth Moss Kanter, *When Giants Learn to Dance: Mastering the Challenge of Strategy, Management and Careers in the 1990s* (New York: Simon and Schuster, 1989). Mel Horwitch, *The Emergence of Post-Modern Strategic Management* (Cambridge, Mass.: Sloan School of Management, MIT, 1987).

12. Michael J. Piore, "Corporate Reform and the Challenge to Economic Theory," in Thomas J. Allen and Michael Scott Morton, eds., *Information Technology and the Corporation of the 1990s* (New York: Oxford University Press, 1994), pp. 43–60. Nitin Nohria and Robert G. Eccles, *Networks and Organizations: Structure, Form, and Action* (Boston: Harvard Business School Press, 1992).

13. James P. Womack, *The Machine that Changed the World* (New York: Rawson Associates, 1990).

14. The literature on this subject is reviewed in Eileen Appelbaum and Rosemary Batt, *The New American Workplace: Transforming Worksystems in the United*

States (Ithaca, N.Y.: Industrial and Labor Relations Press, 1994); and U.S. Department of Labor, *High Performance Work Practices and Firm Performance* (Washington: Office of the American Work Place, U.S. Department of Labor, 1993).

15. Paul Osterman, *Employment Futures: Reorganization, Dislocation, and Public Policy* (New York: Oxford University Press, 1988), pp. 85–89.

16. Edgar H. Schein, *Innovative Cultures and Organizations* (Cambridge: Sloan School of Management, MIT, 1988).

17. Michael J. Piore and Charles F. Sabel, "Italian Small Business Development: Lessons for U.S. Industrial Policy," in John Zysman and Laura Tyson, eds., *American Industry in International Competition* (Ithaca, N.Y.: Cornell University Press, 1983), pp. 391–421. Roger David Waldinger, *Through the Eye of the Needle* (New York: New York University Press, 1986), and *Ethnic Entrepreneurs: Immigrant Businesses in Industrial Societies* (Newbury Park, Calif.: Sage, 1990). Thomas R. Bailey, *Immigrant and Native Workers: Contrasts and Competition* (Boulder, Colo.: Westview Press, 1987).

18. There is a further twist in the problem that makes it even easier to confuse the quality and cost strategies. The high-quality approach seeks cost reduction as well, but it views organizational reform as the route to cost reduction. It expects its suppliers to introduce these reforms and, as a result, expects its supply costs to decline without threatening supplier profits. It generally seeks contracts with suppliers that create incentives for them to proceed along this route. Where successful, the contracts have two components: one is a stick, which specifies the price concessions expected over time; the other is a carrot, in the form of a tutelage arrangement in which the mother company helps its suppliers to introduce the reforms requisite to cut costs pari passu with these price declines and, hence, to maintain their profits. In the hands of the cost faction, the stick is wielded and the carrot neglected.

19. Richard S. Belous and Jonathan Lemeo, *NAFTA as a Model of Development* (Washington: National Planning Association, 1993), p. 2.

20. Harley Shaiken and Stephen Herzenberg, *Automation and Global Production: Automobile Engine Production in Mexico, the United States and Canada,* Center for U.S.–Mexican Studies, University of California, San Diego, Monograph Series no. 26 (La Jolla, 1987). Harley Shaiken, "Advanced Manufacturing in Mexico: A New International Division of Labor?" *Latin American Research Review* 29, no. 2 (1994): 39–72.

21. Robert B. Reich, *The Work of Nations: Preparing Ourselves for Twenty-First Century Capitalism* (New York: Knopf, 1991). Laura d'Andrea Tyson, *Who's Bashing Whom? Trade Conflict in High Technology Industries* (Washington: Institute for International Economics, 1993).

22. Christopher Jencks and Paul E. Peterson, eds., *The Urban Underclass* (Washington: Brookings Institution, 1991).

23. Michael J. Piore, "Jobs and Training," in Samuel H. Beer and Richard Barringer, eds., *The State and the Poor* (Cambridge, Mass.: Winthrop Publishers, 1970),

pp. 53–83. Peter B. Doeringer, Penny H. Feldman, David M. Gordon and Michael Reich, *Low-Income Labor Markets and Urban Manpower Programs: A Critical Assessment,* Harvard University, Program on Regional and Urban Economics, Discussion Paper no. 62 (Cambridge, Mass., 1969).

24. Doeringer et al., *Low-Income Labor Markets.* See also Richard Edwards, Michael Reich, and David M. Gordon, *Labor Market Segmentation* (Lexington, Mass.: D. C. Heath, 1975); David Gordon, Richard Edwards, and Michael Reich, *Segmented Work, Divided Workers: The Historical Transformation of the U.S. Labor Market* (New York: Cambridge University Press, 1982); Bennett Harrison, *Education, Training and the Urban Ghetto* (Baltimore: Johns Hopkins University Press, 1972); Thomas Vietorisz and Bennett Harrison, *The Economic Development of Harlem* (New York: Praeger, 1970); David M. Gordon, "Class, Productivity and the Ghetto: A Study of Labor Market Stratification" (Ph.D. diss., Harvard University, Department of Economics, 1971).

25. Claude Brown, *Manchild in the Promised Land* (New York: Macmillan, 1965). Nicolas Lemann, *The Promised Land: The Great Black Migration and How It Changed America* (New York: Knopf, 1991).

26. Michael J. Piore, *Birds of Passage: Migrant Labor and Industrial Societies* (Cambridge and New York: Cambridge University Press, 1979), pp. 141–166.

27. Emmett Jay Scott, *Negro Migration During the War* (1928; New York: Arno, 1969).

28. On growing up black in the South, see J. L. Chestnut Jr. and Julia Cass, *Black in Selma: The Uncommon Life of J. L. Chestnut Jr.* (New York: Farrar, Straus, and Giroux, 1990); Ralph Ellison, *Invisible Man* (New York: Modern Library, 1952); and John Dollard, *Caste and Class in a Southern Town* (New York: Harper, 1949).

29. Piore, *Birds of Passage,* p. 160.

30. Brown, *Manchild in the Promised Land.* Malcolm X and Alex Haley, *The Autobiography of Malcolm X* (New York: Ballantine, 1973). Richard Mastel, ed., *The Black Ghetto: Promised Land or Colony?* (Lexington, Mass.: D. C. Heath, 1972). Floyd Borboun, *The Black Sixties* (Boston, P. Sargent, 1970).

31. Piore, *Birds of Passage,* pp. 141–166.

32. Ibid.

4. A Cognitive Approach to Economics

1. I will use the term *liberal individualism* to refer to what outside the United States and in political philosophy more generally is known as the liberal tradition. In the American context that tradition is more often referred to as *conservative;* the term *liberal* is usually reserved for left-wing politics that favors a stronger role for the state, although part of the argument is that liberalism in the European sense of the term infuses American political thought across the political spectrum.

2. Again, the terminology here is tricky. I have chosen to use the term *competitive economics* to refer to the whole body of theory that has grown out of the

study of perfectly competitive markets (in the technical sense of the term) and general equilibrium theory. But, as will become clear below, much of that theory has been taken out of the context in which it was originally developed and applied to economic problems more generally. Other terms used in the literature to refer to this body of thought are *neoclassical economics* and *conventional economics*.

3. Richard Nelson and Sidney Winter, *An Evolutionary Theory of Economic Change* (Cambridge, Mass.: Harvard University Press, 1982). Also Duncan K. Foley, "Rationality, Action, and Probability," Department of Economics, Barnard College (manuscript).

4. See, e.g., Oliver E. Williamson and Sidney Winter, eds., *The Nature of the Firm: Origins, Evolution and Development* (New York: Oxford University Press, 1991). Also Jean Tirole, *The Theory of Industrial Organization* (Cambridge, Mass.: MIT Press, 1988).

5. See, e.g., Jon Elster, ed., *Rational Choice* (New York: New York University Press, 1986). Also Robert Nozick, *Philosophical Explanations* (Cambridge, Mass.: Harvard University Press, 1981); Michael Bratman, *Intention, Plans, and Practical Reason* (Cambridge, Mass.: Harvard University Press, 1987).

6. Hans G. Furth, *Piaget and Knowledge: Theoretical Foundations* (Englewood Cliffs, N.J.: Prentice-Hall, 1969), pp. 71–75.

7. See, e.g., Gary Becker, *The Economic Approach to Human Behavior* (Chicago: University of Chicago Press, 1976).

8. The following account draws especially upon Furth, *Piaget and Knowledge;* Howard Gardner, *The Quest for Mind: Piaget, Levi-Strauss, and the Structuralist Movement* (New York: Knopf, 1973); and Gardner, *The Mind's New Science: A History of the Cognitive Revolution* (New York: Basic Books, 1985). Also Peter L. Berger, *The Sacred Canopy: Elements of a Sociology of Religion* (Garden City, N.J.: Doubleday, 1967); and Berger and Thomas Luckmann, *The Social Construction of Reality: A Treatise in the Sociology of Knowledge* (Garden City, N.J.: Doubleday, 1966).

9. Berger and Luckmann, *Social Construction of Reality,* pp. 47–52.

10. Berger, *Sacred Canopy,* pp. 4–5, 23, 85, 94.

11. Furth, *Piaget and Knowledge.*

12. Jean Piaget, *The Moral Judgement of the Child* (New York: Free Press, 1965).

13. Lawrence Kohlberg, *Moral Stages: A Current Formulation and Response to Critics* (Basel and New York: Karger, 1983).

14. Marshall Sahlins, *Culture and Practical Reason* (Chicago: University of Chicago Press, 1976), pp. 51–52. Claude Lévi-Strauss, *The Savage Mind* (Chicago: University of Chicago Press, 1979), pp. 30–37.

15. W. J. Cash, *The Mind of the South* (New York: Vintage, 1969), pp. 30–60.

16. Daniel Patrick Moynihan and Nathan Glazer, *Beyond the Melting Pot* (Cambridge, Mass.: MIT Press, 1963). Oscar Handlin, *Children of the Uprooted* (New York: G. Braziller, 1966).

17. Roberto Mangabeira Unger, *Knowledge and Politics* (New York: Free Press, 1975), pp. 104–144.

18. Although the economies of scale in mass production create an incentive for the producer to try to influence the consumer's consumption pattern, an incentive that is not present in a perfectly competitive economy.

19. Michel Crozier, *The Bureaucratic Phenomenon* (Chicago: University of Chicago Press, 1964).

20. Joseph Schumpeter, *Capitalism, Socialism and Democracy* (New York: Harper and Collins, 1950), pt. 2.

21. B. Joseph Pine II, *Mass Customization: The New Frontier in Business Competition* (Boston: Harvard Business School Press, 1993).

5. *An Interpretative Approach to Cognition*

1. Oliver Sacks, *Seeing Voices: A Journey into the World of the Deaf* (Berkeley: University of California Press, 1989).

2. See Olivier Faverau, "Probability and Uncertainty: After All Keynes was Right," *Economia*, no. 10 (October 1988): 133–167. The points developed in the text reflect discussions with Faverau on this theme.

3. George Lakoff, *Women, Fire and Dangerous Things: What Categories Reveal about the Mind* (Chicago: University of Chicago Press, 1990).

4. Fernando Flores and Terry Winograd, *Understanding Computers and Cognition: A New Foundation for Design* (Reading, Mass.: Addison Wesley, 1987). Richard E. Palmer, *Hermeneutics* (Evanston, Ill.: Northwestern University Press, 1969).

5. The following discussion draws upon Hubert L. Dreyfus, *Being-in-the-World: A Commentary on Heidegger's Being and Time, Division 1* (Cambridge, Mass.: MIT Press, 1991).

6. Hannah Arendt, *The Human Condition* (Garden City, N.J.: Doubleday, 1959), and *Lectures on Kant's Political Philosophy,* ed. Ronald Beiner (Chicago: University of Chicago Press, 1982).

7. For Arendt's view of action in economic life, see especially Hannah Arendt, *On Revolution* (New York: Viking, 1963), pp. 278–279. My characterization here of the relationship of labor and work to modern economic activity is somewhat oversimplified. Arendt actually believed that modern life abridged the distinction between the public and private realms in terms of which the Greek activities were defined. To develop this point here would constitute a considerable digression.

8. The following discussion of the narrative draws upon Jerome Bruner, *Acts of Meaning* (Cambridge, Mass.: Harvard University Press, 1990).

6. *The American Repertoire*

1. Drew R. McCoy, *The Elusive Republic: Political Economy in Jeffersonian America* (Chapel Hill: Published for the Institute of Early American History and

Culture, Williamsburg, Va., by the University of North Carolina Press, 1980). Bernard Bailyn, *The Ideological Origins of the American Revolution* (Cambridge, Mass.: Harvard University Press, 1967).

2. J. G. A. Pocock, *The Machiavellian Moment: Florentine Political Thought and the Atlantic Republican Tradition* (Princeton: Princeton University Press, 1974).

3. "Symposium: The Republican Civic Tradition," *Yale Law Journal* 97, no. 8 (July 1988): 1493–1793. Michael Piore and Charles Sabel, *The Second Industrial Divide* (New York: Basic Books, 1984), pp. 303–307. Robert N. Bellah et al., *Habits of the Heart, Individualism and Commitment in American Life* (Berkeley and Los Angeles: University of California Press, 1985). Other writers influential in the renewal of the American republican tradition include Michael J. Sandel, *Liberalism and the Limits of Justice* (New York: Cambridge University Press, 1982); and Michael J. Walzer, *Radical Principles: Reflections of an Unreconstructed Democrat* (New York: Basic Books, 1980).

4. Nick Salvatore, *Eugene Debs: Citizen and Socialist* (Urbana and Chicago: University of Illinois Press, 1982).

5. Ronald Reagan, *An American Life* (New York: Simon and Schuster, 1990), pp. 19–27.

6. See, e.g., James D. Watson, *The Double Helix: A Personal Account of the Discovery of the Structure of DNA* (New York: Atheneum, 1968).

7. See Waldinger, *Ethnic Entrepreneurs*. Also Alejandro Portes, *Latin Journey: Cuban and Mexican Immigrants in the United States* (Berkeley: University of California Press, 1985).

8. David Brody, *Steelworkers in America: The Nonunion Era* (Cambridge, Mass.: Harvard University Press, 1960).

9. Renato Rosaldo, *Culture and Truth: The Rethinking of Social Analysis* (Boston: Beacon Press, 1989).

10. Steven A. Holmes, "Abortion Issues Divide Advocates for Disabled," *New York Times,* July 4, 1991, p. 11. E.g., Midge Decter, "The Boys on the Beach," *Commentary* 70, no. 3 (Sept. 1980): 35–48, and Letters, *Commentary* 70, no. 6 (Dec. 1980): 6–20. Cindy Patton, *Inventing AIDS* (New York: Routledge, 1990). "Becoming a Spectacle: Lesbian and Gay Politics and Culture in the 1990s," *Radical America* 24, no. 4 (give date: special issue).

11. John Boswell, *Christianity, Social Tolerance and Homosexuality: Gay People in Western Europe from the Beginning of the Christian Era to the Fourteenth Century* (Chicago: University of Chicago Press, 1980). Michel Foucault, *Histoire de la sexualité,* vol. 2, *L'essaye des plaisirs* (Paris: Gallimard, 1984). David M. Halperin, *One Hundred Years of Homosexuality* (New York: Routledge, 1990). See also David F. Greenberg, *The Construction of Homosexuality* (Chicago: University of Chicago Press, 1988).

12. For the comparable debate in the literature on the deaf see Oliver Sacks, *Seeing Voices;* David M. Perlmutter, "The Language of the Deaf," *New York Review of Books* 38, no. 6 (March 28, 1991): 65–72. See also Edward Dolnick, "Deafness

as Culture," *Atlantic* 272, no. 3 (Sept. 1993): 37–53. The flavor of the debate in the feminist literature is suggested by Michelle Zimbalist Rosaldo and Louise Lamphere, eds., *Woman, Culture, and Society* (Stanford: Stanford University Press, 1974), esp. the chapters by Rosaldo and Lamphere themselves, pp. 1–42; Jane Duran, *Toward a Feminist Epistemology* (Savage, Md.: Rowman and Littlefield, 1991); Jane Sawicki, *Disciplining Foucault: Feminism, Power and the Body* (New York: Routledge, 1991); Sandra Harding, *Feminism and Methodology: Social Science Issues* (Bloomington: Indiana University Press, 1987), esp. pp. 181–192; Kathy E. Ferguson, *The Feminist Case Against Bureaucracy* (Philadelphia: Temple University Press, 1984).

13. See, e.g., James March and Johan P. Olsen, *Ambiguity and Choice in Organizations* (Bergen: Universitetstorlaget, 1979).

14. How this squares with economics and the economists' perspective on public policy is a little unclear. Conventional economics incorporates the traditional engineering assumption that the production process is constrained in a distinct and meaningful way by the environment in which it operates. But, as noted in the preceding chapter, this presumption operates through the assumption that economic agents make their decisions within a given cognitive structure, or model, connecting means and ends. One way of understanding the essentialist/constructionist debate is that it replaces that assumption with a new realm of inquiry about where that model comes from and how it evolves. Understood in this way, it could simply be added to the economists' conventional concerns without displacing the understandings that were already there.

The discipline has a second space for the new discourse in the distinction it makes between consumption and production. Strictly speaking, economics has adopted the engineering view only in its understanding of production. Production is treated as a means; its decisions are objectively determined by the ends that are given to it and the constraints of the environment in which those decisions are made. But consumption is governed by taste; decisions in that realm are subjective; and the discipline attempts to explain them in only a very limited way.

The separation between consumption and production is enhanced by the assumption that the income that constrains consumption but that is generated and distributed in the production process can be *redistributed* without affecting the production process after that process is completed and before consumption takes place. The claims of the social constructionists would be relatively easy for the discipline to absorb in the theory of consumption so long as they were limited to tastes. Indians may eat dogs and worship cows while Americans consume cows and treat dogs as pets, but the production of both animals is more or less the same, and the difference between the two countries in this regard would not affect economic analysis to the point where the discipline felt compelled to understand the origins of the two sets of tastes.

It seems doubtful, however, that the new discourse can be confined, and absorbed, in these ways. The assumption about the redistribution of income that separates consumption and production seems increasingly untenable, but even if it could be maintained the implications of the constructionist view are not easily confined to the realm of consumption. Indeed, it seems to imply that the very distinction between the two realms upon which it was built, and the broader separation of means and ends that lies behind it, are social constructions that are problematic. Tastes, it would appear, as Halperin's analogy between sexual preferences and the preferences for different kinds of meat suggests, are themselves the fulcrum for categories through which we organize and understand society; and they, in turn, influence the way we interpret our physical environment.

Thus, ultimately, the issues raised by the new managerial approaches may prove very troubling indeed to the conventions of economics. The questions the new identity groups have led us to pose for them, it would seem, do lead into a community of discourse that stretches well beyond the bounds of these groups themselves, well beyond their immediate concerns and the issues they pose for society. But the links this creates to wider and more general concerns also imply other divisions in the deep structure of thought that undergirds the social fabric, divisions that in the long run may prove even more divisive than the groups themselves.

15. Yiorgos Mylonadis, "The Green Challenge to the Industrial Enterprise Mindset: Survival Threat or Strategic Opportunity?" (Ph.D. diss., MIT, 1993).

16. Paul Leslie Swain, "Labor Market Contracting and the Provision for Work Place Hazards: A Historical Study" (Ph.D. diss., MIT, 1980).

17. Jonathan R. Macey and Geoffrey P. Miller, "The Plaintiffs' Attorney's Role in Class Action and Private Litigation: Economic Analysis and Recommendation for Reform," *University of Chicago Law Review* 58, no. 1 (Winter 1991): 1–118.

18. Abram Chayes, "The Role of the Judge in Public Law Litigation," *Harvard Law Review* 89, no. 7 (May 1976).

19. Stephen C. Yeazell, *From Medieval Group Litigation to the Modern Class Action* (New Haven: Yale University Press, 1987).

20. See Albert O. Hirschman, *Exit, Voice, and Loyalty: Responses to Decline in Firms, Organizations, and States* (Cambridge, Mass.: Harvard University Press, 1970).

21. For the recent American debate on corporate governance see Marc J. Roc, "Political and Legal Restraints on Ownership and Control of Public Companies," *Journal of Financial Economics* 27 (Sept. 1990): 7–41. Also Michael Usecom, *Executive Defense: Shareholders' Power and Corporate Reorganization* (Cambridge, Mass.: Harvard University Press, 1993); Robert A. C. Monks, *Power and Accountability* (New York: Harper Business, 1991); Margaret M. Blair, ed., *The Deal Decade* (Washington: Brookings Institution, 1993).

22. For a related proposal see Charles Heckscher, *The New Unions: Employee Involvement in the Changing Corporation* (New York: Basic Books, 1988).

23. Secs. 8(e) and 8(f) of the NLRA. See Harry A. Millis and Emily Clark Brown, *From the Wagner Act to Taft Hartley: A Study of National Labor Policy and Labor*

Relations (Chicago: University of Chicago Press, 1950), pp. 401, 436, 474–476, 467–468.

24. Millis and Brown, pp. 138–155.

7. Toward a Politics of Common Understanding

1. This notion of leadership as interpretative, or hermeneutic, is captured in the idea of the "rhetorical presidency"; see Jeffrey K. Tulis, *The Rhetorical Presidency* (Princeton: Princeton University Press, 1987). For the contrasting notion of leadership in rational choice see Richard Neustadt, *Presidential Power: The Politics of Leadership* (New York: Wiley, 1961). As Tulis defines it, however, the concept of the rhetorical presidency excludes the second aspect of hermeneutic leadership, which I have called orchestration. And the relationship between rhetorical politics and the kind of politics I am advocating is quite complex. As Tulis notes, the rhetorical presidency was actually quite alien to nineteenth-century American politics. This was in part because the politics of that period was much closer to the civic republican tradition. To the extent that it actually involved civic republican practice, however, it was a republic of politicians, not a republic of citizens. In other words, the "conversations" of the political process were conversations among professional politicians and representatives in the capital, not among the members of the electorate. At its best, the rhetorical presidency would involve presidential leadership of conversations among citizens.

2. Robert Lalonde, "Evaluating the Econometric Evaluations of Training Programs with Experimental Data," *American Economic Review* 76, no. 4 (Sept. 1986): 604–620.

3. This is very similar to the argument made by James Heckman in "Randomization and Social Policy Evaluation," National Bureau of Economic Research Technical Paper no. 107 (Cambridge, Mass., and Stanford).

4. Cf. John S. Nelson, Allen Megill, and Donald N. McCloskey, eds., *The Rhetoric of the Human Sciences: Language and Argument in Scholarship and Public Affairs* (Madison: University of Wisconsin Press, 1987).

5. For an example of this approach to policy see Robert Boyer, ed., *The Search for Labor Market Flexibility: The European Economies in Transition* (New York: Clarendon Press, 1988), esp. pt. 2. Also Office of Technology Assessment, U.S. Congress, *U.S.–Mexico Trade: Pulling Together or Pulling Apart?* ITE-545 (Washington: U.S. Government Printing Office, 1992).

6. Yiorgos Mylonadis, "The Green Challenge to the Industrial Enterprise Mindset: Survival Threat or Strategic Opportunity?" (Ph.D. diss., Sloan School of Management, MIT, June 1993).

7. James Womack, Daniel T. Jones, and Daniel Roos, *The Machine That Changed the World* (New York: Rawson Associates, 1990).

8. Robert D. Putnam with Robert Leonardi and Raffaella Nanetti, *Making De-*

mocracy Work: Civic Traditions in Modern Italy (Princeton: Princeton University Press, 1993).

9. AnnaLee Saxenian, *Regional Advantage: Culture and Competition in Silicon Valley and Route 128* (Cambridge, Mass.: Harvard University Press, 1994).

10. Blanca G. Silvestrini, "Assessing Identity and Claiming Rights: Latinos Search for Public Space in a Multi-ethnic Community," paper presented to the Law and Society Association Meeting, Madison, Wis., 1989.

Index